FINANCE PEOPLE

An Introduction to Their World and How They Think

MICHAEL J. SCHILL

DARDEN BUSINESS PUBLISHING

Charlottesville, Virginia

To all those curious about and intimidated by finance

Darden Business Publishing

© 2023 by the University of Virginia Darden School Foundation

All rights reserved. Permission may be obtained by writing to
permissions@dardenbusinesspublishing.com.

Printed in the United States of America on acid-free paper

First published 2023

978-1-61598-212-7

Library of Congress Control Number: 2023944071

Cover art: Tatjana Jovic

Contents

Acknowledgments

I am deeply grateful for the profound contributions of many who have left important imprints on the pages of this book. The foundational content has emerged from years of collaboration with my colleagues at the Darden School of Business, including Rus Abuzov, Yiorgos Allayannis, Bob Bruner, Susan Chaplinsky, Bob Conroy, Ken Eades, Bob Harris, Marc Lipson, Elena Loutskina, Pedro Matos, Matt McBrady, and Ting Xu, as well as the school's remarkably dedicated students. The crafting of the manuscript has been a labor of love by Staci England, Emily Gray, Skyler Gray, Erin Facer, and Skyler Clark-Hamel, who have fine-tuned the text to keep it true to its purpose and emerged as triumphant finance people. Lastly, the book has benefited profoundly by my partnership with the team at Darden Business Publishing, including Jennifer Hasher, Leslie Mullin, Sherry Richardson, Elliot Leflar, Charlotte Walker, and Andy Dahl, along with graphic designer Julia Grammer, and in particular my editor, Jane Haxby, whose dedication to this project just may surpass my own. As I am solely responsible for any errors, please send any recommendations for improvements directly to me.

Preface

A travel book can be tremendously helpful at orienting a traveler to the unique aspects of the places, people, culture, and language of a new land. This book, like a travel book, is designed to orient you to a unique people—finance people—and their profoundly important way of thinking.

This book will refer to finance people as those within the broad culture of finance and business. Their key characteristic is that they understand and appreciate the important connections and interactions among financial markets, investors, and business. They share a common language, a way of thinking, and an appreciation for an important part of society that impacts all of us. This book seeks to introduce the most fundamental elements associated with the language, the way of thinking, and the markets orientation of finance people—enabling you, the reader, to understand, interact with, and assimilate with them.

This book is meant for those who don't know much about the land of finance but are thinking of embarking there, maybe for a class or a job. It is meant for those who want to build a broad exposure to and appreciation for finance and its people, but may be intimidated by the journey. The book recognizes that while building comfort with finance and its people may take some time and generate some anxiety, finance can be approached, understood, and celebrated by anyone. Finance people do not have to stay foreign.

Following the model of a travel book, the focus is on introducing the most important and foundational concepts that define how finance people think about business decisions. These concepts are organized into five major sections within the book: the lay of the land, performance benchmarks, performance measurement, valuation, and business financing. The first section lays out the most foundational concepts to give you the building blocks of the language and provide a sense of what finance is—and is not—about. The second section introduces principles finance people use to discriminate good investments from bad ones, including such concepts as inflation, risk, diversification, and the opportunity cost of capital. The third section transitions to the metrics finance people use to measure performance, including such concepts as financial accounting, cash flow, and financial modeling. The fourth section explores principles of valuation and how finance people use them to value all sorts of stuff, such as loans and businesses. The final section examines principles finance people use to fund their business operations, including such concepts as the cash cycle, leverage, and the sources and uses of cash. These core concepts of performance benchmarking, performance measurement, valuation, and business financing provide the necessary foundation for thinking like a finance person and effectively using the tools of finance.

Since finance is commonly taught with an orientation toward business finance rather than personal finance, this book will follow a similar path: most of the situations and decision-makers will be businesses and business people. While it is fine to read this book "on site" (once you are on the job or in class), the book is most effective if read prior to the "trip." It is designed to build your intuition with a set of core concepts, so you are prepared to effectively grapple with traditional and more challenging finance material and thinking. This is not a comprehensive handbook of finance concepts, but rather a broad introduction to only the most foundational ideas in finance.

The tone of the book is lighthearted, and the presentation is simple and focused on settings that are diverse and easy to relate to, featuring down-to-earth decision-makers. For simplicity and ease of engagement, all the people and settings presented are fictitious and constructed so that the central concepts are easy to grasp and readily meaningful. Still, it is important to appreciate that the book requires substantial mental energy. Despite the attempt to make these concepts approachable, the ideas are still challenging and will take some effort to grasp and process. Don't get discouraged if an idea takes some time to come together! If you struggle at first, that doesn't mean you don't have what it takes to understand. Keep moving along and do your best to gain a broad grasp of each idea. Eventually, as when you are learning a language or navigating an unfamiliar city, the concepts will clarify and you will begin to understand.

Each chapter provides practical examples from the perspectives of business decision-makers. The end of each chapter contains some "get out your pencil" practice problems to review your understanding. Engaging with these review problems is critical to absorbing the key principles and methods in each chapter. As a check for your understanding, some good answers to the review problems are provided in **Appendix 1** at the end of the book. While the examples and review problems are filled with lots of calculations, you should appreciate that the core, nonquantitative concepts are most important to understand. Since we learn best by doing, the technical calculations are here to help solidify the core concepts. In each chapter, these core concepts are highlighted near the beginning in a section called "Concept" and again at the end in a "Concept Wrap-Up" section. Understanding and internalizing these key concepts defines one as a finance person, just as becoming fluent in a new language is a key part of integrating into a new culture. To facilitate your comfort with the language and math of finance, two additional appendixes (**Appendixes 2** and **3**) are provided as a go-to location for many of the terms and equations introduced over the course of the book.

Happy reading, and have a great trip!

SECTION I
THE LAY OF THE LAND

What should I expect of a trip to the land of finance? Which of my preconceived notions are true and which are not? Is the language difficult to learn, or is it easier than I expect? What are the important things to see? To give you an appreciation of the lay of the land, we'll start with an overview of finance in the first three chapters.

As with people of all types, there are all sorts of stereotypes and misconceptions about finance people. What motivates them? What do they care about? Do they have a good impact on society or a bad one? What do they do that is interesting? The first chapter explores all sorts of common misunderstandings and misconceptions about finance and finance people. This overview is just the thing to give you a quick understanding of why finance and its people are so important to society—and why they are worth understanding.

As in any foreign culture, finance people speak their own language. This language of finance can be terribly intimidating. The second chapter discusses finance in its own words and helps you begin to get acquainted with some of the key terms and phrases. The chapter is the first step in a long-term commitment to getting to know the language of finance.

The third chapter introduces the foundational conceptual theme of finance—*economic value creation*. This concept provides the fundamental motivation for a finance frame of mind. The theme of economic value creation will keep coming up throughout the book, and throughout your larger journey into finance.

The combination of these three chapters will provide a survey of the land that will prepare and orient you to all that is coming later.

1

Fly Fishing and the Intimidating World of Finance

NYMPHS IN THE NEVERSINK

The early spring sun was rising on the Neversink River in New York's Catskill Mountains. The benthos were busy, and abundant groups of stoneflies sheltered on the glistening river rocks. A southern breeze added warmth to the valley as the rattling call of a belted kingfisher cut through the light haze.

Protected by well-used waders and with fly-fishing rods in hand, Joan Fox and her husband Lee stepped into the cool mountain water. Joan had settled on a rig that included a size 18 tan caddis nymph for a dropper fly and a gold-beaded pheasant-tail dry fly as an indicator, along with a small split shot. Despite Lee's insistence that woolly buggers would prove to be the nymph of the day at attracting the stream's trout, Joan trusted in her own rig selection. With an easy side-arm cast that dropped her fly expertly on the surface, she worked the soft, slack water in the riffles, letting the fly ride down along a seam. Within seconds, the indicator disappeared, and she instinctively flicked her Scott G Series fly rod to set the hook in the lip of an unseen fish. With a strong sweep of the tail, a glistening arc of spray shot up and caught the morning light. "What a fighter!" Joan shouted as she worked the fish back and forth in the channel while maintaining steady pressure on the line with the deeply bending Scott G.

After a minute of skilled work, she reached down with her hand net to secure a spectacular 16-inch speckled wild brown trout. Lee nodded at his wife's catch as she proudly displayed the impressive fish. As Joan knelt down to release it, Lee discreetly switched out his woolly bugger.

CONCEPT

To the uninitiated, fly fishing is intimidating and saddled with misconceptions. Why is that? Is it because of uncertainty around how to secure the appropriate equipment? The mystery of fashioning a fly in just the right way? The challenge of mastering the endless terminology? The ambiguity of learning to effectively read the river? Or could it be the elusive—and iconic—art of the rhythmic back-and-forth casting technique? Maybe all these characteristics—the theory, the language, and the skills—build barriers that elicit trepidation among the inexperienced. One might say with a sigh, "Fly-fishing people are simply born fly-fishing people, and I'm not one of them."

Yet despite the barriers, for those who dare to assist an expert tying a Copper John fly, or follow a friend holding a rod out in the water, or even read one of classic fly-fishing books, the wonder of it all tends to break down those initial barriers and settle itself in the psyche. A person who knew very little about the sport soon becomes a novice, and a fly-fishing novice quickly appreciates that an entire world opens up once they come to understand a few simple principles.

To the uninitiated, finance is also intimidating and saddled with misconceptions. "Finance people" seem different, unapproachable, and with their own foreign culture.[1] The terminology, institutions, and lore all serve as formidable barriers that elicit trepidation among the inexperienced. One might say, "Finance people are simply born finance people, and those who don't get finance and its culture will never be comfortable in the land of finance."

---

[1] While the term *finance people* can be defined in many ways, this book will refer to finance people as those within the broad culture of finance and business professionals. Their key characteristic is that they understand and appreciate the important connections and interactions among financial markets, investors, and business. Since finance is commonly taught with an orientation toward business managers and business investors, this book will take a similar lead and think about finance people as business managers and business investors.

Yet despite the barriers, for those who dare to assist an expert in working through a discounted cash flow analysis, follow a friend into the pricing of traded securities, or simply read a book like this one, the wonder of it all tends to break down those initial barriers and settle itself in the psyche. A person who knows very little about finance culture soon starts to learn stuff. This book is designed to open up the world of business finance to the uninitiated by introducing a set of simple principles and core skills that form the subject's foundation. These principles and skills are introduced in accessible contexts that emphasize broad understanding over technical detail. Each chapter includes simple learning opportunities to practice these principles. The focus of the book is introducing how finance people think. Like those who understand the principles of fly fishing, finance people understand and are comfortable with the core finance principles. The objective of this text is to ease the uninitiated into the land of finance—it is not to make you an expert in all things finance. Reading it will expose you to those concepts and ways of thinking that help you be conversant, comfortable, and interested in finance and its people.

We will explore problems people experience all over the globe—problems associated with everything from football teams to bus driving and from horticulture to food trucks. From these everyday contexts, we'll find simple principles that are foundational to finance. We will examine the intuition behind such topics as financial analysis, financial modeling, cash flow, the cash cycle, inflation, valuation, return benchmarks, diversification gains, trade credit, and financial leverage. Our discussion won't go deep into those topics but will examine them enough to encourage a basic intuition of the key principles and lines of thinking that form the foundation of the topic.

To get things going, in this first chapter we'll review some of the commonly held misconceptions around finance and finance people. We'll use these misconceptions to consider what finance is and what it is not. As we seek to find our way in the land of finance, it will be important to break the misconceptions about its culture and about finance. Demystifying the concept by distilling what it is from what it isn't is the first step to opening up the remarkable world of financial decision-making.

MISCONCEPTION 1
Finance people just buy low and sell high—their decisions benefit only themselves.

It is true that the buying and selling of financial securities get lots of attention in society. News outlets emphasize the daily ups and downs of the stock market. A fortune can be made and lost in one bold trade. Such trades generate lots of drama. But finance is a lot more than stock trading. It is a lot more than extracting wealth from society by buying assets cheaply and selling them dearly. Instead, finance is fundamentally about the creation of wealth for all of society.

One of society's primary responsibilities is to oversee the productive assets of the world economy. By the productive assets of the world economy, we mean all the productive resources in society, including all the financial wealth, all the stores of natural resources, the entirety of the physical facilities and equipment across the globe, and all the world's labor. Each day, society—made up of billions of individuals making their own decisions—chooses how to deploy those assets. The world's assets can be deployed for tremendous gain or tremendous waste. In broad terms, the theory and practice of finance provides a set of governing principles meant to guide society in using the productive assets of the world economy. Getting the practice of finance right is of vast import for all of society.

At the heart of how finance people think is this foundational principle: *economic value creation beats economic value destruction.* Economic value is created when the total value of the expected benefits created by the decision exceeds the total value of the resources expended. Economic value is destroyed when the total value of the expected benefits created by the decision is less than the total value of the resources expended. When the resources expended exceed the long-term expected benefits, society is worse off and finance people say that value is destroyed. This principle is key to everything finance. This principle dictates how finance people make decisions.

Suppose that Pierce David is considering investing his family fortune into building a children's hospital. Each year, Hospital Design A can serve 1,000 children but consumes USD1 million in cash.[2] Hospital Design B is similar to Hospital A in that it also serves 1,000 children; but unlike Hospital A, Hospital B generates an excess profit of USD1 million in cash. Which design should David accept? The principle of economic value creation implies that Hospital A is inferior, because even though it helps lots of children, it consumes economic wealth. It is self-destructive: it can't economically sustain itself and requires someone to continuously inject cash (USD1 million per year). It runs by burning wealth—wealth that could be used to do more good in society. Alternatively, Hospital B helps a lot of children *and* generates rather than consumes cash. Because Hospital B generates cash, it is self-sustaining (no one has to continue to feed the fire). Hospital B generates additional wealth that can be used to accomplish more good for society—like building more children's hospitals. Financial theory holds that assets deployed in ways that produce rather than consume wealth will, over both long-term and short-term periods, produce more gains for society.

One important challenge in investment decisions is the large uncertainty in outcomes. Because of this outcome uncertainty, it is important to work hard to identify and understand the expected and potential economic gains and losses associated with investments. A big part of finance is learning to properly identify and understand the value-creation process for any decision. Not surprisingly, it is not easy. The process takes tremendous care and discernment. Yet, by understanding and applying general financial principles, finance people become skilled at clarifying and incorporating the value implications in their business decisions.

The creation of value is thus a critical difference from the simple rule, "buy low and sell high." "Buy low, sell high" is a zero-sum game where one person's gains are another person's losses. Instead, the principle of economic value creation implies wins for society in total, because the total value of the expected benefits created exceeds the total value of the resources expended. It is a powerful principle that creates discipline and adds rigor to decision-making by keeping as a cardinal goal that decisions create welfare for society.

---

[2] USD = US dollars.

Finance asserts that economic value creation beats economic value destruction. Economic value is created when the total value of the expected benefits created by the decision exceeds the total value of the resources expended.

MISCONCEPTION 2
Finance people do their own thing off in a remote corner of society.

Finance is kind of like weather—it's pretty hard to avoid. While people can temporarily choose to stay sheltered indoors, few people can stay indoors forever. The weather finds and affects us all, both directly and indirectly. Similarly, finance finds everyone and affects us all on a very regular basis.

Finance and its people are a core foundation upon which society is built and operates. Finance is how society funds commerce, trade, infrastructure, housing, and wealth, while easing uncertainty and poverty. Finance determines how society's resources are managed over time. Finance so permeates society that living in society means we will interact with finance regularly, whether we intend to or not.

This book focuses on the financial decisions of business managers. Business managers not only can't avoid finance—they are swimming in finance. According to the norms of standard business ownership structure, those who fund the assets of a business (the investors) own the business. Ownership gives ultimate decision-making privilege—owners can override any business decision. Generally, owners ascribe to finance principles, meaning they want their business to create, rather than consume, wealth.

In many organizations, business managers are appointed by the owners to make day-to-day decisions, with the understanding that their decisions must please the owners. Let's consider the example of Martine Banza, who runs Leonard Motors, an automobile manufacturer owned by the five Mabika brothers. As the managing director, Banza is highly influential in company policy. If she wants to double the price of her cars, she can make that happen. If she wants to paint all the cars pink and purple, she can do that too. If she wants to produce and market a car-boat-plane combo vehicle called the Banza Awesome Extreme 300Z, she can also do that. However, if her decisions displease the Mabika brothers—the owners of Leonard Motors—Banza's time at the helm of Leonard Motors will be short. Business managers decide business policy only at the pleasure of the business owners. The preferences of the Mabika brothers, the investors in Leonard Motors, should always pervade Banza's decision-making. She is the steward, not the owner. Finance people advocate that Banza, like any business manager, should always have an "investor or owner perspective." A good business manager is able to think like an owner or investor.

Because of their ultimate decision-making privilege, investors (or owners of the business) are critical stakeholders for any business manager. In truth, managers who fail to please their investors, regardless of how well they please other business stakeholders (such as customers or employees), will at some point be removed. Because of this reality, it is essential that all business managers, regardless of their functional focus, know how to think like investors. Thinking like long-term investors is the same as thinking like finance people. In the business finance context, finance people have an abiding appreciation for value creation and why it matters to business investors (and therefore owners). Finance people are able to think like long-term investors—the kind who care about economic value creation.

But finance matters to managers for reasons other than just pleasing investors. The principle of value creation is fundamental to any manager interested in the wise use of resources—whether the organization is a for-profit enterprise or a not-for-profit charitable organization (an enterprise that doesn't have profit-oriented investors). Managers of not-for-profit institutions are still motivated to follow standard principles of finance if they want to maintain a healthy organizational "cash flow" and avoid squandering enterprise capital. *Cash flow* measures the net amount of cash that the organization generates. Positive cash flow allows an organization to operate; it is the lifeblood of any organization. Finance helps managers measure and maintain that cash flow lifeblood. In addition, finance people understand the uncertainty associated with their organization and the inherent risk they face. Finance helps managers balance the sources of value in their organization against the inherent risks and scrutinize a business proposal to improve decision-making. A business manager who appreciates the importance of cash flow and has the ability to think like an investor is a better manager than one who cannot. Because finance is everywhere in society, a strong background in finance is broadly applicable to all sorts of decision-making roles in business and society. Finance people are center stage because finance pervades decisions throughout society.

Finance so permeates society that living in society means we will interreact with finance very regularly, whether we intend to or not.

MISCONCEPTION 3
Finance people calculate "right answers."

Many new to finance believe that if you do the right calculation in finance, you always get the right answer. While this may be true for some finance problems (like calculating the correct payment on a car loan), it is not true for most financial decisions. A striking characteristic of real-world business decisions is that they don't tend to have straightforward, black-and-white answers. Because of the complex nature of business decisions, the goal of finance is not necessarily to output the "right" answer, but instead to help people build the judgment they need to effectively approach highly nuanced decisions.

Finance gives people tools that add rigor to their judgment. It helps people identify the sources and magnitudes of both concern and opportunity. It helps them appreciate the risks they face and understand the perspectives and needs of investors. In truth, because of the ambiguity embedded in real-world problems, there are lots of right answers and lots of wrong answers.[3] Finance helps people distinguish between the two.

Finance people use a simple set of frameworks to provide powerful intuition and judgment across a wide range of business situations. For the most part, a finance decision is more like a coach's decision about whether

---

[3] The characteristic of lots of right and wrong answers is not so dissimilar to other real-world ambiguous problems, such as, "What should I wear tomorrow?" or, "What should I do to make a living?" These are the kinds of questions, like those in finance, that have lots of right answers and lots of wrong answers.

to acquire a particular player for the team than it is like a statistician's calculation of that player's correct field goal percentage. Finance is not so much about the math as it is about the judgment.

Let's consider the example of Pei Lin, a manager at a major retailer in Shanghai. Lin is pondering two decisions: which stores her company should selectively upgrade, and which of a number of proposed new store sites should be opened. Finance provides Lin with a host of tools and frameworks she can use to focus her attention on the things that matter most in these important decisions. In one instance, for example, she is able to identify the precise increase in store traffic needed to justify a proposed store upgrade expenditure. Because of this observation, she reflects on the probability that she can achieve that level of traffic increase and considers how prudent it is to make the upgrade expenditure. Nothing is certain, but her financial analysis is able to give her an informed view. For a proposal for a new store, she connects the store's viability to the outcome of a road development that is under discussion. She uses this analysis to focus her attention on the likelihood of specific development outcomes and their influence on her decision-making. These observations are invaluable to Lin in building the judgment she needs to make these decisions. Although her financial analysis gives her valuable information, she does not expect it to tell her specifically what to do. It is still uncertain whether it is best to upgrade Store X or open Store Y. This is because real-world decisions can be ambiguous. Finance helps Lin make decisions in a world filled with ambiguity.

Finance people deal with nuanced decisions more often than decisions with simple "right answer" calculations. Finance is not so much about the math as it is about the judgment.

MISCONCEPTION 4
Nobody knows the future. Financial forecasts
are useless for decision-making.

Although finance people spend a lot of time working on financial forecasts, they fully appreciate that their forecasts are frequently wrong.

Society and the world are too uncertain to forecast the details of the future with any real precision. But despite the inevitable failure of the specific details of financial forecasts, finance people use them to gain critical insights into what matters across the highly uncertain bets they make. Such forecasting or "modeling" is not unique to finance people. People commonly consider, model, or predict what traffic might look like when they leave the house. Depending on the time of day, they use their forecast to consider what time they need to leave in order to arrive somewhere on time. There may be unexpected events—a car crash, a change in weather, a flat tire, a late bus—but their mental model allows them to anticipate the future and make an educated decision. Finance people use similar, albeit more sophisticated, models or forecasts to understand the drivers of business economics, so they can better establish probable ranges for forecasted outcomes and use these ranges to improve their understanding of business linkages and performance. The process of disciplined forecasting is highly valuable to business managers who constantly make important decisions in a highly uncertain environment.

Suppose Sandeep Habersham, who works for a big toothpaste company, is thinking about the long-term prospects of marketing a toothpaste to the elderly. He uses his understanding of trends in the target population, the macroeconomy, the industry dynamics, and the company strategy to model a base-case forecast of product demand, profit, and investment. In order to get a sense of which of his model's assumptions are important, he adjusts them to identify those elements that are most impactful to the forecast. For example, Habersham discovers that the forecasted business profit is relatively unaffected by the cannibalization of existing company toothpaste brands.[4] This is because the profit margins of the different toothpastes are similar, so it doesn't matter which of his company's toothpaste brands customers buy. In contrast, the forecast

---

[4] *Cannibalization* is a term toothpaste people and finance people use to measure the amount that sales of one product erodes the sales of another in-house product. For example, if elderly people begin to buy the new toothpaste brand but stop buying one of the company's other brands of toothpastes, the new brand is cannibalizing the sales of the company's other toothpaste brands.

profit is highly sensitive to the number of new customers he is able to attract (this is because the lifetime gains associated with attracting new customers are much higher than the costs of attracting them). Habersham's analysis helps him appreciate what matters and what does not. Through the analysis, he discovers the strategic importance of using a financial model to understand how the toothpaste brands and customers interact in his business. This insight helps him maintain better judgment in the decisions he makes as a manager.

Finance people face highly uncertain bets. Given such uncertainty, financial forecasts and models are critical to understanding which assumptions matter.

MISCONCEPTION 5
Financial markets follow the whims of traders, so they don't offer much information to thoughtful managers.

Investors make lots of big money decisions. Because of the magnitude of the money at stake, finance people pour tons of analysis into these bets, and this analysis moves prices. Through the forces of supply and demand in markets, the prices of financial securities aggregate and reflect the combined wisdom of all that analysis across the entire globe.[5] If the price of a security becomes a little high or a little low based on existing information, finance people swoop in to compete away any such mispricing. With all this swooping in to trade on any information about a company's stock, for example, the stock's price will adjust to fairly reflect the information out there. In other words, the stock will be fairly priced, because the price will fairly reflect the aggregate information investors have about the stock. The concept of financial security prices adjusting to reflect the information in the market is known as *market efficiency* or *an efficient market*. The phrase "the market is efficient" implies that the forces buying and selling in the

---

[5] *Security* is a term finance people use to denote the financial contracts, such as share of company stock or loans and bonds. These financial securities are often bought and sold in financial markets.

market are such that the market prices reflect the true available information about the value of financial securities. The buyers and sellers in an efficient market compete against each other in a way that neutralizes the effect of false information and reflects the value of true information in market prices.

Because of the competitive forces that maintain financial market efficiency, financial market prices reflect all of society's aggregate wisdom. Through this information-aggregation process, financial markets provide a remarkable array of highly scrutinized information that is readily available to managers making business decisions. Market efficiency maintains that the price of any financial security, such as a stock or a bond, reflects the combined analysis of all the market's participants around the world. Market efficiency is a strong statement about the rationality of markets and varies considerably from a view that market prices are dictated by the whims and manias of market psychology.

Consider Rodrigo Flores, who operates a manufacturing facility in central Mexico. Flores is considering purchasing a new piece of equipment for his manufacturing business. Through improvements in product quality and manufacturing efficiency, he expects that the new equipment will generate an 8% return on investment. He questions whether 8% is a good return, and decides to do some financial analysis to figure that out. Financial markets can provide great assistance. Not surprisingly, this is not the first time investors have seen manufacturing equipment risk. By looking at current prices in financial markets, Flores learns that investors in Mexico's financial markets think the rate of return needed on investments of comparable risk is about 9%. Therefore, the 8% rate of return that Flores anticipates is insufficient to justify the manufacturing equipment purchase. By gleaning information from investors in financial markets to benchmark his investment decisions, Flores is able to recognize that he needs to find ways to improve the return on the proposal above 9%. The benchmark of 9% that he uses doesn't come out of thin air. Rather, it is grounded in what investors in markets today think is a sufficient return for the risk taken. Flores decides that before moving forward with the investment, he needs to think harder about how to take better advantage of the virtues of the equipment, so he can improve the expected returns of the project.

Because of financial markets' incredible ability to aggregate information through competitive forces, financial markets provide a remarkable array of highly scrutinized information that is readily available to aid managers in making business decisions.

MISCONCEPTION 6
Finance people think business growth is always good.

In fact, some growth is good and some growth is bad—it depends on whether the growth creates or destroys value by generating or draining the company's resources. Investment proposals for business growth generally involve flows of money over multiple years. Those fluent in finance know how to evaluate such multiyear bets by assigning different values to money across time. They recognize that receiving money sooner is worth more than receiving money later and that the precise difference in relative value depends on relevant rates of return. Finance people think hard about measuring and identifying the potential gains and returns from any investment. They look beyond projected profits to identify the financial impact on investors. Good growth happens when the expected total returns compensate investors for the risk they take by investing. Through these principles, finance helps managers distinguish good growth from bad growth.

Suppose that Jane Bates is considering adding a car wash to the gas station she owns with her brother Jack. She expects that the car wash will cost USD50,000 to set up and will generate annual net profits of USD10,000 for six years. Since the car wash is expected to be profitable, Jane tells Jack, "Get me some water, Jack! The car wash will make money, and growing our gas station is of course good." But Jack thinks like a finance person. He recognizes that there are lots of things he and Jane could do with USD50,000. Based on his assessment of financial markets, he explains to Jane that they can earn 7.0% on investments of similar risk. "My calculation, Jane, is that the car wash business only generates an expected 5.5% return on investment,"[6] Jack says. "Let's look at some other opportunities before we build it. There may be smarter ways to grow our business that help us earn at least 7.0% on our money. Or maybe we should do something else, like selling snack food. Maybe we should try running the numbers on that?"

Finance people believe that not all growth is good. Some growth is good because it creates economic value and makes society better off with more resources, and some growth is bad because it destroys economic value by draining society's resources.

MISCONCEPTION 7
Finance people think fooling investors is good for business.

Business is filled with smoke-and-mirror activities—maneuvers that may dazzle initially but prove empty of any true value. Because they produce no long-term value, finance people recognize that it is in their best interest to avoid paying for them. Finance people have frameworks to see through the smoke and mirrors and isolate those activities that are truly meaningful. In this way they pay only for real value creation. Scrutinizing smoke-and-mirror activities is particularly relevant in financial policy decisions such as a business's appropriate level of borrowing, level of cash, and level of dividends.

Suppose Zeeshan Omar, the chief financial officer (CFO) at a large software company, is considering initiating a EUR1.00 annual cash dividend where the company sends a check for EUR1.00 for every share that they own.[7] His intent is to boost the company's EUR20.00 stock price by

---

[6] The 5.5% return estimate is obtained by calculating the internal rate of return (IRR) on the USD50,000 investment. This concept is discussed in chapter 12.

[7] EUR = euros.

increasing the returns to shareholders. Omar wonders how appreciative and impressed shareholders will be by the cash they might start receiving. The naive view is that Omar has just given his shareholders an extra 5% return on their investment (5% = 1.00/20.00), and that investors will bid up the share price as shareholders try to get a piece of this new, bigger dividend. But when considered from a thoughtful finance perspective, it becomes clear that the investors own that cash both before and after the dividend. The investors already own all the business's assets. Shareholders don't necessarily gain when cash is distributed and comes out of the company. The astute shareholder recognizes that, by gaining the EUR1.00 cash dividend, the company has reduced the value of company assets by EUR1.00. In effect, cash has simply moved from the shareholders' stock portfolios to the shareholders' bank accounts. The overall wealth of a shareholder is no different than if she moved a coin from one pocket to another. If this is the interpretation of investors in the market, Omar should expect his dividend announcement to create very little reaction in stock price appreciation.

Finance people pay only for activities that create real value. And scrutinizing smoke-and-mirror activities is particularly relevant in financial policy decisions, such as a business's appropriate level of borrowing, level of cash, and level of dividends.

CONCEPT WRAP-UP

Finance is filled with all sorts of misconceptions. This chapter offers counterarguments to many of them and emphasizes that gaining an understanding of finance and learning to take a finance perspective is worth the effort. Core finance principles include the following:

Principle 1. Finance asserts that economic value creation beats economic value destruction. Economic value is created when the total value of the expected benefits created by a decision exceeds the total value of the resources expended.

Principle 2. Finance so permeates society that living in society means that we will interact with finance very regularly, whether we intend to or not.

Principle 3. Finance requires nuanced decisions more often than decisions with simple "right answer" calculations. Finance is not so much about math as it is about judgment.

Principle 4. Finance involves highly uncertain bets. Faced with such uncertainty, financial forecasts and models are critical to understanding which assumptions matter.

Principle 5. Because of financial markets' incredible ability to aggregate information through competitive forces, financial markets provide a remarkable array of highly scrutinized information that is readily available to aid managers in making business decisions.

Principle 6. Not all growth is good. Some growth is good because it creates economic value and makes society better off, and some growth is bad because it destroys economic value by draining the resources.

Principle 7. Only activities that create real value should be pursued and paid for. Scrutinizing smoke-and-mirror activities is particularly relevant in financial policy decisions such as a business's appropriate level of borrowing, level of cash, and level of dividends.

This book is meant to build your interest in, comfort with, and intuition for the marvel that is finance. Reading it will allow you to better appreciate how finance helps people think in a valuable way and learn to think in these ways yourself. Let's grab a pole, head into the water, and see what we catch.

2

The Basics of Speaking Finance

Finance speak:

PE firm ASB is offering 15 times EBITDA to buy out CloudX share-holders. Despite its recent surge in revenue and profit, CloudX maintains a serious cash flow problem. Given its increasingly levered balance sheet, stockholders are punishing the share price to demand more premium despite the strong debt tax shield the company enjoys. Consistent with rising yields and credit spreads in the broad market, the company's bond prices have also fallen substantially.

Translation:

ASB, a firm that invests in private businesses, is offering to pay a fairly high price to acquire the company CloudX from its owners. Despite its recent surge in sales and profit, CloudX hasn't been generating much money for investors. CloudX's stock investors are getting worried about all the debt the company has despite the fact that the interest payments reduce the income taxes the company pays. Due to the general rise in interest rates, the market value of CloudX's debt has fallen substantially.

CONCEPT

Finance people—like Korean people, Brazilian people, Italian people, and American people—speak their own language. While speaking finance facilitates communication among finance people, it creates sizable barriers for those who don't speak the language. Finance language can be baffling, unintelligible, and unapproachable. With such imposing language barriers, it can be struggle to navigate finance society. Some expect finance to come easily because they know the language of math and think finance is mostly math. But while it is true that finance uses lots of numbers, in reality, finance is more a language of terms and concepts than an exercise in number crunching. The bottom line is, when approaching any culture—including finance—you've got to learn the language to communicate with the people.

Gaining comfort with a few key words and phrases in a foreign language goes a long way toward meeting the basic needs of navigating a foreign society. Knowing key words and phrases like "Gamsahabnida"; "Posso tomar um sorvete?"; "Due biglietti per favore"; and "Where is a bathroom?" makes all the difference: with these, one can thank people in Korea, order ice cream in Brazil, buy tickets in Italy, and find a restroom in the United States. Initial efforts to learn a language add a great deal of comfort and enjoyment to traveling in a foreign land. The same is true of speaking finance. A lot can be gained by learning a few simple finance terms and phrases. A little effort will quickly help you become comfortable in finance society and understand how finance people think.

This chapter and the accompanying appendix introduce the basic terms and phrases that are critical to learning conversational finance. As with any language you're trying to learn, at the beginning, the words of finance can be intimidating. Experiencing these terms and phrases can make your brain hurt. Yet, with practice and patience, the language will soon become familiar and the phrases will settle into your normal vocabulary. Eventually, you might find finance words rolling off your tongue as if you were a Wall Street native.

In this chapter, we'll introduce some foundational finance words. This section introduces just eight terms to get things going; we'll introduce many more in subsequent chapters. A complete list of finance terms highlighted in this book is provided in **Appendix 2**. Don't be afraid of **Appendix 2**! It is a section of the book that you can dive into as often as you need, and one that you may find yourself returning to even after you've finished this book and completed all the review questions. Consider it a resource like a phrase book you'd study before a trip and also keep in your back pocket while walking the streets of a foreign country. In this chapter, a brief description of each term or phrase is provided. For now, a broad understanding of these words is sufficient. In the subsequent chapters, many of these words will be explained in more detail and given relevant context and examples. As you look at these terms, you may be tempted to skip them because you think you already know what they mean. Read through the definitions anyway: you may find that you don't know what they mean as much as you think you do.

Let's learn to speak a little finance.

TERMINOLOGY

Corporate governance. Finance people care a lot about who gets to decide all the stuff having to do with a business. Lots of people have an interest in the affairs of a business: one term for all these people is *stakeholders*. Stakeholders are all those who care about the business outcomes. These stakeholders include managers and employees, customers, suppliers, investors, the government, and community members. As you might imagine, the varying stakeholders have varying ideas about what should be done with the business. Corporate governance deals with the rules, laws, and norms about who gets to decide what the business (or firm or company—all synonyms) does.

Investors. Finance has lots of terms for investors. Investors provide the money that firms need to operate. If a firm needs a warehouse or a truck, investors put up the money. If a firm needs a pile of inventory to sell, investors put up the money. If a firm needs to fund the development of a drug or a computer system, investors put up the money. To compensate investors for all that money, firms issue *claims* on the business to investors. These claims promise two things: (1) various monetary payouts and (2) influence on firm decisions. The investor arrangement works well for both parties—the business gets the money it needs to operate, and the investors exert power over the business decisions and get a share of the profits.

Debt holders. Debt holders (also called *debt investors*) are one type of investor. In exchange for lending money to the business, debt holders have the following two claims: (1) a promise of a set of fixed future payments and (2) the right to exert control over the assets of the business in the event that the promised fixed payments are not paid. Suppose Boris gives USD1 million to Jumbo Airlines in exchange for a promise of annual interest payments of 10% of the USD1 million loan for 10 years, plus a return of the USD1 million at the end of the 10-year loan. As a debt holder, Boris can expect to receive annual payments of USD100,000 every year for the next 10 years. As long as those payments are made, Boris has no right to exert influence on the company's business decisions. But if Jumbo Airlines fails to make its promised payment, Boris is assured that he will have influence. The structure of the debt contract gives the debt holder assurance that others in the company won't take advantage of them.

Equity holders. Equity holders are another type of investor. The term *equity holder* is synonymous with the terms *equity investor, stockholder,* and *shareholder.* Equity holders are residual claim holders, meaning that each period they get what is left over after everyone else has been paid. In exchange for their investment in the business, equity holders maintain the following two claims: (1) the right to exert control over how the assets of the business are used as long as the promises to other claim holders (i.e., debt holders) are made and (2) the right to the residual profits of the business. Suppose Ivana gives USD1 million to Jumbo Airlines for a promise of shared equity in the company—meaning she shares the equity with people who have similar claims—and a promise of the residual profits. As an equity holder, Ivana can expect to have voting rights on company policies and the leadership of Jumbo Airlines. If she doesn't like the decisions the board of directors is making, she can vote the board members out. The company provides cash payments to Ivana through board-approved cash *dividends* (cash payments made to equity holders where each share of stock entitles the shareholder to a certain cash payment) and through equity buybacks (cash payments made to equity holders where shareholders who want to sell their stock back to the company can do so for a certain price). Both cash dividends and stock buybacks are ways to deliver cash back to equity holders. If the company is acquired or liquidated, Ivana gets her share of what is left over after all other claim holders are paid. The structure of the equity contract gives the equity holder assurance that others in the company won't take advantage of them. Sometimes it is good to be a residual claim holder and sometimes it is not. In times when things go well for the business, the equity holders get to keep all the upside gains; in times when things go poorly for the business, the equity holders bear the downside losses. Both debt holders and equity holders are investors in the business, and investors choose what type of investor they want to be (i.e., what type of contract or claim on the business they want to have).

Management. In some small businesses, there is a single owner and employee, and all decisions are made by one person. But as businesses get larger, it is common for there to be a separation of ownership (the investors) and management (the people who make the day-to-day decisions). This makes sense because (1) growing businesses are better served by pooling the resources of lots of investors, and (2) the skills required to invest in a business may be very different from the skills needed to run a business. It is typical for the management team to serve at the discretion of the equity holders. If the management team works hard and impresses the equity holders, the equity holders keep them on. If the management team loafs around or makes lots of bad decisions that frustrate the equity holders, the equity holders step in and find a new management team.

Board (board of directors). Some businesses have very few equity holders, while other businesses have millions. When there are lots of equity holders, it is common for the equity holders to elect a body of people responsible for overseeing the management team and big company policy decisions. These board members represent all the equity holders and often come from a wide range of backgrounds.

Default. When a company does not pay its promised payments to debt holders, the company is in default. Default typically triggers specific conditions that are written into the debt contract. Default can be messy, as debt holders and other claim holders battle to maximize their payout. To protect the firm from a disorderly unraveling as claim holders look out for their own best interests, the board of directors may seek the more orderly process of bankruptcy protection.

Bankruptcy. When a company is not able to make the payments it has promised to debt holders (an impending default), the board may file for *bankruptcy protection*. Bankruptcy protection means that a legal court organized by the local government becomes the arbiter with the power to renegotiate the claims by the claim holders. In the extreme example (chapter 7 bankruptcy in the United States), a trust appointed by the bankruptcy court liquidates the assets of the company and distributes them, as negotiated by the court, to all the claim holders in the company, including employees, suppliers, customers, debt holders, and possibly equity holders. In the more common example (chapter 11 bankruptcy in the United States), the company continues to operate while the bankruptcy court renegotiates the claims of the claim holders. For example, it may be determined that debt holders will do better if they simply miss a couple of interest payments to allow the business to get back on its feet and begin repaying its debt. In this case, the board and management team may continue to run the company, or the court could decide that it is best for the management team to be replaced.

CONCEPT WRAP-UP

You've now reviewed some foundational words in finance. These words are important to understanding the rules under which finance people operate. As we move forward, please remember that finance people speak a different language. The words they use reflect the things that are important to them. The more words they have for a concept or a metric, the more important that concept or metric is likely to be. In order to understand finance people, we need to be able to speak their language. Fortunately, as with any foreign language, anyone can learn to speak finance with practice and patience. While practice and patience can be trying, a lot is gained with just a few simple finance terms and phrases.

This chapter has introduced a few select terms that are used in many of the foundational ideas in finance. Many more terms are provided in **Appendix 2**. You are encouraged to dive into this appendix as soon as possible. **Appendix 2** should definitely be your friend throughout the book.

Now that you know a little bit of lingo, let's begin our journey.

3

Economic Value Creation and Sustainability at Camp Big Fish

A DISCUSSION AT THE NATURE LODGE

It was a hot summer day at the Nature Lodge at Camp Big Fish. Katie Korb, a camp staffer, was standing in front of a chalkboard on which she'd written "Sustainability." After a brief pause to ensure that she'd spelled it correctly, she turned to a group of six exceptional summer campers, all of whom were either 12 or 13, and asked if they had heard of this word. All acknowledged that they had. She then asked, "So what does it mean? How would you define it?"

Brian Huff, a camper who went by the camp name First Aid and had an uncanny ability for finding unique ways to get injured, was the first to raise his hand. "Sustainable means not using natural resources."

"Thanks, First Aid. That's a good answer. What does everyone else think?" asked Korb.

"Too restrictive," countered Chantelle Hardy, a camper who went by the camp name Soap because she hadn't touched a bar of the stuff since arriving at camp. "Eventually everything comes from natural resources. If sustainability means not using natural resources, that's not sustainable—since we all die. I think sustainability is more about finding a good balance."

"Yeah, I think that's right," agreed Rich Everett, a camper who went by the camp name Swamp and aspired to maximize his camp time at the waterfront. "I see sustainability as more about using natural resources at the right rate. It's like the lake. If the amount of water leaving the lake is greater than the amount of water entering the lake, then we are going to end up with an empty lake. The rate isn't right. Sustainability is using natural resources at a rate at which they can be replenished. Maybe there can be short periods of depletion, but if the long-term outflows exceed the long-term inflows then there are going to be problems."

"Okay, maybe Soap and Swamp are right," Huff said. "But I think it makes sense to add that sustainability means leaving the world at least as good as you found it. This happens when resources are replenished at least as fast as they are consumed."

"I like it. I think another part of the definition is the ability to endure," offered Aimee Meunier, a camper from France who went by the camp name Pluie and made it a bit too clear that her life's aspiration was to one day work at the Nature Lodge. "If forests operate sustainably, each of the species in the forest lives in such a way that the forest system doesn't deplete the resources it needs. Instead, each species in the forest supports other species' ability to endure."

"Another aspect of sustainability is the efficiency of the system—like how it compares to alternative ways of doing the same thing," piped in Larry Slade, a camper who went by the camp name Sunrise because of his fixation with waking the camp each morning by playing full-blast trombone tunes. "Let's say you are considering installing a wind turbine that you think can generate electricity at a cost of 20 cents per kilowatt-hour. Alternatively, you could build a solar-powered system at a similar cost that would be expected to predictably generate electricity at a cost of 15 cents per kilowatt-hour. Which system would you pick? While both systems might be thought of as sustainable, the solar system is more sustainable because it is more cost efficient. It isn't clear that the more expensive wind system can endure."

"Excellent discussion," Korb said, smiling. "Maybe one of you will one day have a job at the Nature Lodge." After a few feigned chuckles and a sigh from Meunier, Korb explained that the group had brought up a number of key attributes of sustainable systems. She added the following to the board:

What is sustainability?

1. Sustainability considers replacement rates. Systems are not sustainable if the depletion rate exceeds the replacement rate.
2. Sustainability is the ability to endure or continue. Sustainable systems can maintain themselves. They do not exhaust the resources they require.
3. Sustainability considers alternative ways to generate the same effect. If one approach generates an effect by inefficiently consuming more resources than another, the inefficient approach is abandoned.
4. Sustainability considers total long-term effects rather than just short-term or partial gains. Sustainable systems maintain resources for the long term.

"Obrigado," exclaimed Esperta Silva, a camper from Portugal who went by the camp name Doctor because of her interest in medicine and perceived ability to treat Huff's injuries better than the camp infirmary. In addition to her interest in medicine, Silva was from a family that owned a large conglomerate of businesses in Europe, and it was rumored that Silva was already exerting managerial influence on the family businesses. "I feel we've learned a lot about sustainability for natural resources, but it occurs to me that these principles can also be applied to other forms of sustainability, such as economic sustainability."

"Economic sustainability?" echoed Huff. "What does that have to do with Camp Big Fish?"

"Believe me, First Aid," responded Silva, "everything has to do with economic sustainability. Camp Big Fish exists only because it is economically sustainable."

The eyes of the other campers turned to Silva—and even Korb began taking notes. "I believe that economic sustainability also has a number of key attributes," Silva explained. With a nod of thanks to Korb, she added another list to the board:

1. Economic sustainability considers replacement rates. Economically sustainable organizations maintain cash inflow that exceeds cash outflow. Sustainable enterprises are built to replenish financial resources over the very long term, not to run out of cash.

2. Economic sustainability is the capacity of an organization to endure or continue. Sustainable enterprises are able to maintain themselves. They do not exhaust the financial resources they require.

3. Economic sustainability considers alternative ways to generate the same effect. If one approach generates something by consuming more resources than another approach, it would be best to abandon the inefficient approach. In evaluating production efficiency, sustainable organizations also consider the risk associated with the process.

4. Sustainable enterprises consider total long-term effects rather than just short-term results or partial gains. Enterprises that consider long-term viability are more likely to endure for the long term.

Silva handed the chalk back to Korb, saying, "Organizations that are economically sustainable create economic value by generating economic benefits that exceed economic costs."

Silence embraced the Nature Lodge as Korb and the six campers considered the relevance of these principles of sustainability across a vast swath of society. Each member of the small group serenely absorbed this profound summer camp truth and insight into world affairs, until Everett lifted his face to the heavens and split the tranquility with a hearty bellow: "Cancerous corn dogs, dudes, it's lunchtime!"

CONCEPT

This chapter introduces *economic value creation* as the motivating principle of finance. As Silva observed, the notion of economic value creation shares many principles with sustainability. The outcome of any decision should be the creation of economic value—where value is defined as decisions where the expected long-term economic gains created exceed the expected long-term economic costs of the resources consumed. This principle entails a number of key attributes:

- The economic gains and costs include all the incremental organizational economic value effects that are impacted by the decision. If the enterprise is made better or worse off in any way by a decision, the economic value of that effect should be included in the calculation of economic value.
- The economic gains and costs are measured in expectation. That means that while one might not know specifically how a decision is going to affect the organization, one includes the *expected* economic value of that effect. Sometimes people mistakenly think that economic value is only measured as near-term financial effects, but the expected financial effects should be measured over the very long term. Economic value creation is *not* a measure of short-term impact.
- The economic cost of using a resource is measured in terms of the loss of the opportunity to use it in another way. In chapter 4, this way of valuing things will be called an *opportunity cost*.
- Economic value creation ensures that the organization is economically sustainable.
- Decisions based on economic value creation safeguard that decision-makers improve society by creating rather than destroying economic wealth for society. While surprising stuff might happen along the way, value creation requires that the decision be expected to make society better off economically.

TERMINOLOGY

Economic value. When making a business decision, economic value is the difference between the value of the long-term gains created and the value of the long-term resources consumed. Economic value is created when the expected long-term economic gains created by a decision exceed the expected long-term economic costs of the resources consumed by that decision. Economic value captures the economic gains accrued to owners by any decision.

THE FIRST AID CARE CENTERS

Brian Huff wanted to do good in the world. With a nature and comportment that made him highly accident prone, Huff had spent a substantial portion of his life in emergency departments and urgent-care facilities. Now, 20 years after his days at Camp Big Fish, at the age of 33, Huff's experience with acute health care had inspired a business concept he called First Aid Care Centers. His plan entailed the broad placement of very small offices in which patients would receive quick treatment, at low cost, for acute physical ailments. Each center would be staffed by just two people: a clerk to handle the flow of patients and clerical work and a skilled technician to handle patient testing and treatment. With the assistance of the technician, each patient would be evaluated by an off-site physician connected to the center electronically. Improvements in remote health technology made online evaluation and diagnosis substantially more efficient, and physicians could cover many small First Aid Care Centers at the same time. Huff predicted that wait times at his centers could be cut by over 50% compared to existing urgent-care facilities; he thought lowering wait times for acute health care had the potential to do a lot of good in the world.

Huff didn't care if the centers operated as part of a for-profit organization or a tax-exempt not-for-profit. His goal was to do good. Huff had a sizable nest egg of USD5 million that he anticipated would be enough to start up a constellation of centers in his home town.

But there were other demands on his resources. One Friday evening, he found himself at a fundraising dinner that his old camp buddy Aimee Meunier had organized to support the Nature Lodge at Camp Big Fish. Sitting between Soap (Chantelle Hardy) and Swamp (Rich Everett) at the dinner, Huff talked through his concept for the First Aid Care Centers.

"Sounds interesting," offered Everett, who now worked as an engineer at an energy company that made turbines for offshore wind farms. "What are you hoping to accomplish with this venture?"

Huff looked up from his half-eaten vegetable pesto lasagna and considered how to respond. "It may seem cheesy, but I'm actually hoping to do some good. I've been fortunate in my career, and I want to use the proceeds of my good fortune to help people. I think improving the efficiency of health care delivery is a real need in society, and I'm hoping my centers make impact."

"Good for you, my friend," responded Everett respectfully. "There's a lot of need out there in the world, and I'm glad that you feel the call. You don't want to squander the opportunities that come your way."

"Yes. Nice work, Huff," added Hardy, who now ran a nonprofit that combated food insecurity in rural communities. "I assume you've run some numbers on this initiative. What do the expected cash flows look like? Do you expect the inflows of cash for the centers to exceed the outflows?"

Huff gave a brief overview of the market research he had conducted and explained how it had helped him build a financial model for the project. Opening a file on his tablet, he confessed that the cash inflows he expected to bring in were likely to be below the projected cash outflows he expected to pay out.

The expected cash shortfall, due to cash exiting the business faster that it was entering, was a cause of concern for Everett. "That's good to know. Do you expect that shortfall in cash to be temporary?" he asked.

"No, if I'm honest, I expect the cash shortfall to get larger as other providers respond to the inroads my centers are hopefully making on the competition," Huff acknowledged.

"It looks like you've done great research. Well done," Hardy congratulated him. "But if I were anticipating cash losses like that, even if I really believed in the cause, I'd go back and rethink the rollout of the centers."

"You're being a stickler, Soap," Everett cut in. "What does it matter if the enterprise loses money? It's First Aid's money, and he can always make up for the shortfall by hosting fundraisers like this dinner, can't he?"

"Sure, it is his money," Hardy replied. "But just because you're running a nonprofit doesn't mean you don't care about profitability. I live in the world of charitable organizations, and believe me, donors care about organization sustainability. Few donors want to invest in a building that's on fire, no matter how much good it is doing. They want to know that the organization has staying power—that it has a business model that is sustainable. They don't want to put their hard-earned money in a short-term flameout. No, they want to know that the management team has a plan for their capital to do long-term good. You've built yourself a nice pile of cash, Brian. I think you owe it to yourself to build a sustainable model for accomplishing what you believe in, so that it will last over the long term."

"Thanks, Chantelle," said Huff. "I do appreciate you looking out for my long-term best interests. Have you been in contact with Doctor recently? Your whole sustainability talk reminded me of what she said that one time back at Big Fish!"

"Sadly, it has been a while since Doctor and I talked, but yes, that talk of hers stuck with me. It has been a bedrock of how I've built my career," Hardy said. "Her principles are at the heart of the concept of economic value creation. Economic value represents the net economic benefits associated with an economic decision. If the expected economic benefits of a decision exceed the expected costs, then the decision is said to create economic value. If the expected economic benefits of a decision are outweighed by the expected costs, then the decision is said to destroy economic value. Economic value is a measure of how much better society is economically because of the decision made. Economic value measures the net increase in economic resources of any sort. And economic value creation is strongly tied to the economic sustainability of an organization."

"Okay, Soap. I get that economic value creation is important for any organization," admitted Everett. "But what is Huff supposed to do, walk away from his dream?"

"No, he doesn't need to walk away from it, but he should think harder about his financial model."

"Makes sense," Huff acknowledged with a smile. "I have noticed that there are significant cash outflows associated with acquiring and maintaining the imaging equipment in each of the centers. I wonder if there is a different model where I could consolidate imaging into a couple of special centers—that might improve the cost efficiency of the portfolio."

"Bravo!" Hardy cheered. "That's exactly the kind of thinking that will help you successfully build out your network of centers and really improve the delivery of medicine. I'll bet you could benefit from a long chat with Esperta. She actually is a doctor now, you know. I know she'd be interested in your concept and would have some good ideas."

"Thank you both for talking me through this dream of mine," Huff said. "I really need to think through the sustainability implications."

"My pleasure," said Everett, who had long since finished his plate of lasagna and had just noticed the team of servers coming out with trays of small plates. He suddenly stood, lifted his face to the heavens, and interrupted every conversation in the place with a hearty bellow: "Cancerous corn dogs, dudes, it's dessert time!"

CONCEPT WRAP-UP

Finance people care about how wealth is allocated. They are enthusiastic about decisions that create economic value and they are opposed to decisions that destroy economic value. The notion of economic value creation is at the center of the financial decision-making paradigm.

Economic value measures the difference between a project's expected gains and expected losses. Finance people go to great lengths to estimate and value the associated expected gains and losses of any decision. In fact, a lot of what goes into finance is this estimation process, which includes scrutinizing the specific gains and costs of any activity and coming up with ways to value those effects. Because economic value is so central to finance, this book will spend a lot of time focusing on understanding, measuring, and anticipating it.

REVIEW QUESTIONS

Question 1.   A well-respected report defines sustainability as "meeting the needs of the present without compromising the ability of future generations to meet their own needs."[8] How does this definition of sustainability help define the focus in finance on economic value creation?

Question 2.   Why is economic value creation such a good decision metric for finance people?

---

[8] *Our Common Future* (Oxford University Press, 1987), published by the United Nations in recognition of the work of Gro Harlem Brundtland, Chair of the World Commission on Environment and Development.

SECTION II
PERFORMANCE BENCHMARKS

Society has lots of *benchmarks*, meaning signals that discriminate good performance from bad performance. For example, a relevant benchmark for students is the performance metric that separates those students who pass a class from those who do not. A student whose performance is above the benchmark receives good grades and one whose performance is below it does not. A relevant benchmark for farmers is the quality metric that discriminates a crop that is okay to sell from one that is not. A relevant benchmark for building contractors is the standard that determines safe and satisfactory building quality. A relevant benchmark for air traffic controllers is the weather-risk metrics that define safe conditions for a plane to land and take off. In all these cases, the benchmark provides the performance standard.

Finance people also think a lot about benchmarks. A particularly important benchmark in finance is the performance metric that discriminates good investments from bad ones. Finance people tend to care a lot about benchmarks because they put so much money into investments and recognize how critical it is to discriminate the good from the bad. This whole section is about understanding benchmarks in finance. To do this, we'll consider the following questions:

What metrics do finance people use to discriminate between investments and activities that create economic value from those that destroy value?

Why do finance people think so much about investment risk? How do they measure risk in performance outcomes?

How and why do finance people adjust their benchmark performance metrics to account for the various levels of risk?

Before we begin this section, it's important to keep a couple things in mind. First, when finance people consider an investment opportunity, they don't tend to look at it in isolation. Instead, they evaluate it in comparison to the potential outcomes they can get from alternative investments. These performance benchmark rates are based on prevailing capital market rates—what investors can expect to get if they put their money in investment opportunities that exist today in the market. For example, suppose you were considering an investment in Roy's Wonder Boots—the combat boots that feel like bedroom slippers. In evaluating the investment, you would want to consider what you could earn if you invested the same money in a reasonable alternative investment, such as a portfolio of shoe company stocks. This comparison adds rigor to the evaluation: it encourages you to think like an investor by considering what is called the *opportunity cost* of the investment. This concept was introduced in chapter 3, with the exploration of economic value creation, and will be furthered in chapter 4, with the consideration of alternative investment opportunities called the *opportunity cost of capital*. The notion of opportunity cost of capital is also the basis of chapter 5, in which we learn about how investors include inflation rates (declines in the purchasing power of money) in their benchmarks. They do this because they need to be compensated for the opportunity cost of money inflation when considering investment opportunities.

Second, finance people think a lot about ways to understand the uncertainty, or *risk*, related to their investment outcomes. It's important to think about risk because investments are usually fairly uncertain—or risky—and a lot of money rides on this risk. Chapters 6 and 7 introduce foundational concepts related to risk and how they relate to establishing

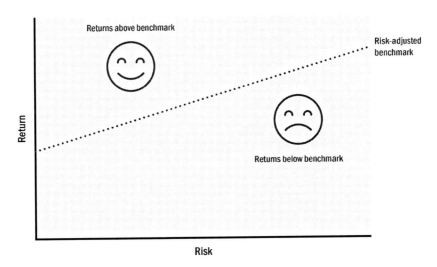

FIGURE II.1. Risk-return graph.

Source: Unless otherwise noted, all figures and tables created by author.

benchmarks. The framework for this section is the ubiquitous "risk-and-return" graph that identifies the appropriate tradeoff between investment risk level and the return required to compensate for the risk. The graph in **Figure II.1** shows the theoretical dotted line that represents the risk-adjusted benchmark. This risk-adjusted benchmark line identifies the level of return that is satisfactory for the relevant level of risk. If investments have high risk, then the benchmark return is high, as investors require a high expected return. If investments have low risk, then the benchmark return is low, as investors require only a low return. The risk-adjusted benchmark is the bright line that distinguishes good investments from bad ones. Investments above the line are deemed "good" because their expected return exceeds the benchmark return. Investments below the line are deemed "bad" because their expected return falls below the benchmark return.

Figure II.1 provides the basis for establishing economic value creation. Investments expected to earn returns above the dotted line are said to create value because their returns exceed the risk-adjusted benchmark. This region is identified with a smiley face. Investments expected to earn returns below the dotted line are said to destroy value because their returns fail to meet the risk-adjusted benchmark. This region is identified with a frowny face. The risk-adjusted benchmark discriminates between good expected performance and bad expected performance. Since this benchmark is so important to financial decision-making, a lot of time is spent thinking about and estimating the risk-adjusted benchmark (the dotted line). It is a pursuit that is central to thinking like a finance person.

4

Opportunity Cost of Capital and Wait Times at the DMV

THE LINE AT THE DMV

Despite the fact that there were 200 people seated throughout the large room, everything was quiet and subdued. At the front of the room were 10 desks, 2 of which were occupied by clerks of the local Department of Motor Vehicles (DMV) office, who processed all the automobile registration, licensing, and titling needs of local citizens.

Fifteen-year-old Russell Rozbic looked down at his phone. "Wow, Mom. It's 2:15! I've totally missed my econ class. I think I'll probably miss chemistry too and not have to go back to school," he said, not so softly, to his mother, Zuzanna Rozbic, who was seated next to him. The pair was waiting to be called to one of the front desks, where the clerk would set Russell up with a written driving test. If Russell passed, he would receive a learner's permit allowing him to practice driving with an adult. The wait was approaching the two-hour mark.

"Let's not worry about that yet, Russy," Ms. Rozbic replied with determination. "I'm hoping you'll be called next."

"I don't know, ma'am," said a gruff voice nearby. "Maybe we should all worry about it." The two turned to see a well-dressed man who was working on a laptop computer in the row behind them. "I don't think Russell's going to make his chemistry class. I'm still waiting and I've been here since 11:00!"

"Sorry to hear that," offered Ms. Rozbic, before introducing herself and her son to their DMV neighbor.

"Very nice to meet you," the man replied. "I'm Rashid. You know what's wrong with this place?"

"Endless waiting?" suggested Russell.

"Yes, of course, endless waiting," Rashid responded. "But you know, I believe the heart of the problem is a lack of proper understanding of the concept of opportunity cost."

"Opportunity cost?" echoed Russell. "Hey, I think that's on my econ test next week!"

"Well, good. What do you think is the opportunity cost of not having more DMV clerks?"

"I don't know. The cost of their salary?" offered Russell. "Maybe USD20 per hour?"

"Nice thinking, Russell," acknowledged Rashid. "The opportunity cost is the value of the next-best alternative that is given up by making a specific decision. So, the cost to the DMV of hiring another clerk is the cost of their salary. But defining the opportunity cost in that way ignores the opportunity cost to the community. The opportunity cost to the community is the value of the time spent by all the people in this room, time that would be freed up if there were more clerks. Ignoring the full opportunity cost of choosing to staff the DMV with just two clerks is what leads to this mess. What do you say we make use of our time here and figure out the opportunity cost to the community, huh?"

"That's okay. I think I'd rather sit here and zone out while I study for my driving test," answered Russell.

"Russell!" Ms. Rozbic exclaimed. "Where are your manners? How about we politely go along with this kind man's line of inquiry?"

"Thank you, ma'am," answered Rashid. "Now, look around the room. We have all sorts of people here. Students like you, Russell. Parents like you, Ms. Rozbic, missing work to sit and wait. Other working people like me, trying to make the most of the terrible Wi-Fi to get my work done. What would you guess is the average value of an hour of each of these people's time?"

"I'd guess USD40," Ms. Rozbic said.

"Good, that seems reasonable to me too," Rashid said. "So let's work the math. What's USD40 times the 200 people in this room?"

"That makes USD8,000," replied Russell so quickly that it brought a smile to his mother's face.

"Eight thousand dollars! Do you see the injustice, Russell?" replied Rashid in a voice so loud that everyone in the room turned to him. "Are you telling me that the DMV, by not hiring a few more clerks, is extracting USD8,000 per hour from our community? How does our government justify that? How does the government let this go on when it doesn't make a shred of economic sense?"

"I think the government is simply ignoring the opportunity cost of all our time," responded Russell with a tone of indignation his mother had never heard before.

"Darn right!" Rashid encouraged. "If the government took the time to consider the USD8,000-per-hour opportunity cost of our time, it would rethink its policy of saving USD20 per hour for another DMV clerk."

"I wish I made USD20 an hour," offered one of the DMV clerks. "Neither of us makes more than USD18!"

"I think I'm going to write my state delegate," expressed Russell with a tone that presaged a future in activist politics.

"You don't have to, Russell," responded a middle-aged woman who was standing at the side of the room waiting to get new plates for her SUV. "I am the state delegate. My name is Nita Patel."

The crowd quieted. All eyes turned toward Patel—all except Russell's, who was writing something in his school notebook. Once he was finished, he walked over to her and held up the notebook for all to see. The phrase he had written on it was "DMV Opportunity Cost Bill."

Russell announced, "I'd like to propose that you put forth the DMV Opportunity Cost Bill—a bill designed to transform our state's DMV staffing by recognizing the opportunity cost of the time for all the citizens who spend far too long waiting at the DMV."

"I'd be honored to introduce this bill in the next session," Patel said graciously.

Everyone cheered the news. Russell posed for several photos with Rashid, Patel, and some of the most popular people in his school, who were also waiting to take their driving tests and now thought Russell was cool. The feeling in the room was significantly more hopeful, at least until the two DMV clerks announced their shifts were finishing in 15 minutes and only one person was coming to replace the two of them.

CONCEPT

Opportunity cost is an important concept in economics and finance. The opportunity cost is the value of what is given up when one alternative, such as a particular investment, is chosen over other alternatives. The opportunity cost is the benchmark that helps a person figure out whether they've made a good decision.

For example, consider the claim that Maria Diaz is the best fisher in all of Spain, based on her ability to deliver mackerel at a price of EUR8 per kilogram—a price far below what other Spanish fishers are able to offer. In fishing markets, fishing conferences, and at local drinking establishments, Maria brags that her low prices are due to her uncanny ability to identify and exploit the most productive fishing beds. All the attention she has received has made her the pride of the Diaz family.

However, if you quietly asked her sister Angelica, you would hear a different story. Angelica would say that Maria's low prices are due not to her fishing abilities but rather to a generous grandfather and an ignorance of the principle of opportunity cost. Angelica would reveal that Maria has free access to all her grandfather's fishing equipment and boat. Because her grandfather doesn't charge Maria to use his equipment, she has a distinct advantage over other fishers, who need to maintain higher prices to cover the cost of their equipment. If pushed, Angelica would estimate that the opportunity cost of the equipment is equal to the price at which the equipment could be rented out, which Angelica estimates would be about EUR7 per kilogram of mackerel caught. By allowing Maria to take the fishing boat out, the family is forgoing the opportunity to rent it to another fisher, or to sell it and make money on the proceeds. This forgone amount is the opportunity cost. Even though Maria doesn't pay anything to use the boat and equipment, she should properly add in the extra EUR7, because the family is missing out on the EUR7 by letting her take the boat out for free. In considering this opportunity cost, Maria would do better to price her catch at EUR15 per kilogram (her normal price of EUR8 plus the opportunity cost of EUR7). As Angelica recognizes, this EUR15 price happens to be EUR3 above the going market rate for mackerel. While she wouldn't ever say it, Angelica knows her sister's fishing isn't anything to brag about.

Or consider Theodore Husker, the man who turned half of his Nebraska corn farm into the world's largest Frisbee field. When asked why, Husker said, "I was tired of corn farming, so I went down to half production two years ago. Since half of my field was just sitting there doing nothing, the kids and I decided to play a lot of Frisbee—140 acres' worth."

Husker's neighbors figure he hasn't thought through the opportunity cost of the Frisbee field. The neighbors say they'd be willing to buy the land, or at least rent it for farming, at USD200 an acre. "We figure the Huskers must like their Frisbee," say the neighbors. "'Cause it is costing them USD28,000 a year." When asked, one neighbor explained his USD28,000 estimate as the rental income Husker is forgoing by not claiming the USD200 per acre for his 140 acres.

Opportunity cost is a powerful tool for decision-making because it helps people make sensible decisions. Since finance people are concerned about allocating capital, the opportunity cost measure they most frequently use is the *opportunity cost of capital*. In the Maria Diaz example, the opportunity cost of capital is reflected in the value the Diaz family has invested in the fishing equipment and boat. In the Theodore Husker example, the opportunity cost of capital is reflected in the value Husker has invested in the farmland. The opportunity cost of capital recognizes that Husker's investment in that 140 acres of land has a productive value of USD28,000 per year. In this chapter, we'll explore additional intuition around and implications of the concept of opportunity cost of capital.

TERMINOLOGY

Required return. When making investment decisions, investors weigh the expected return on investment (ROI) with the risk associated with the investment. The required return is the expected ROI that compensates the investor for the risk they are undertaking. The higher the risk, the higher the required return. Because of the importance of this concept in investment decision-making, there are many terms that finance people use for the required return. These synonyms include the *opportunity cost of capital*, the *cost of capital*, the *hurdle rate*, and the *discount rate*. All these terms refer to the benchmark rate that distinguishes returns on investment that are good (above the benchmark) from those that are bad (below the benchmark).

PROPELLERS TURNING AT CCAW

A warm breeze greeted Mihir Hava as he left a small office building in western India on his way to lunch. Hava worked as a research analyst at CCAW, a medium-sized industrial company that specialized in manufacturing propellers for the shipping industry. Financial performance had been mediocre, and several prominent investors in CCAW were having a fit.

The managing director, Parth Patavaar, had been stoic in his defense of company performance to investors last week. "Shipping is a difficult business. Low financial returns are the grim reality of the industry, and we can't be expected to make mango juice from rice. The fact is we're still making a positive profit, which is better than most of our peers."

With a board meeting coming up the next week, Hava had been charged with crafting a presentation that described the company's most recent financial performance in a way that would resonate with the investor base. Needing some fresh perspective, he invited his friend, Nita Patel, to join him for lunch at a local restaurant.

"Why so gloomy?" asked Patel as Hava sat down at the table.

"Sorry," Hava said. "I said I needed to talk, but I didn't realize it showed so prominently on my face."

"Is Patavaar giving you a hard time?"

"No, not at all. It's not Patavaar. It's our investors. We've got a board meeting next week and I've got to justify our performance."

"Let me guess—they think the returns in shipping are lousy," predicted Patel.

"Yes, that's exactly it," replied Hava. "I mean, we're a shipping supplier, so what are we supposed to do? It's a tough, competitive business. We do good work, and I believe our cost structure is as efficient as anyone's. There's just not a lot of money in shipping these days. The investors don't seem to appreciate how hard we are working."

"So, why do you think your investors are frustrated?"

"I don't know," Hava said. "None of us do! I think it is time they accept reality."

The two paused the conversation while they gave their food orders to the waiter. Then Patel said, "Maybe it would help to consider it from their perspective. Investors are about investing."

"Yeah, that's helpful!" Hava said with a sardonic smile.

"Just wait," Patel said. "Investing is about putting up money or capital, and anticipating a return on that capital. So what should a good investor do when that return ends up being poor?"

"Accept the sad reality that it was a bad investment?"

"Maybe, but remember that the investor isn't locked into the investment. They can always sell out. An investor always has an alternative opportunity to invest in something else. If an investor can earn 10% investing in something else, why would she keep her capital deployed in a business that earns only 5%?"

"I don't know."

"Exactly," Patel said. "It's nothing personal, but managers need to appreciate that investors always have alternative opportunities. They can shift their capital to something else. That's why it is important for managers to always appreciate the reality of capital flight. Investors can't just be ignored once they've invested. Business managers need to appreciate the importance of beating alternative return benchmarks. If they can't justify keeping the capital invested in their business, it is only reasonable that the capital migrate to the alternative. In practice, this benchmark is called the *opportunity cost of capital*. The opportunity cost of capital is the return investors can get by investing in the next-best alternative."

"So are you telling me that we shouldn't be satisfied if CCAW is simply generating positive profit?" Hava asked.

"Yes, that's right. A positive profit is not the benchmark that CCAW needs to beat. That's not the benchmark investors are thinking about. They surely have other, better investment opportunities that are expected to earn well above just being positive. You need to be hungrier."

"But how can we be hungrier in an industry with poor economics?"

"Well, maybe shipping is not where you belong?" Patel suggested.

Hava frowned. "What?"

"Like, yeah, maybe there are other areas where your business can do better?"

"Where?"

"Remember the old Indian saying, 'You can't change the direction of the wind but you can adjust the sails,'" Patel counseled. "Ever thought about wind energy?"

"No."

"There are excellent returns in wind turbine construction these days. Maybe the investors are right, and CCAW is squandering its resources manufacturing ship propellers. If CCAW pivoted to wind propeller manufacturing, you might make a killing."

"Ah, what a fascinating proposition! I suppose it wouldn't be all that costly to shift to producing an alternative propeller. No wonder the investors are disgruntled. Their money is tied up in shipping when it could be doing something much more profitable."

"You got it. Since investors wisely have the opportunity cost of capital at the front of their minds, business managers need to keep it at the front of their minds too. The cost of capital is the bright line that establishes whether performance is good or bad and keeps investors from squandering their capital."

"Got it. I love the wind idea," Hava said. "Do you mind if I share it with Patavaar?"

"No, not a bit," Patel replied.

"Great. Feel free to eat my meal when it comes. I'm heading back to the office. I've got some work to do, learning about wind turbines. Oh, and thanks for the insight. I keep forgetting how smart you are, Nita. You know, some day you should run for political office or something."

CONCEPT WRAP-UP

Finance people think like investors. Investors appreciate that there is a wealth of alternative investments—and that the cost of any chosen investment is the effect of forgoing its alternative. The concept of opportunity cost encourages the decision-maker to consider the cost of not doing the alternative. The approach helps investors to consider the true cost of decisions.

The concept of opportunity cost is front and center in financial decision-making. A fundamental aspect of financial benchmarks is the opportunity cost of alternative uses of investment capital.

REVIEW QUESTIONS

Question 1.   What is the opportunity cost of the following activities in your life?

a) Going on a trip in a car this weekend.
b) Going on the same trip in a plane this weekend.

    c) Spending the evening watching a movie instead of studying for a test.

    d) Adopting a pet.

    e) Spending a year as a full-time student.

Question 2. Investors have invested INR30 million in Saba Motors.[9] If the opportunity cost of capital is 8% per year, what amount of annual profit do investors need in order to exceed their opportunity cost?

---

[9] INR = Indian rupees.

5

Inflation and Returns at Cackling Hen Collectibles

CACKLING HEN COLLECTIBLES

It was another night of combat at the site of Cackling Hen Collectibles, a warehouse that housed old collectibles for long-horizon investment profit. Jane Yellen, also known as "the Bird," was the owner of this successful collectible trading business that spanned the gamut of popular American collectible toys. Standing in the boss's office and vying for recognition were two eager traders, Andy Burns and Peter Volcker, both claiming to have identified and be holding the better collectible investment. Baby Beans, held by Burns, was a toy doll with a plastic head, a fuzzy, bright-yellow body filled with dry beans, and a yellow hood with lace that looked like it had been sucked on a few too many times. Dizzy Duck, held by Volcker, was a brightly painted metal wind-up toy duck whose head rotated randomly and plunged down as if looking for food. Manufactured in the 1940s, Dizzy Duck was 100% mechanical.

"Dream on, Volcker," sneered Burns. "eBay has Beans trading at 26 bucks. That's money city. No way you're besting me for investment value."

"Not so fast, Burns," answered Volcker. "Duck may be going for just USD20.00 now, but don't forget about his entry price. Duck sold for just USD0.95 back in 1940. Your Beans doll, on the other hand, cost a whopping USD3.49 in 1970. And don't question me on that—she's still wearing the price tag!"

"Cut it out!" interjected Yellen. "Let's take a minute to think."

Burns and Volcker stood, squabbling with each other quietly for several full minutes while Yellen did some calculations.

"Get out of here!" Yellen hollered once her calculations were complete. "Neither of you deserves another minute in this office."

Both Burns and Volcker stood facing her, their faces elongated and their eyes drooping. "Why, Jane, what is wrong with our investment return?" they pleaded, not understanding her complete dismissal.

"I'll sum it up in one word," she offered condescendingly. "Inflation. I never pay for inflation gains."

CONCEPT

Inflation is the tendency for money to be worth less over time. For example, in 2022, the annual currency inflation rates were 3% in Switzerland, 5% in South Korea, 6% in the Philippines, 7% in the United States, 18% in Nigeria, and 95% in Argentina. The 95% rate in Argentina means the buying power of the Argentine peso declined by 95% in 2022; in other words, one Argentine peso at the end of the year bought 95% fewer goods and services than it did at the beginning of 2022. As a consequence of the decline in value of the peso, prices for goods and services in Argentina increased on average by 95%—they effectively doubled. A similar story follows for the other currencies. Prices in Nigeria were up 18% over the year, while prices in the United States were up 7%. In all six countries, positive inflation effects meant that all the currencies declined in their purchasing power.

The effects of inflation are not uncommon. This chapter is about the importance of inflation in evaluating investment returns. The chapter will introduce some technical details, such as how to calculate the compound annual growth rate (CAGR)—a common calculation in finance—and then explain the underlying importance of recognizing the effect of inflation in investment returns and of being compensated for it.

TERMINOLOGY

Inflation rate. Inflation is a general rise of prices for goods and services in the economy. It results from the same amount of money buying less over time—it is a decline in the purchasing power of money. Inflation occurs in an economy when the supply of money grows faster than the demand for goods and services. For example, inflation may result from government efforts to stimulate the economy or employment by giving money to businesses through stimulus checks, tax breaks, or low interest rates. The inflation rate measures the percentage increase in prices, which is the same as the percentage of a currency's reduction in purchasing power. If the inflation rate is 10% over the course of the year, then it takes 10% more money this year to buy the same basket of goods as it did last year. In other words, the value of the currency has declined by 10%. A common measure of inflation in many countries is the Consumer Price Index (CPI). The inflation rate matters to investors as they seek returns that compensate them for declines in purchasing power. By choosing to invest their money, investors are, by definition, deferring their ability to spend that money. In order to convince investors to spend their money later rather than now, it is necessary to compensate them for expected inflation in prices.

    Nominal rates versus **real rates.** Nominal rates include inflation; they tend to be how people think about rates of price or value changes in everyday living. Real rates are adjusted nominal rates that exclude inflation. Inflation is baked into nominal rates but removed from real rates. For example, suppose that over the year, the price of lumber has increased 10%. This rate of 10% is considered a nominal rate because it is the rate of increase that people see in lumber prices. If the general currency inflation rate was 4%, then the real rate of increase for the lumber price was 6% [the 10% nominal rate less the 4% inflation rate]. This real rate of 6% excludes inflation, as it means that the rate of price increase is 6% above the general inflation rate of money. Finance people would say that nominal lumber prices are up 10% and real lumber prices are up 6%. Nominal figures have inflation baked in, while real figures have it removed.

Compound annual growth rate (CAGR). There are two standard ways to average growth rates over multiple periods: the *average annual growth rate* and the *compound annual growth rate* (CAGR—often pronounced *cay-grr*). The CAGR is the annual rate that, when compounded over the relevant number of years, changes the beginning amount to the ending amount. For example, suppose that the price of chocolate is USD10 in Year 1, then grows by 50% to USD15 in Year 2, and then declines by 20% to USD12 in Year 3. The average annual growth rate is calculated by simply taking the average of the two annual growth rates (+50% and −20%), which gives an average annual growth rate of 15%. The *compound* annual growth rate, which we can call R for *return*, is calculated by finding what growth rate would grow USD10 (the start point) to USD12 (the end point) over two years, if compounded for those two years. That amount is calculated by finding the R that makes the following equality true: USD10 $(1 + R)^{2 \text{ years}}$ = USD12. Note that the "two years" value is an exponent, as $(1 + R)$ is raised to the power of 2. When solving this equation for R, we get $(\text{USD}12/\text{USD}10)^{1/2} - 1$, which is equal to 9.5%. This means that if we start with USD10 and grow it for two years at a CAGR of 9.5%, we can expect to have USD12 in two years. See **Figures 5.1** and **5.2** for graphic illustrations. To calculate the CAGR for any series, one divides the ending value by the starting value and then takes that value to the power of 1 over T, which is the same as taking that value to its Tth root, where T is the number of years. In the above example, we found the 9.5% CAGR by finding the square root of 12/10 and then subtracting 1.

CACKLING HEN AND INVESTMENT RETURNS

After seeing tears well up in her traders' eyes, Yellen invited the two to have a seat on her beanbag chair and "get the word from the Bird."

"Let's start with some investment return math, shall we?" Yellen asked.

Both Burns and Volcker looked enthusiastic.

"What do you know about calculating CAGR?"

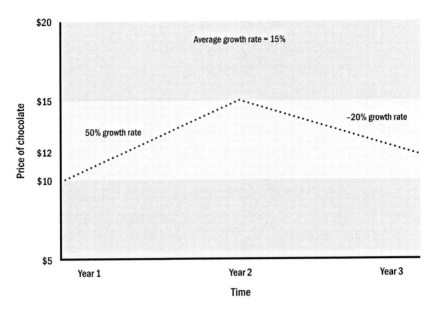

FIGURE 5.1. Average annual growth rate.

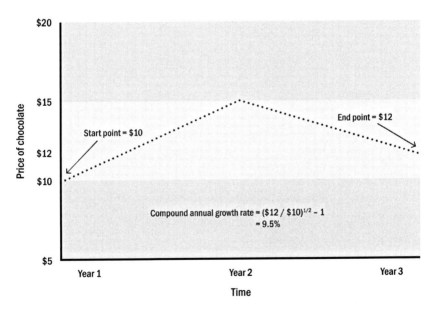

FIGURE 5.2. CAGR.

"Oh, that's easy," Volcker said. "To calculate the CAGR for any series, you divide the ending value by the starting value and then take the Tth root of that ratio, meaning raise the ratio to the power of 1 over T, where T is the number of years."

"Impressive," returned Yellen. Burns began sucking on Baby Beans's lace hoodie. "Let's go through that more slowly, with an example," Yellen continued. "You showed me all the market value histories for your toys. Duck sold in 1940 for USD0.95, but now in 2022 he's worth USD20.00. To understand how the investment has performed, it is helpful to calculate the average annual return. By that, I mean what is the annual compounded return that someone would have earned over the 82 intervening years if they had bought Duck in 1940 and sold him in 2022?"

Burns perked up and grabbed a piece of paper. "So what you are saying, Jane," he offered, "is that the CAGR is one way to calculate the annual return that an investor would have received. To calculate the CAGR for Duck, I have to solve for the return, R, that satisfies this relation." Burns wrote the following on a piece of paper:

$$USD0.95(1+R)^{82} = USD20.00.$$

"Is that right?"

"That is exactly right, Andy," Yellen replied, impressed with the two traders' mathematical skills. "We are trying to figure out what annual rate R would get USD0.95 to become USD20.00 if compounded annually over 82 years. As you said, we need to solve your equation for the rate of return R. Got it?"

"Got it," they both replied.

"To do that algebraically, we divide both sides by USD0.95 and take the 82nd root, to get the following relation. This is the standard formula for calculating CAGR:

$$R = \left(\frac{USD20}{USD0.95} \right)^{1/82} - 1.$$

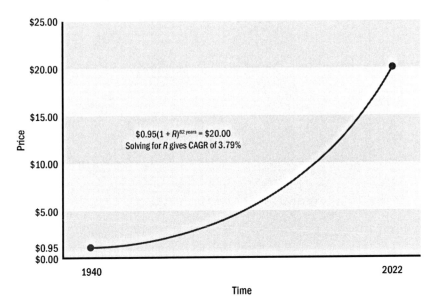

FIGURE 5.3. CAGR for Dizzy Duck's price.

"If you calculate that out," Yellen continued, "you'll find the rate R must be 3.79%. So 3.79% is the annual return that an investor earned by paying USD0.95 in 1940 for Duck and then selling him for USD20 in 2022." Yellen illustrated the concept with a figure that showed how the CAGR gave the rate that would have been needed to grow the investment from USD0.95 to USD20 over 82 years (see **Figure 5.3**).

"Far out," Burns said. "Can I calculate my compound annual return from USD3.49 to USD26.00?"

"Sure, let's see you do it on your own," encouraged Yellen.

Picking up the pen, Burns worked through the math. He first wrote the setup relation:

$$USD3.49(1+R)^{52} = USD26.00.$$

"Where did you get 52?" asked Volcker.

"It's the number of investment years from 1970 to 2022," responded Burns, and then he drew a figure similar to Yellen's that showed the annual

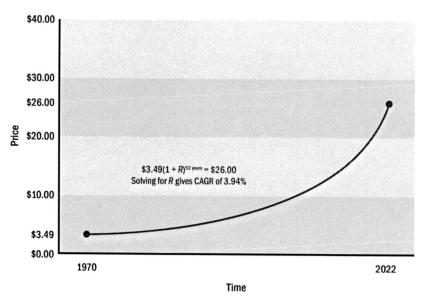

FIGURE 5.4. CAGR for Baby Beans's price.

appreciation rate that grew the price from USD3.49 to USD26.00 in 2020 (see **Figure 5.4**).

"Got it," replied Volcker.

"Let's do it. Let's crank out a CAGR!" shouted Burns. Rearranging the relation for *R*, he got the following:

$$R = \left(\frac{USD26.00}{USD3.49} \right)^{1/52} - 1.$$

"Gadzooks, you are good," Yellen said. "What does that imply *R* must be?"

Tapping on the calculator on his phone, Burns solved for *R* and responded, "3.94%. Beans generated a return of 3.94%. Is the debate over? It seems to be clear that Baby Beans's return of 3.94% was better than Dizzy Duck's return of 3.79%!"

"Not necessarily, Andy—it all depends on how those returns compare to a relevant benchmark," Yellen said. "In this case, the benchmark return I am considering is modest—it's just the inflation rate. I want to be sure that

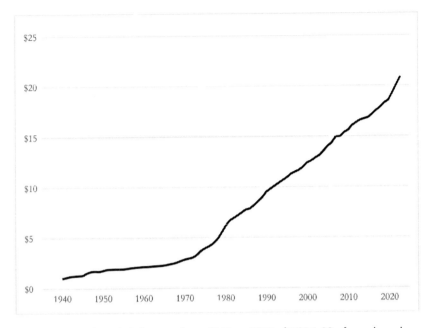

FIGURE 5.5. The US dollar cost from 1940 to 2022 of USD1.00 of goods and services from 1940.

Note: This figure uses a government statistic called the US Consumer Price Index (CPI), reported by the US Bureau of Labor Statistics from 1940 to 2022 using end-of-year values.

Source: Author analysis of CPI Data from US Bureau of Labor Statistics, December 2022, https://bls.gov/cpi/tables/supplemental-files/home.htm (accessed Apr. 14, 2023).

the investment returns I get are at least higher than the rate of inflation. In other words, I want to be sure that the investment is at least compensating me for the rate of inflation. To understand that, let's start with a definition of inflation. Inflation is a general rise of prices for goods and services in the economy. It results from the same amount of money buying less over time—it is a decline in the purchasing power of money. Inflation occurs in an economy when the supply of money grows faster than the demand for goods and services. To give you a sense of the power of inflation, have a look at this." Yellen picked up a graph she had lying on her credenza (see **Figure 5.5**).

"This shows changes in the value of one US dollar, over the period from 1940 to 2022," Yellen said. "If you compare the value of a dollar in 2022 to a dollar in 1940, consumers in 2022 required USD21 to purchase the same amount of goods and services that cost USD1 in 1940. The effect of inflation over the years means that dollars in 2022 buy 95% less than dollars did in 1940. The steepness of the line shows the amount of prevailing inflation. We see the slope steepen in the 1970s as the required amount increases from USD2.84 to USD6.15 from 1970 to 1980. We also see a lot of inflation in the early 2020s as the line gets steep again there. Another way to see this is by looking at the annual inflation rates. The annual inflation rate is the rate by which the currency has declined in value over the course of the year. This graph provides a plot of the annual inflation rate over the same time horizon. Here again, you see the high rates of inflation in the 1970s and early 2020s, but also a short period of high inflation in the 1940s. Inflation in the United States has had a powerful erosive effect on the purchasing power of currency. Because of that effect, investors always want to be compensated for the erosive effects of inflation." (See **Figure 5.6**.)

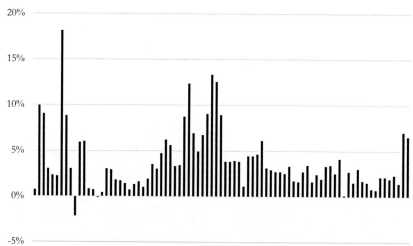

FIGURE 5.6. The annual US dollar inflation rate, 1940–2022.

Note: This figure uses a government statistic called the US CPI, reported by the US Bureau of Labor Statistics from 1940 to 2022 using end-of-year values.

Source: Author analysis of CPI Data from US Bureau of Labor Statistics, December 2022, https://bls.gov/cpi/tables/supplemental-files/home.htm (accessed Apr. 14, 2023).

"As you can tell, inflation is something I care about, as I always want to be sure that my investments returns are compensating me for the declines in purchasing power caused by inflation," continued Yellen. Burns and Volcker seemed to be really interested in her inflation graphs, so she pulled out a table. "Here's another of way of seeing the same thing. Each row in the table contains a starting-point year and each column contains an ending-point year. So for example, the top right cell is USD21.15. This means that what one could buy for USD1.00 in 1940 (the row header) costs USD21.15 in 2022 (the column header). The bottom right cell is USD1.14. This means that what one could buy for USD1.00 in 2020 costs USD1.14 in 2022." (See **Table 5.1**.)

"The US dollar sure has plenty of inflation effects," suggested Volcker, based on his observations from the table.

"I would definitely agree. I'm glad that you are gaining some respect for the important effects of inflation," acknowledged Yellen. "Now that you appreciate the need to consider inflation in your analysis, let me introduce you to two important inflation vocabulary terms: nominal values and real values. A *nominal* value is measured in terms of its current monetary value. Nominal values tend to be the way we think about values in everyday living. A *real* value is measured in terms of buying power for goods and services. Real values are pegged to the value of goods and services, which means they are adjusted to remove the effect of inflation. Real values are calculated by pegging the values to money values at a particular time. Inflation is baked into nominal values but removed from real values. For example, the price quotes of USD3.49 and USD26.00 for Baby Beans are nominal prices— since USD3.49 and USD26.00 are the actual amount of money that was required to purchase Baby Beans at two points in time, 1970 and 2022."

"I think I follow," said Burns. "In a sense, nominal prices are not fully comparable over time because the value of the dollar to buy Baby Beans was different in 1970 than it was in 2022. Because the value of the dollar was different in those two years, the USD3.49 and USD26.00 prices are not really comparable. But real values are comparable over time, because the effect of inflation is stripped out of them."

"Yes, that is exactly right. In order to calculate the real price for Baby Beans in 1970, we would need to increase the USD4.95 purchasing price to remove all the inflationary reduction in a dollar's value over time, since dollars in 1970 bought more goods and services than they did in 2022. If both prices are quoted in 2022 buying power, so-called real values, then they are comparable since the inflation differences in nominal values is removed," explained Yellen.

"Can we do that?" asked Volcker. "Can we put both prices in 2022 dollars?"

"Sure, but you are not going to like it," warned Yellen.

"Huh?"

"Okay, let's do it for your own good," Yellen continued. "From the table (see **Table 5.1**), you can see that the value of a 1970 dollar was USD7.45 in 2022. That means the buying power of the dollar has declined by a factor of 7.45—meaning it takes USD7.45 in 2022 to buy the same thing you could buy for USD1.00 in 1970. To adjust the 1970 nominal price, we'll need to multiply the 1970 nominal price by 7.45, to reflect its greater

TABLE 5.1. The US dollar cost of one dollar of goods and services in a past year (left column) compared to the amount required in a later year.

What one dollar buys in this year . . .	. . . required this many dollars in this year.				
	1990	2000	2010	2020	2022
1940	9.52	12.38	15.61	18.56	21.15
1950	5.38	6.99	8.82	10.48	11.95
1960	4.48	5.82	7.34	8.73	9.95
1970	3.35	4.36	5.50	6.54	7.45
1980	1.55	2.01	2.54	3.02	3.44
1990	1.00	1.30	1.64	1.95	2.22
2000		1.00	1.26	1.50	1.71
2010			1.00	1.19	1.36
2020				1.00	1.14

Note: This table uses a government statistic called the US CPI reported by the US Bureau of Labor Statistics from 1940 to 2022 using end-of-year values.

Source: Author analysis of CPI Data from US Bureau of Labor Statistics, December 2022, https://bls.gov/cpi/tables/supplemental-files/home.htm (accessed Apr. 14, 2023).

buying power in 2022. So, if we multiply USD3.49 by 7.45, we get a curious value: USD26.00. This USD26.00 value is a real value—it's a 1970 price brought to 2022 dollar values."

"What is so curious about USD26.00?" asked Burns.

"It is curious because both the 1970 real price and the 2022 real price are exactly the same: USD26.00," Yellen replied. "That means that the real value of Baby Beans hasn't changed over those 52 years. The amount of buying power one has to give up to buy a Baby Beans today, at USD26.00, is exactly the same as the amount of buying power one had to give up in 1970, at a USD3.49 nominal price and a USD26.00 real price. The total return that an investor in Baby Beans earned by holding her over the 52 years was simply keeping up with inflation. Another way to say that is the 3.94% compound annual return you earned is exactly the same as the compound annual rate of inflation over the same time period. In terms of buying power, an investor would be no better or worse off by having purchased Baby Beans in 1970 and holding her to 2022."

"I guess that return isn't much to brag about," confessed Burns. "Beans didn't really increase in value at all."

"No, I'm afraid you are right. What about Dizzy Duck?" asked Yellen. "Do you think Peter did any better with his 3.79% return, going from USD0.95 to USD20 over 82 years?"

"Well, let's see. Based on the figures in the table (**Table 5.1**), the value of a dollar went from USD1.00 in 1940 to USD21.15 in 2022," began Volcker. "Another way to think about that is this: to buy the same amount of stuff as you could buy in 1940 with USD1.00, you'd need USD21.15 in 2022.

"So, to get a real price for the 1940 price, we multiply the USD0.95 1940 price by an inflation factor of 21.15. Hmm, what does that give me?" Volker started to work the math out on paper.

"Or," Burns added, "an alternative way to compare the investment returns for Ducky is to calculate the compound annual inflation rate and compare that to the 3.79% investment return."

"Yes, both approaches are correct," Yellen said. "You can compare nominal investment returns with the inflation rate or compare the real prices."

"Okay," continued Burns. "I can do that by putting the nominal prices in the CAGR formula over the 82 years from 1940 to 2022." He smiled to himself as he used finance people's pronunciation of the acronym for compound annual growth rate: *cay-grr*.

$$R = \left(\frac{\text{USD21.15}}{\text{USD1.00}} \right)^{1/82} - 1.$$

Burns took a moment to calculate the implied return, and what he found was illuminating. "The rate is 3.79%—a rate we've seen before. Yes, I'm afraid that the 3.37% compound annual inflation rate is again the same rate of return that Ducky earned with his price going from USD0.95 to USD20 over 82 years."

"Yeah, I'm afraid I'm getting the same thing," confessed Volker. "The real value of the USD0.95 purchase price in 2022 dollars is exactly USD20—the same as the nominal value in 2022. It seems that our toys both end up returning the same thing. Neither of them has done anything for investors except keep up with inflation."

"That is correct. Today's buyers seem to value these toys as much as buyers did when they first came out," Yellen confirmed. "The bad news is that I am looking for collectibles that return much more than just keeping up with inflation. So, as I said before, 'Get out of here! Neither of you deserves another minute in my office!'"

CONCEPT WRAP-UP

The inflation rate provides a relevant benchmark return for investors. If an investor is losing 5% of the purchasing power of their money each year, they surely want to be compensated in expected return for that expected loss in value—meaning that an investor would not be happy getting less than a 5% expected return if the expected inflation rate is 5%. Having an appreciation for expected inflation is relevant for setting benchmarks, as investors will always hope to achieve expected returns that at least keep up with inflation (no one will be satisfied with their expected purchasing power declining).

The calculation of annual inflation rates gave us the opportunity to introduce the tool of average annual growth rates and compound annual growth rates. Finance people commonly use these different approaches to characterize annual growth rates. Reflecting growth rates on an annual basis is a norm in finance. Whenever an interest rate or growth rate is expressed, it is assumed to be annual—meaning it reflects the amount of change that is expected to happen over the course of a year.

In the course of examining the effects of inflation, we have used two forms of the compounded return equation. In the first form of the compounded return equation, a past value is transformed into a future value:

$$\text{Value in Year } 0(1+R)^T = \text{value in Year } T.$$

This equation shows that the value of a thing in a past year (i.e., Year 0) increases by compound returns to its value in a future year (i.e., Year T) by being multiplied by the factor $(1 + R)^T$, where R is the periodic compound rate and T is the number of periods. If the past value is the price of Baby Beans in 1970 and the future value is the price of Baby Beans in 2022, then R is the compound annual inflation rate 3.94% and T is the 52 years between 1970 and 2022. We can use this equation to solve for any missing component of the equation, such as the inflation rate, the past price, or the future price.

The second form of the compounded return equation is a rearrangement to solve for the CAGR, R. This form is called the CAGR formula:

$$\text{CAGR} = \left(\frac{\text{value in Year } T}{\text{value in Year } 0} \right)^{1/T} - 1.$$

This formula will help you identify the implied growth rate, inflation rate, or rate of return implied by two values over time. The review questions provide an opportunity to revisit these equations.

REVIEW QUESTIONS

Question 1. The inflation rate over the past year was 5%.

> a) If a pizza was priced at USD10 a year ago, what do you expect it to be priced at this year?
> b) What are the nominal prices and real prices for the pizza? Has the real price of pizza changed?
> c) What is the value of one dollar today in terms of the value of one dollar a year ago?

Question 2. The price for similar new cars has increased from USD20,000 five years ago to USD28,000 this year.

> a) What appears to be the compound annual inflation rate for new cars?
> b) If the annual inflation rate had been half of that, what would be the implied price of new cars this year?

Question 3. Your business pays USD30 per meter for an important raw material. You read that the raw material is supposed to increase in price by 4% per year over the next three years. What do you anticipate the price per meter to be in three years?

Question 4. A stock investment increased from USD30 per share to USD50 per share over the past 10 years. The annual inflation rate was 6% over the same 10 years. What was the nominal return on the stock investment (the return implied by the two nominal prices)? What was the real return on the investment (the return above the inflation rate of 6%)?

6

Return Benchmarks and the Bus Driver Leaderboard

RISK-ADJUSTING BISON COUNTY

"Good morning, Liam!" announced Joe Yellowtrout with his customary cheer as he opened the bus door to allow three-foot-five-inch Liam Jonas to climb on board. "How are you feeling? Last week of kindergarten!"

Yellowtrout was employed as a school bus driver for Bison County Public Schools in southwestern North Dakota. After years of yearning to one day drive a school bus, he had been overjoyed a year before to have been offered a position and presented with his own bright-yellow bus. In his first year, Yellowtrout had demonstrated that he was well suited for the job. The households on his routes gave him rave reviews, his safety record was impeccable, and his bus maintenance log received the highest marks. Still, Yellowtrout wasn't satisfied. The school district maintained a bus driver leaderboard, and he was in the middle of the pack. Using these rankings, the district would soon present its annual Driver of the Year award, and Yellowtrout suspected—as did most drivers in the county—that Donna Zimmerman's name would once again be engraved on the trophy.

The county bus driver leaderboard ranked drivers based on the average time each driver took to complete their elementary school bus route over the year. The assigned bus routes had been designed with the expectation that they should all take about the same time to drive under optimal conditions. Yellowtrout was a naturally competitive person, and his ranking on the bus driver leaderboard frustrated him. His time stood at 49.07 minutes, which put him at 39th place. Zimmerman, on the other hand, stood above all others at 43.57 minutes, 30 seconds ahead of her closest rival. In an effort to find ways to improve his performance, Yellowtrout hired an 11th grader, Rex Raven, to use his pickup truck to track Zimmerman and some of the other competitive bus drivers and learn their trade secrets.

The next week, Raven and Yellowtrout texted each other with updates.

YELLOWTROUT: What's the scoop on Zimmerman?

RAVEN: it's simple, dude. she's got the lowest drive-time uncertainty risk route on the board.

YELLOWTROUT: What do you mean she's got the lowest risk?

RAVEN: c'mon follow me here, dude. drive-time uncertainty risk means things that make the driving time uncertain or variable. drive-time uncertainty risk might be something that makes the drive time shorter, but usually it makes the trip longer. traffic lights are an example of a risk item since you don't know if you'll hit the red light or the green light. the driving time for a route with lots of traffic lights will be highly uncertain since you might get lots of greens or you might get lots of reds. since the student pickup schedule keeps a driver from finishing early, drive-time uncertainty risk tends to make average driving times slower.

YELLOWTROUT: Got it. So you mean drive-time uncertainty risk is route features like the amount of busy traffic streets, number of pickup stops, and of course the number of occasionally late kids?

RAVEN: yeah that's it, dude. zimmerman's got none of that. she's got mostly back roads to neighborhoods where large numbers of kids get on all at the same time. the lady's got no drive-time uncertainty.

YELLOWTROUT: But that's totally unfair. My route is filled with risk! Traffic lights, tons of stops with kids who are sometimes late, roads that keep going under construction. How am I expected to compete head-to-head with her when she's driving a riskless route?

RAVEN: can't be done, dude. the problem is that the county needs to benchmark the drive times in a risk-adjusted way. the transportation board should evaluate driving times with a risk-adjusted benchmark that compares performance to a longer expected time for routes with high drive-time uncertainty risk and to a shorter expected time for routes with low drive-time uncertainty risk. such a system would recognize the higher driving risk on some routes and allow for more drive time in the benchmark.

YELLOWTROUT: I knew this competition was catawampus! Maybe my only path to the Driver of the Year award is to finagle a route swap. I hate to do that 'cause I'd miss the kids on my route.

RAVEN: no worries, dude. i'm already working on changing the county's ranking system. i built a computer model to simulate all the bus routes in the county, including estimates of driving time uncertainty based on the risk profile of each route. using my estimates, i've derived risk-adjusted benchmarks for every bus driver. i compare those benchmarks to their average times to identify which drivers are beating their benchmark time. i've written up a whole proposal for an adjusted performance measurement and submitted it to the transportation board for adoption.

YELLOWTROUT: You did what? That's genius.

RAVEN: dude, i'm just applying simple finance theory.

YELLOWTROUT: No matter. Am I top on the adjusted leader board?

RAVEN: sorry, dude. on a risk-adjusted basis you are ahead of zimmerman, but floyd wanner, who happens to be my driver, is ahead of you by 30 seconds. dude's got a terrible route. dude's got me.

CONCEPT

Risk-adjusted benchmarks are used to discriminate good performance from poor performance. If you beat the benchmark, you are doing well. If you miss the benchmark, you are doing poorly. For finance people, investment returns that exceed their risk-adjusted benchmark create economic value, in that the expected return exceeds the respective risk-adjusted opportunity cost. Conversely, investment returns that are below the risk-adjusted benchmark destroy economic value, because the expected return on the project is less than what is expected for investments of similar risk. **Figure 6.1** provides a graphic illustration. Finance theory recommends benchmarks that are defined as the opportunity cost (or best alternative rate of return) for the funds that investors commit to a business investment. As such, this benchmark reflects the best rate of return that investors expect to achieve on investments of similar risk and horizon. Value-creating investments are above the risk-adjusted benchmark, and value-destroying projects are below the risk-adjusted benchmark.

When a person considers investing in financial securities such as stocks and bonds, they consider both the expected return and the risk of the securities. In **Figure 6.1**, the security with the smiley face is at a point where the expected return investors anticipate is better than is required at

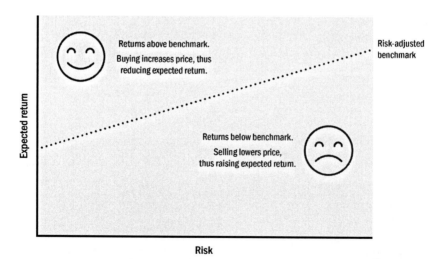

FIGURE 6.1. How risk-adjusted benchmarks discriminate among investment opportunities.

the respective level of risk. As such, this security is attractive to investors, and there will tend to be heavy demand for it. The security with the frowny face is at a point where the expected return investors anticipate is less than is required at the respective level of risk. As such, this security is not attractive to investors, and there will tend to be little demand for it. The heavy market demand for the smiley-face security will tend to push up its market price. At the higher price, the expected returns investors anticipate become lower, because the price of buying into the security is so high. These lower returns push down the placement of the smiley-face security in **Figure 6.1** such that it is closer to the risk-adjusted benchmark line. In an opposite effect, the modest demand for the frowny-face security will tend to push down its market price. At the lower price, the expected returns investors anticipate become higher because the price of buying into the security is so low. These higher returns push up the placement of the frowny-face security such that it is also closer to the risk-adjusted benchmark line. Finance theory suggests that market forces of buying and selling securities will tend to move the prices of securities such that they tend to cluster around the risk-adjusted benchmark line. The investor invests in securities when the expected return compensates for the associated risk. Investors expect the same discipline when business managers make real asset investments in new business projects. With such discipline in mind, new business projects are justified only when the expected returns compensate investors for the associated risk.

The *benchmark rate* or cost of capital (as was discussed in chapter 4) is thus not arbitrarily defined, but rather set by market forces based on prevailing rates of return in financial markets. Since investors consider real asset investments in the context of prevailing returns in financial markets, financial theory demands that managers set hurdle rates that reflect the prevailing cost of capital. It is helpful to note that there are many names for the benchmark rate. These include *hurdle rate, cost of capital,* and *discount rate,* but they all mean the same thing—the risk-adjusted benchmark return that helps discriminates good from bad performance.

TERMINOLOGY

Risk premium. Finance people believe that investments with more risk need to earn greater return than investments with less risk. They call this the *risk-return relation*. The risk premium measures the steepness of that relation. The risk premium is the amount of additional return that is required with greater risk. As an example, stocks have historically earned greater returns than bonds when examined over long periods of time. This additional return makes sense to finance people because of the risk premium. Because stocks are considered riskier than bonds, the additional return associated with investing in stocks is considered an example of a risk premium. Finance people say "the greater the risk, the greater the return" to emphasize the concept of the risk premium. A subtle point to appreciate is that the concept of a risk premium is true only in expectations—before the outcome. Since higher-risk investments are, by definition, riskier, the outcome may be that they may or may not pay out with high returns. This is the risk of holding a high-risk investment—you expect higher returns on the investment, but there is no guarantee. If you want a guaranteed return, you'll have to forgo the high-risk premium associated with high-risk investments and accept a low-risk premium on a low-risk investment. The mechanism for achieving the risk premium is the market price of the investment. Low-risk investments will tend to be attractive to investors, so their prices will be bid up such that their subsequent returns will be relatively low (because investors have had to pay so much). On the other hand, high-risk investments will tend not to be as attractive to investors, so their prices will be bid down such that subsequent returns will be relatively high (because the investors have had to pay so little).

Risk-free rate. The term *risk-free rate* is used to denote the return investors can achieve without bearing risk. In **Figure 6.1**, the risk-free rate is the y-intercept of the risk-adjusted benchmark line—the amount of return investors require for investments whose risk is zero. The risk-free rate is a baseline rate, as other required rates of return should always be at least as high as the risk-free rate (since that is what you get without bearing any risk). Government bond yields or interbank rates are used in practice as examples of risk-free rates. To obtain an estimate of the required rate of return, one commonly adds a relevant risk premium to the prevailing risk-free rate.

ZIMMERMAN SCHOOL VAN SERVICE

With one of the best reputations in Bison County and a shelf full of Driver of the Year awards, Donna Zimmerman sensed it was time to launch her venture. In her downtime, Zimmerman had concocted a plan for a private bus service that she believed would meet important needs of county residents. Her plan was to purchase a dozen 12-passenger vans. With the fleet of vans and some cherry-picked drivers, she intended to offer a high-end school shuttle service that would compete head-on with the county school bus service. The concept was a premium-priced quick and efficient door-to-door shuttle service for children. The service would include comfortable seating, a safe travel environment, intellectually engaging in-van discussions, and optional warm meals en route. The service would operate on a subscription model and target affluent households in the county. Zimmerman was somewhat of a celebrity in Bison County, and she believed her reputation would attract interest in the venture and add credibility to her claims that the service would be safer than the county busing service. To leverage her name, the business would be called Zimmerman School Van Service or "Zim Van."

Zimmerman was determined that the business be financially viable. She had significant wealth aspirations and she did not want to drain her financial reserves to subsidize the school shuttle needs of the county's wealthy. Leveraging her knowledge of the industry and testing most of the assumptions with customer and driver survey methods, she constructed a five-year forecast of financial performance for the venture. The van fleet acquisition would require a USD400,000 capital expenditure. Comparing the forecasted profits to the required investment, she anticipated that the business would generate a return on investment of about 9%.

Not knowing what to make of the 9% figure, she confided in her long-time friend and driving colleague Floyd Wanner and asked for his impressions of the viability of an 9% return. Wanner had previously worked as the CFO at a large Chicago food-processing company and had returned to North Dakota to be near his aging parents. He had been instrumental in the development of Zimmerman's shuttle concept and was happy to help estimate an appropriate benchmark for the anticipated return figure.

"In order to evaluate the 9% expected return figure, you need a benchmark or hurdle rate against which to compare," explained Wanner. "Now, out in the world of corporate finance, there are two types of hurdle rates: the arbitrary ones and the objective ones. Which would you like?"

"I suppose an objective one?" questioned Zimmerman.

"Good answer, Zim!" exclaimed Wanner. "You'd be surprised at how many benchmark rates used out in the world are completely arbitrary figures with no market reality. As an alternative to simply pulling a number out of thin air, an objective rate seeks to establish what return an investor might expect to earn today on securities in financial markets with similar risk."

"Got it. So the idea is to establish what other return I might achieve if I invested the USD400,000 today in the market in a similar investment."

"Yes, that's it. This rate is called the *opportunity cost of capital*. If your USD400,000 can do better in alternative investments, it doesn't make sense economically to pursue the shuttle bus venture, and it would be better to put your money in alternative investments in the market. The most common way to establish such a benchmark is to identify the returns that investors are simultaneously experiencing with publicly traded securities. For example, based on today's market prices, if an investor purchased a 10-year government bond today, she could expect to achieve a return of 4% per year over the life of the bond (i.e., 4% is the yield to maturity on the bond). This 4% rate provides a potential benchmark for your 9% return on Zim Van. Is it helpful to know that your 9% rate is better than what investors can achieve through investing in government debt?"

"Well, I'm glad to see that my venture is expected to do more than twice as well as what you can get investing in government debt," Zimmerman answered thoughtfully. "But something tells me that Treasury bonds aren't the right benchmark. Isn't my shuttle bus venture riskier than government bond investments?"

"Good question," said Wanner. "Good benchmarks should be matched on risk profile. Since investors require greater returns for bearing greater risk, one should expect that the returns associated with riskier investments should require higher returns. What would be a good comparable business to Zim Van?"

"How about, say, Uber? To some extent I think of this venture as the Uber of school busing."

"Excellent example, Donna," responded Wanner. "I agree. I've had a look at the interest rate that both Uber and Lyft are paying for their debt. The rate for both companies is about 6%. So what do you think of 6% as a benchmark for your venture?"

"It feels better. I know that 6% is the rate quoted to me on a loan I was offered for financing part of my fleet."

"Good. The prevailing borrowing rate represents the opportunity cost that you would pay on borrowing the money you are investing. This rate is called the *cost of debt*. Still, it doesn't capture the full extent of the risk in the venture returns. Why not?"

"I'm not sure. Is it because debt financing is only part of the financing?"

"Yes, that's exactly it," responded Wanner. "The risk of your venture returns is divided between two sets of investors—*debt holders* and *equity holders*. The debt holders don't take on much risk, as they require that a certain interest rate be paid. The equity holders take on significantly more risk, as their return is what's left of the profits after the debt holders have been satisfied. An appropriately risk-adjusted hurdle rate should reflect compensation for *all* the risk of the project—both debt holder risk and equity holder risk."

"So what kind of return do Uber's equity holders expect?" Zimmerman asked.

"There are a number of ways to estimate the cost of equity. Using one standard approach, I estimate that Uber equity holders maintain a relatively risky position and have priced Uber shares in order to achieve an expected return of about 12% per year," Wanner replied.

"Okay, so let me figure this out," Zimmerman said. "The Uber debt holders are requiring 6% per year for the risk they are taking on. The Uber equity holders are requiring 12% per year for the greater risk they are taking on. Since Uber is financed with about half debt and half equity, I expect that 9%—the average of 6% and 12%—represents the appropriate opportunity cost of capital."

"That is exactly the right idea. We use the weighted average between the cost of debt and the cost of equity to approximate the opportunity cost of capital for the comparable company. It turns out that the equity weight is a little more than 50%, and the cost of debt is a little less than 6% due to a tax shield, but you are right that 9% is what I also get for the Uber rate. I did the same calculation for Lyft and also got about 9%."[10]

"So I take it that you agree that 9% is a reasonable, objective, market-oriented benchmark against which to evaluate the returns of my van transport venture?" asked Zimmerman.

"Yes, that is correct."

"Okay, so since my venture is expected to earn a return of only 9%, I take it that the market is telling me that after all my effort to launch this shuttle service, I can expect to generate approximately the same return as if I were to simply passively invest in Uber or Lyft?" asked Zimmerman.

---

[10] Government tax policy commonly subsidizes certain actions by reducing business or individual taxes in order to encourage or subsidize certain activities. The value of the reduction in taxes resulting from such tax policy is called a *tax shield*. One type of tax shield is associated with debt financing. In order to stimulate the acquisition of assets, governments commonly allow individuals or businesses to deduct their interest. Because of the tax shield's ability to deduct interest payments from taxable income, it reduces the cost of borrowing. For example, suppose that Jumbo Airlines buys some assets using debt financing and pays USD1 million in interest. Since the interest payments Jumbo makes are tax deductible (meaning that Jumbo is able to reduce its taxable income by the amount of the interest payments), the net cost of the debt financing is less than the interest payment. Instead, the true net cost of the debt is equal to the amount of interest paid less the tax payments that the interest deduction saves the company. The value of the tax savings from interest deductions is the value of the tax shield.

"Yes, that is exactly what the opportunity cost of capital gives you," responded Wanner. "You may get lucky and do better, or you may get unlucky and do worse, but given what you've told me, your expected returns are the same."

"Well, I can tell you one thing. There's no way I'm going through a huge effort just to break even. I think I'll go back and think harder about the assumptions. Do you know anyone who could help generate some good ideas to increase the expected returns on my venture to 12%?"

"You are one smart lady!" encouraged Wanner. "That's exactly the right response. This doesn't mean that your idea is a dud. It simply means that you've got to adjust your business in such a way as to make it more viable. There's this kid who rides my bus who I believe could help you. Here's his number. When you text him, forget about capital letters."

"Got it."

CONCEPT WRAP-UP

Benchmarks discriminate good performance from poor performance, and this chapter advocates for those benchmarks to be risk adjusted. When risk is properly incorporated, investment returns that exceed their risk-adjusted benchmark create economic value, and investment returns that are below the risk-adjusted benchmark destroy economic value (**Figure 6.1**). Finance theory recommends benchmarks that are defined as the opportunity cost (or best alternative rate of return) for the funds that investors commit to a business investment. As such, this benchmark reflects the best rate of return investors expect to achieve on investments of similar risk and horizon. The benchmark rate or cost of capital is set by market forces based on prevailing rates of return in financial markets. Finance people use many names for the benchmark rate, including *hurdle rate, cost of capital, required return,* and *discount rate.*

The following concept extension section provides a couple of additional principles for best practice in estimating benchmark rates.

CONCEPT EXTENSION

In estimating the appropriate benchmark rate for any investment decision, the following finance principles provide valuable guidance:

Principle 1. Good benchmark measures focus on the opportunity cost for investors today.

Suppose a firm is paying 4% on a loan it took out three years ago, but interest rates have since risen such that the business would have to pay 6% if it took out the loan today. What is the appropriate cost of debt for such a firm? The novice analyst would set the cost of debt at 4%, since this is the actual cost the firm is paying on its debt. The experienced analyst recognizes that the cost of debt is not intended to measure the *actual* cost of funds, but rather the opportunity cost of those funds. The same logic is behind how you might feel if you lent a baseball card to your brother when it was worth very little but, now that the player on the card has been named a surprise league MVP, the card is worth a lot. You would want your brother to consider the current opportunity cost of the baseball card, not its value when you lent it to him, because you know its value. The same is true of debt holders who have lent money to the business. Astute managers appreciate the current opportunity cost of the capital they have borrowed from investors. While in the example of the firm paying 4%, it is true that the actual cost of funds is 4%, the benchmark cost of debt more appropriately focuses on the opportunity cost of debt holders today, so the opportunity cost of debt should be the return that debt holders require today. The benchmark that is most useful in decision-making reflects the returns investors require today, not historically. As such, 6% is the appropriate cost of debt in this example because it measures the opportunity cost of those funds rather than the actual cost of debt that the firm has contracted to pay them.

Principle 2. Good benchmark measures incorporate the prevailing risk premium for traded securities of comparable risk.

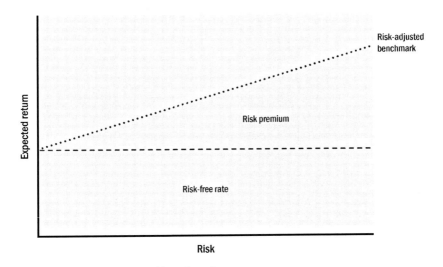

FIGURE 6.2. Risk-adjusted benchmarks.

Note the composition of both the nominal risk-free rate and a risk-adjusted risk premium.

Expected return is composed of two parts: a nominal risk-free interest rate (that sufficiently compensates the investor for expected inflation) and a risk premium (that rewards investors for the investment's riskiness). To obtain an appropriate risk premium for the investment under consideration, analysts commonly look to the risk premium for investments of similar risk. If one observes that the expected return is 9% for firms in a business similar to that of the investment under consideration, a 9% return may provide an appropriate market-based risk-adjusted benchmark to use in evaluating investment returns. This 9% rate includes an appropriate risk-matched risk premium on top of the nominal risk-free rate. In **Figure 6.2**, we can see that the risk-adjusted benchmark is composed of two parts: a risk-free rate that is the same no matter what the risk premium is, and a risk premium that increases as the risk increases. These two parts come together to ensure that the benchmark reflects both the nominal risk-free cost of capital (including the prevailing inflation expectations) and an appropriate risk-matched risk premium.

The cost of capital is commonly estimated using an approach called the *weighted average cost of capital*. This approach uses the prevailing expected return for debt and equity claims on the firm and then takes a weighted average of those components to obtain a weighted average estimate of the cost of capital. In debt markets, credit ratings provide one common estimate of the riskiness of bonds. For equity markets, measures of market comovement are a common measure of risk. The notion of comovement risk (also known as beta risk, market risk, or systematic risk) is considered in the next chapter.

REVIEW QUESTIONS

What is problematic about the following statements regarding hurdle rates? Recall that *hurdle rate* is just another term for benchmark rate or cost of capital.

Question 1.   Mick: "We use 10% as our company hurdle rate. It is simple and clear. It has always worked."

Question 2.   Yua: "We did a ton of analysis five years ago to establish an appropriate cost of capital of 8.4% for our business. At some point we will review it, but for now we are just focusing on building the business."

Question 3.   Miguel: "Business forecasts always have optimistic bias built into them. You'd be a fool to take a forecast at face value. In order to combat that bias, I add 2% to the cost of capital to neutralize the optimism before evaluating any project."

7

Diversification Gains and Profit Risk in Katanga

THE GREATNESS OF AS SOLEIL

Soleil team star Jacques Kasongo began to exit the stadium after a decisive victory in the Congo Premier League football championship match. With a 3–1 victory over rival AC Dilimaso, Congolese football team AS Soleil had just won its third title in as many years.

A news reporter approached Kasongo and asked, "What makes Soleil so good?"

Kasongo had considered this question many times and decided that now was the time to give a thoughtful response. "Soleil is filled with a lot of great football players, but the greatness of this team cannot be pinned on any one player. We are not great because Niemba is such a great striker or because Wawa is such a strong keeper. The reality is that any of us can have a bad day. The best proof of that is me. You all saw how poorly I played in the semifinal. The greatness of Soleil comes from our ability as a team to cover each other. When I had a bad day last week, Ndey happened to have a spectacular day. That day, our team rode on his shoulders despite my performance. Every game is like that, including today. What makes Soleil so good? It is because as a team we overcome the ups and downs that each of us has individually."

"Thank you, Jacques, and congratulations," responded the reporter, followed by audible expressions of gratitude from the other media representatives in the crowd.

The next day, the lead article of a national newspaper covering the team's win had the headline, "The Power of Diversification."

CONCEPT

The more risk investors bear, the more expected return they will require. This risk-return relation is a fundamental concept in finance. Understanding the risk-return relation requires an understanding of how to think about both risk and the associated risk premium.

This chapter introduces an important concept related to risk: some risk matters more than other risk. Consequently, investors should think about some risk differently that they do other risk. Finance people recognize that some risk is easy to eliminate through *diversification*. In Kasongo's words, "What makes Soleil so good? It is because as a team we overcome the ups and downs that each of us has individually." The performance risk of the team is not the same as the performance risk of any individual player. Individual players can have good days and bad days. The team doesn't have to follow the same pattern as long as the ups and downs in performance by one player are offset by the ups and downs in performance of another player. Because of this offsetting effect, the performance risk of the team can be substantially reduced through bundling players together. In an individual sport, the risk reduction of bundling is impossible: the outcome of a singles tennis match is due only to the individual performance of the individual player. Individual sport players face more performance risk than teams because they are unable to rely on their teammates to make up for their poor individual performance due to injury, illness, distraction, or just bad luck.

An important parallel exists in investing. A bundled portfolio of investments has less risk than an investment in a single security or asset. In bundled portfolios, wide swings in individual investment performance are offset by opposing swings in other investments in the portfolio. This effect is called diversification. Because of diversification gains, investors have a strong incentive to bundle investments together in portfolios: this bundling reduces overall risk. Investors who concentrate all their wealth into a single investment face risk that could be eliminated with diversification.

In this chapter, members of the Kasongo family explore different metrics for risk and related considerations for investors. We consider how return correlation affects portfolio volatility, discover the difference between systematic risk and idiosyncratic risk, and learn how diversification reduces idiosyncratic risk. These concepts are at the foundation of *portfolio theory* and the associated risk premium known as the *capital asset pricing model* (CAPM).

TERMINOLOGY

Volatility. Volatility is a measure of risk. It considers the amount of variation in performance outcomes. Statistical measures for volatility include *variance* and *standard deviation*. To calculate the variance of a set of outcomes, one calculates the average of the set and then adds up the squared differences between the outcome and the average and divides by the number of observations less 1. For example, if the goals in two games are the numbers 3 and 7, then the average goal is 5 and the variance in goals is 8. This variance value of 8 is calculated by first finding the variation between each number of goals and the average number of goals, as follows:

Game 1 variation: Difference between outcome of 3 and average of 5 is −2.

Game 2 variation: Difference between outcome of 7 and average of 5 is +2.

Next, we square the values of the two variations to get numbers that are always positive, and add them up. By squaring the −2 and +2, we get a positive measure of variation that we add up to get 8 $[8 = (-2)^2 + (+2)^2]$. Since the number of observations is just 2, dividing by 1 doesn't change the answer. To calculate the standard deviation of a set of outcomes, we calculate the square root of the variance. In the above example, the square root of 8 is 2.83. Thus, a measure of volatility for the number of goals in two games (3 and 7) is variance 8 and standard deviation 2.83. These statistics provide a measure of risk or volatility. If, alternatively, the set of outcomes are 1 and 1, then variance is zero and the standard deviation is zero. This set of numbers has no variance or volatility.

Systematic risk. Systematic risk measures susceptibility to common risk factors. A firm is considered to have high systematic risk if it is highly susceptible to the risk factors that affect other firms. A firm is considered to have low systematic risk if it is not all that susceptible to the risk factors that affect other firms. As an example, firms that are highly affected by bad world outcomes such as military conflicts, pandemics, or energy shortages are considered to have high systematic risk. Firms that are minimally affected by these bad world outcomes are considered to have low systematic risk. Common alternative terms for systematic risk include *market risk, covariance risk,* and *beta risk.* These terms are used interchangeably in finance.

Idiosyncratic risk. Idiosyncratic risk measures the risk that is not associated with common risk factors. Suppose the value of a pharmaceutical firm depends mostly on the outcome of a drug trial. If the trial shows the drug to be effective at treating a certain illness, the firm is worth tons. If the trial shows the drug to not be effective at treating a certain illness, the firm is worth nothing. In that case, the firm has lots of idiosyncratic risk, since the outcome of the firm's drug trial is not likely to be a risk factor for other firms in the economy. Common alternative terms for idiosyncratic risk include *nonmarket risk* and *firm-specific risk.* These terms are used interchangeably in finance.

Capital asset pricing model (CAPM). The CAPM (often pronounced *cap-em*) is a specific equation for the risk premium required by investors. It is a theory for the risk-return relation. This theory says that investors insulate themselves from idiosyncratic risk through their tendency to diversify their investment portfolios. Because of the diversification effect, investors only care about systematic or nondiversifiable risk. The theory uses the term *beta* as a measure of systematic risk: beta measures how the prices of any investment comove with the prices of other investments. According to the CAPM, the fair risk-adjusted return investors should expect of any investment opportunity should be reflected in the following formula:

$$\text{Expected return} = \text{risk-free rate} + \text{beta risk of investment} \\ \times \text{market risk premium.}$$

THE KASONGO BROTHERS' DILEMMA

Following his departure from football, Jacques Kasongo built a sizable business producing and exporting ski sweaters made of Congolese wool. The business allowed his family of six to live comfortably for many years in the Democratic Republic of the Congo's capital city of Kinshasa before he passed the business to his children.

Jacques's sons, Daniel and Julian, ran the ski sweater business for a number of years and then made the professional pivot of their lives when they sold it and invested the proceeds in a new business. Lured by the investment achievements of their two sisters, the brothers purchased separate mining rights in Katanga, in the eastern part of the country. Daniel developed the Boule de Neige cobalt mine, and Julian developed a neighboring copper-mining operation called Ours Polaire. While they owned and operated their mines independently, they shared the dream of developing a viable small-scale artisanal mining operation that was community minded and met family financial needs.

Both brothers had begun to appreciate the volatility of mining profits. While some months brought great gains, others brought large losses, and in others, they just broke even. Business revenue, costs, and output were all highly unpredictable. **Table 7.1** provides a monthly history of the profits for the two mining operations over the past two years of operation. The

TABLE 7.1. Operating profits to date for Boule de Neige and Ours Polaire.

	Year 1		Year 2	
	Boule de Neige	Ours Polaire	Boule de Neige	Ours Polaire
January	2,127	1,337	(980)	(1,236)
February	(1,354)	1,542	(276)	922
March	2,594	(509)	(1,281)	(1,034)
April	1,561	(2,067)	(1,357)	1,099
May	2,909	1,475	(1,016)	1,194
June	(1,780)	614	1,936	(3,757)
July	1,359	(1,915)	(1,184)	605
August	284	1,007	648	3,181
September	(545)	1,833	2,046	1,974
October	620	(1,446)	470	(324)
November	(2,297)	(3,196)	(1,227)	(515)
December	1,416	(38)	1,973	2,301
Total	6,893	(1,364)	(248)	4,411

US dollar was commonly used in Katanga, so business profits were reported in US dollars. The first month of operation (January, Year 1) went well, with both brothers pulling in more than USD1,000. Then in February, Boule de Neige lost over USD1,300 while Ours Polaire brought in more than USD1,500. But fortunes quickly reversed in March, with Boule de Neige up over USD2,500 while Ours Polaire's profits were negative; and Ours Polaire went even more negative in April.

By the end of Year 1, Boule de Neige had made positive profits of nearly USD7,000 and Ours Polaire had lost USD1,364. But in Year 2, Boule de Neige experienced losses and Our Polaire made over USD4,000.

The business volatility bothered both Daniel and Julian and caused them to begin to restrict further investment. Independently, they each increased their hurdle rates (meaning the expected investment return they required to approve investment projects). When they discussed this issue, they agreed that they both felt the need to preserve their capital and were uncomfortable deploying additional resources in such risky ventures. Limiting investment seemed like the right thing to do.

Their sisters, Lilian and Madeleine, thought otherwise. Over a group dinner one evening, the subject of investment risk came up in conversation.

While Daniel and Julian complained about the disconnect between their desires to grow their mines and their inability to stomach the monthly booms and busts in business profits, Lilian interrupted with the question, "Have you thought through the source of your business risk?" Not getting a response, she continued, "Can you go through the main factors that contribute to your business volatility?"

Julian was quick to answer, "Of course. Our mining costs are actually fairly predictable, so our volatility in costs is driven mainly by transportation costs. Our transportation costs change constantly with fuel-price and transportation-supply variation. Our revenue is volatile, with variation in the market price of metal and variation in the richness of the veins we discover. Lastly, there are plenty of other random things that happen. I had a front-end loader break down last week, and Daniel's foreman recently had to move for family reasons. Then of course there is occasional pirating of our shipments. You never really know if a shipment will make it to market. Daniel lost two loads last month, but I got lucky and my shipments all made it."

"Daniel, do you agree with Julian's assessment?" queried Madeleine.

"Yes, that's pretty much it," agreed Daniel.

"Good. We can categorize your business risk into two types: systematic risk and idiosyncratic risk," continued Madeleine.

"Huh?" replied Daniel and Julian in unison.

"Okay, we're trying to understand how much of your risk is common to both mines and how much is independent or unique. We'll go through each source of risk and classify them one by one," answered Lilian. "Let's start with an easy one. Is the monthly variation in the richness of the vein you are working common across the two mines?"

"No," replied Julian. "The richness of our veins is totally independent. Sometimes I am lucky with a rich vein that I'm working and sometimes Daniel is lucky. It just is what it is."

"Good. We'll call vein richness uncertainty an idiosyncratic risk then. *Idiosyncratic* is a fancy word for independent or unique. Let's keep going. How about transportation cost?"

"I think the variation in transportation costs is pretty common," Daniel said. "If the price of transportation is high due to fuel-price effects or driver-supply concerns, it is high for both of us, and vice versa. Transportation cost variation is a macro thing."

"Very good," Madeleine said. "Variation in transportation cost affects both of your mines. So, we'll classify transportation costs as systematic risk, meaning that variation in that factor is common across both your mines. How about the market price of metal?"

"Hmm." Daniel considered this. "That's a tough one because we are selling different metals. Some variation in metal price is common. When the world economy is strong, there is demand for both copper and cobalt, and prices rise. But other variation is more independent, like the effect of some recent rich cobalt discoveries that have independently driven cobalt prices down."

"That's good," offered Madeleine. "We'll put metal price variation as both systematic and idiosyncratic. You said the other factors tend to be random, like breakdowns and pirating. If so, how should we classify those effects?"

"If they are in fact random independent effects, I suppose they must be idiosyncratic, right?" offered Daniel, with some statistical swagger.

"That's right, brother. Mother would be proud," affirmed Lilian. "The good news for both of you is that much of your business risk appears to be idiosyncratic."

"That doesn't sound good to me . . . all this wild, independent, up-and-down unpredictability. What's so good about idiosyncratic risk?" countered Julian.

"What's good about it is that it is easy to get rid of," replied Madeleine with a smile.

"Get rid of it? How? I'd give my three best pickaxes to unload all the idiosyncratic risk I have at Boule de Neige," Daniel said.

"Thank you, Daniel. I could use some good axes," acknowledged Madeleine. "The secret to getting rid of your idiosyncratic risk is simple—diversification. The problem you are both facing is that because you have concentrated all your money into your individual mines, and you each own your own business, you have also concentrated your business risk."

The brothers looked mystified.

"Since I recognize that neither of you are fully following this," Lilian continued, "let me show you a little diversification magic. Let's look back at your erratic profits over the past two years." She worked out some calculations on her phone and produced some additional analysis (see **Table 7.2**). "I've added a couple things. The first thing is the average monthly profit for each mine and each year—I calculate this in the row labeled 'Average.' I've also added another column, called '50-50 Partnership,' on the right for each year. How do I compute this? This 50-50 partnership profit is simply the average monthly profit for the two mines. For example, the USD1,732 profit value in January of Year 1 represents the average of the USD2,127 profit for Boule de Neige and the USD1,337 profit for Ours Polaire. Under the row for 'Average,' I've added a row

TABLE 7.2. Additional analysis of operating profits for Boule de Neige and Ours Polaire.

	Year 1			Year 2		
	Boule de Neige	Ours Polaire	50-50 Partnership	Boule de Neige	Ours Polaire	50-50 Partnership
January	2,127	1,337	1,732	(980)	(1,236)	(1,108)
February	(1,354)	1,542	94	(276)	922	323
March	2,594	(509)	1,043	(1,281)	(1,034)	(1,158)
April	1,561	(2,067)	(253)	(1,357)	1,099	(129)
May	2,909	1,475	2,192	(1,016)	1,194	89
June	(1,780)	614	(583)	1,936	(3,757)	(911)
July	1,359	(1,915)	(278)	(1,184)	605	(290)
August	284	1,007	645	648	3,181	1,915
September	(545)	1,833	644	2,046	1,974	2,010
October	620	(1,446)	(413)	470	(324)	73
November	(2,297)	(3,196)	(2,747)	(1,227)	(515)	(871)
December	1,416	(38)	689	1,973	2,301	2,137
Total	6,893	(1,364)	2,765	(248)	4,411	2,082
Average	574	(114)	230	(21)	368	173
Standard deviation	1,734	1,691	1,271	1,379	1,874	1,217
Correlation	0.10			0.10		

called 'Standard deviation,' which is a measure of total risk. This risk measure tells us how volatile your profits are by measuring how far the monthly profits tend to fall from the monthly average. You can see that Boule de Neige profits were the most volatile in Year 1, with a standard deviation of USD1,734, while Ours Polaire profits were the most volatile in Year 2, with a standard deviation of USD1,874. These values are high relative to your average profits. The statistics confirm what you have been living—you've got a lot of volatility in your businesses."

"But where's the diversification magic?" Julian asked, impatient.

"We're getting there, little brother. Let's suppose you form a partnership with each other to share the profits. In doing so, you are diversifying your investment across two mines rather than one. The monthly payout you'll both receive is the average of the profits of both mines. We can see how this works with my 50-50 column, where I've calculated the average profits each month. So, Julian, walk me through this. How does the partnership turn out?"

"Well, in January of the first year, Daniel had a great month, with a profit of USD2,127, and I had a decent month, with a profit of USD1,337. If we had shared profits, we would each have gotten USD1,732, a good month for both. In February, Daniel had a crummy month with a loss of −USD1,354, while I had another decent month with a profit of USD1,542. In the partnership, my good luck would have offset his bad luck and we would both have broken even, with USD94 each. In March, Daniel did really well and I did poorly, so the partnership would do well, with USD1,043 for each of us."

"You got it."

Daniel quickly followed up with a graph of the three profit outcomes (see **Figure 7.1**). Using the graph, he suggested that the solid "partnership" line was less volatile than either of the single mine lines. "So, what you are proposing," he said, "is that by diversifying our investment, we reduce business risk, because my good months tend to offset my brother's bad months and vice versa. The risk reduction is evident in the lower volatility of the solid 50-50 line."

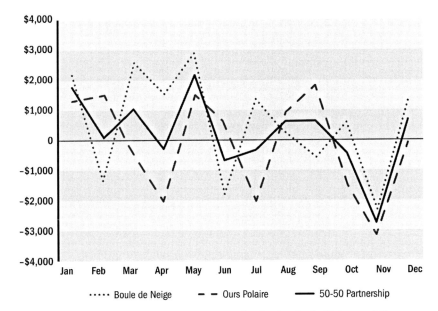

FIGURE 7.1. Graph of Year 1 operating profits for Boule de Neige and Ours Polaire.

"Excellent!" Lilian praised. "You can see the risk-reduction effect in the table with the standard deviation of the partnership. Notice how the 50-50 partnership standard deviation is just USD1,271. The diversification effect has resulted in you both getting the average profit but with substantially less-than-average risk. The diversification magic is the more-than-proportional risk reduction."

"Very impressive!" exclaimed Julian with his customary vigor and back slapping. "It *is* magic. You would think that you would have the average risk with the average returns, but the risk of the 50-50 portfolio is less than the average! It is way less! But help me understand—how does the diversification trick work?"

"To answer your question, Julian, I have a question for you. Is the risk reduction we see in the partnership due to a reduction of systematic risk or idiosyncratic risk?"

"I believe it is the idiosyncratic risk," Julian said. "I notice that we don't get much risk reduction in November. That was a bad month for both

Daniel and me because of the high transportation costs we had to pay. It was a systematic risk event that affected both of us."

"Brilliant!" responded Madeleine. "The strong risk reduction comes from the fact that you both have a large amount of idiosyncratic risk in your business. That means that by diversifying, you are able to eliminate a large amount of that risk by sharing it. With the systematic risk, you don't get the offsetting effect, as you both bear it in the same way. You can get a sense of the amount of systematic risk by looking at the correlation in your returns. Notice the last row I added to your profits (**Table 7.2**), 'Correlation.' The correlation coefficient is a statistic that measures how much correlation there is between the two series—in this case, the series of monthly profits of Boule de Neige and the series of monthly profits of Ours Polaire. A correlation coefficient with a value of 0 means no average correlation, and a correlation coefficient with a value of 1 means proportional correlation—they tend to both go up and down with the same proportions. For both Year 1 and Year 2, the correlation coefficient of your profits was 0.1, which is small, meaning the variation in profits of the two mines aren't meaningfully related to each other."

"That is very helpful. I think I'm beginning to understand what the two of you have done in your own businesses," observed Daniel. "You never really wanted to own a single business. Rather, the two of you, through your investment fund, have bought up small positions in just about every responsibly run business in the country. With small investments in hundreds of businesses, you've reduced your idiosyncratic risk to effectively nothing. All that risk is washed out."

"Yes, now you know our secret," admitted Lilian. "And you should also know that it affects our appetite to invest. Our diversified position eliminates much of the risk in any single investment. So, while investments with high idiosyncratic risk might make you two nervous, Madeleine and I take them on with little concern, because our portfolio of investments works together to reduce risk. Because of the risk reduction, we are more willing to invest our money. While the two of you face considerable idiosyncratic risk, our total risk exposure is substantially less since we have eliminated our idiosyncratic risk through diversification. Because of our diversified position, investments that look poor to you look acceptable to us. Since we are exposed only to the systematic risk, we are willing to accept lower expected returns on investments."

Lilian continued, "As an example, I've done some analysis on a sample of 40 large French stocks. If you pick, at random, any one of those stocks to hold, the standard deviation of your return will be about 28%. But if you combine that stock 50-50 with another random stock, the standard deviation of your 50-50 portfolio return drops to 24%. If you add 8 more random stocks, so that you have 10% invested in 10 of the French stocks, the standard deviation of your portfolio return drops to 19%. And if you simply hold the entire index of 40 stocks, the standard deviation of your portfolio return drops to 17%. As you can see from this graph (see **Figure 7.2**), the more you diversify with additional assets in your portfolio, the lower the total risk of your return becomes."

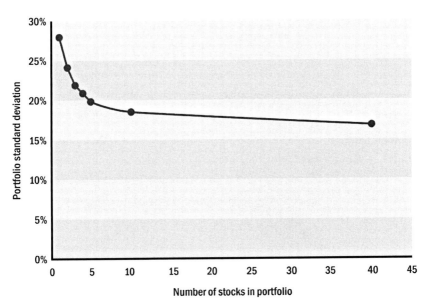

FIGURE 7.2. Portfolio standard deviation of returns for random portfolios of French CAC-40 Stocks (2015–2019).

Data source: Stock return data from Yahoo! Finance.

Madeleine added, "But know that it's not that we don't care about risk, because we do. The difference is that we focus exclusively on systematic risk rather than worrying about total risk (meaning both systematic and idiosyncratic risk). We get nervous about investments where the variation is highly correlated with macro movements. And in those instances, we'll definitely require more return. But idiosyncratic risk? It doesn't bother us."

Daniel filled his sisters' glasses and turned to Julian, saying, "Julian, maybe it is time we stop putting all our eggs in one basket. As father used to say, 'as a team we overcome the ups and downs that each of us have individually.'"

CONCEPT WRAP-UP

This chapter provides a look at how finance people think about risk and illustrates three important principles.

Investment bundling reduces risk. While it might be natural to think about risk in terms of total volatility, some forms of risk or uncertainty matter more to investors than other forms of risk. In particular, the chapter illustrates the power of diversification to reduce idiosyncratic or firm-specific risk. By bundling financial securities or businesses together in portfolios, the investor is able to reduce the total risk of the portfolio, as wide swings in individual investment performance are offset by opposing swings in other investments in the portfolio. This effect is called diversification. Because of diversification gains, investors have a strong incentive to bundle investments together in portfolios. In contrast, investors who concentrate all their wealth into a single investment face more risk than those who are diversified.

Some risk is common and some risk is unique. Diversification gains reduce some, but not all, risk. In the football team context, bundling reduces team performance risk when the risk is individual—Kasongo's performance on the field is unrelated to the other players' performance. But what if just before the match, the flu runs through the team, or word gets out that the team's coach is leaving the team to take another position? Events like these might affect all team players in the same direction. If all players are affected similarly by the event, then bundling will be unable to reduce the team performance risk associated with that event. In finance speak, risk that is common across investments is called *systematic risk* or *market risk*; risk that is independent across investments is called *idiosyncratic risk* (also known as diversifiable risk or nonsystematic risk). Bundling investments together into portfolios reduces idiosyncratic risk, but not systematic risk. Because of the ease with which investors can get rid of idiosyncratic risk, it makes sense for them to be more concerned about systematic than idiosyncratic risk. In finance, systematic risk is expected to matter and justify a risk premium (since investors can't eliminate systematic risk and thus want extra expected return to hold an investment with systematic risk) and idiosyncratic risk is not (since investors can eliminate idiosyncratic risk through diversification and thus don't need to receive extra expected return to hold it).

While systematic risk inherently affects all investments, it affects some investments more than others. Examples of systematic risk events in financial markets include oil price shocks, interest rate shocks, business cycle shocks, and public health shocks. One systematic risk shock could be the unexpected arrival of a deadly communicable disease epidemic. While the epidemic is likely to adversely affect most businesses, it can be expected to affect some businesses more than others. Businesses in travel or public entertainment might be expected to be more affected than businesses in the food or health care sectors, which may be relatively immune to the epidemic or other adverse risk shocks. In finance speak, food and health care businesses have less systematic risk than travel or businesses services because of the lower magnitude of the shock. Because systematic risk shocks create less impact on these businesses, investors in food and health care businesses will generally require less of a risk premium than investors in travel and business services. Savvy investors and managers appreciate that risk assessment is best considered based on an investment's effect within a diversified portfolio, not just its effect in isolation.

TECHNICAL CONCEPT REVIEW

In this chapter, we learned that variance or standard deviation is a common measure of risk. Technically, variance is defined as the average squared individual deviations from the average. This is calculated as taking each of the differences from the average, squaring them, adding them all up, and dividing by the number of observations less one.[11]

$$\text{Variance} = \frac{1}{N-1} \left[\left(x_1 - \overline{x} \right)^2 + \cdots + \left(x_N - \overline{x} \right)^2 \right],$$

where N is the number of observations, $\overline{x}$ is the average of the observations, x_1 is the first observation, and x_N is the last observation. The standard deviation is calculated by taking the square root of the variance. The standard deviation can be interpreted as the average deviation from the average.

But while standard deviation is a reasonable metric for total variation or risk, it overstates the risk to investors who hold portfolios of assets. This is because in portfolios, any risk that is idiosyncratic or independent of the movements of other risky assets can be eliminated through diversification. By adding together different risky assets, any risk that is nonsystematic is washed out, since the random ups of some assets are offset by the random downs of other assets.

Because diversified portfolios have large risk-reduction gains, there is a strong incentive for investors to build large portfolios that collectively eliminate idiosyncratic risk. Because of the ease associated with idiosyncratic risk reduction, according to portfolio theory, investors in equilibrium will not require a risk premium for idiosyncratic risk.

Unlike idiosyncratic risk, systematic risk is the portion of total risk that cannot be eliminated through diversification. This risk is the variation due to systematic factors that affect most risky assets. Because of the difficulty

---

[11] While it may seem that the sum of squared deviations should be divided by N to get the average, statisticians tell us that it is more accurate to use $N - 1$, as there is a redundant observation used in the calculation of standard deviation.

in reducing systematic risk, according to portfolio theory, investors in equilibrium will demand a risk premium for systematic risk only. The CAPM provides a specific equation for the risk premium required by investors that insulate themselves from idiosyncratic risk through their tendency to diversify their investment portfolios. Because of the diversification effect, investors only care about systematic or nondiversifiable risk. The theory uses the term *beta* as a measure of systematic risk: beta measures how the prices of any investment comove with the prices of other investments. According to the CAPM, the fair risk-adjusted return that investors should expect of any investment opportunity should be reflected in the following formula:

$$\text{Expected return} = \text{risk-free rate} + \text{beta risk of investment} \\ \times \text{market risk premium,}$$

where expected return is the required return for the investment, beta is the measure of systematic risk for the investment, and the market risk premium is the risk premium associated with holding a unit of systematic risk. The CAPM makes the bold prediction that the only investment attribute that justifies a risk premium is the measure of systematic risk, or beta. In other words, when an investor considers the expected return associated with any stock, for example, beta captures all the relevant aspects of risk.

REVIEW QUESTIONS

Question 1. In **Table 7.2**, the standard deviation of Year 1 profits is USD1,734 for Boule de Neige and USD1,691 for Ours Polaire. Why is the standard deviation of the profits in the 50-50 partnership not the average of the two, or USD1,713, rather than the standard deviation of USD1,271 reported for the portfolio? How can the standard deviation of the portfolio be less than the standard deviation of either Boule de Neige and Ours Polaire?

Question 2. Suppose that the operating returns on investment for the first three months of Year 3 are as shown in **Table 7.3**.

TABLE 7.3. Operating return on investment (monthly profit/amount of investment).

	Boule de Neige	Ours Polaire
January	1%	3%
February	−1%	1%
March	3%	−1%

a) If the two brothers form a 50-50 partnership on the two mines, what is the monthly return on the partnership for each of the three months (note that the partnership return is the average return for the two mines)?

b) Over the first three months, what is the average monthly return for Boule de Neige, Ours Polaire, and the 50-50 partnership?

c) Over the first three months, what is the standard deviation of monthly returns for Boule de Neige, Ours Polaire, and the 50-50 partnership?

d) Explain the result. How can the 50-50 partnership maintain the same return as either mine, but have a standard deviation that is so much lower than that of either mine?

Question 3. Ski Afrique

A hot, steamy rain poured out of the Congolese sky, hitting the metal roof of the Ski Afrique warehouse. Sisters Lilian and Madeleine Kasongo were helping their father Jacques box up an order for 500 ski sweaters for shipment to Lyon, France. Ski Afrique was a family business in Kinshasa that employed nearly 1,000 workers over an exclusively Congolese integrated supply chain, including every step from sheep farming to sweater production and marketing. While the Democratic Republic of the Congo (DRC) was considered perhaps the world's richest country in terms of natural resources, wool goods production was not common, and in fact Ski Afrique was the only producer in the entire country.

Despite its success, the unique nature of the business had been a source of frequent public debate over the years. The most common question Jacques fielded was "Why?" Why, in a country that has never recorded a single snowflake, would it make sense to pursue a winter-sports business? The Congolese resources had so much to offer in so many other business domains, so why pursue a business that seemed to belong in Scandinavia or New Zealand?

Jacques's response had always been to simply smile and say, "I make ski sweaters because I'm good at it." But that rainy night, after the boxing up was complete, he sat down near the boxes and asked his daughters, "Why does a sweater business make sense for our family?"

"It makes sense because Kasongos are clever," was Madeleine's quick response.

"Oh, are we?" responded Jacques with an unconvinced smirk. "And what makes us so clever?"

"We like cheap money," was Lilian's response.

Using the concept of diversification, explain the intuition behind Lilian's response. Why is a ski sweater business in the DRC arguably less risky, with all sorts of mining investments to consider? Why should investors want to invest in such a business?

SECTION III
PERFORMANCE MEASUREMENT

Finance people, like sports people, care a lot about measuring performance. Both finance and sports people have an intense desire to distinguish future winners from future losers. To do this, they concoct reams of metrics and statistics to measure and scrutinize performance from every possible angle. Despite all their analysis of past performance, both finance people and sports people recognize that forecasting future performance is challenging. Still, both groups commonly use a combination of an analysis of past performance and an understanding of current conditions to forecast future performance. The finance term for scrutinizing past performance is *financial analysis*.

In this section, we will explore the tools and concepts used to conduct financial analysis and performance measurement. These tools include ways to analyze financial statements, financial ratios, and financial models. In this section, we will consider such questions as the following:

How does double-entry accounting work and why is it so useful?

What finance metrics are used to measure business success?

How do finance people identify causes of business underperformance? What metrics are useful in thinking about how to convert underperforming businesses into outperformers?

Why do finance people always say "cash is king"?

In a world with lots of uncertainty, how can a person set up a business for financial success?

This section will consider these and other questions over four chapters. Chapter 8 introduces double-entry accounting and explains how it is used to build financial statements. The chapter motivates why financial statements are so useful for measuring a business's financial performance and financial position. Chapter 9 builds on chapter 8 by exploring financial analysis, the process of analyzing financial statements. Both chapter 8 and chapter 9 are bound to be intimidating because they are packed with an enormous amount of new vocabulary to wade through (remember you are on a trip to a foreign land!). Despite the ridiculous number of new terms to learn, you are advised to push through and do your best to build your comprehension of this material. A basic familiarity with the language and the approach to performance measurement will do wonders not only for this chapter but, importantly, for building a foundation for much of the future material. Chapters 8 and 9 are worth returning to and reviewing several times, as the language is so critical to later chapters.

Chapter 10 introduces the fundamentals of financial modeling. Financial models are the workhorses that finance people use to understand and forecast future performance. The model of sandwiches developed in this chapter is fairly simple and should whet your appetite for the insights that come from building models.

Chapter 11 introduces the concept of cash flow and discusses why it is such an important metric in finance. The chapter contrasts cash flow with profits and introduces the drag that business growth can have on cash flow.

These three concepts—financial analysis, financial modeling, and cash flow—are powerful keys to finance that will help you on your journey to understand and communicate with finance people.

8

Financial Statements and the Music of Chabyon Kwa Daebyon

PROFESSOR BOKFORING'S PRIZE

"Does anyone know what's for lunch?" Charles Bokforing, professor of ancient history, asked with a chuckle as he steadied himself in his usual way. After months of excavating a hillside adjacent to an ancient necropolis above the Nile River valley in Egypt, Bokforing's archaeological team was suddenly on to something big. They had discovered a passageway of carved stone going into the hill. After they had emptied the passageway of packed earth and followed it for 10 meters, their tools had abruptly hit and exposed an elaborately carved doorway. After considerable effort to carefully break the intact seals that held the doorway, Bokforing anticipated in the next minutes what was likely to be the greatest discovery—or disappointment—of his career.

With visions of the historical artifacts that might greet them, the crew slowly rotated the heavy door out into the passageway. A surprisingly fragrant air settled over them. Holding up a light that immediately reflected the glint of gold, Bokforing peered into a spacious room filled with elaborate ancient decor, furnishings, and statuary. Bokforing entered the chamber, making his way past the obvious artifacts and treasure, and proceeded straight for a shelf containing several dozen papyrus scrolls. While the others looked on in silent wonder, Bokforing examined the outside markings, picked up a relatively large one, and laid it out on a large cat-shaped table of pure gold and encrusted gems. Deciphering the ancient hieroglyphics on the cover and the top of the scroll, a broad smile overtook Bokforing's face. "We've found what we're looking for," he proclaimed.

"Huh? What's with the scroll?" asked a bewildered assistant.

"Double-entry accounting, my friend," responded Bokforing as he moved past this group. "With this record of ancient Egyptian financial statements, we're about to discover a whole new perspective on the ancients." And with that, scroll in hand, Professor Bokforing walked out and left the site.

CONCEPT

Since ancient times, finance people have embraced double-entry accounting as the primary tool for keeping track of the financial performance and financial position of a business.

The foundation of double-entry accounting is what is known as the *accounting equation*. In its most basic form, this equation is defined as

$$Assets = liabilities + equity.$$

The fundamental idea is that any asset has two sides. The first is the physical side—what the asset is and what it can do productively (i.e., generate profit). The second is the finance side—how the asset was acquired and what promises were made to investors about its productivity. Suppose that long ago an Egyptian merchant took out a loan to acquire a chariot, with the expectation of providing a delivery service for his papyrus business. The price of the chariot and the amount of the loan was five shat (the existing unit of money in Egypt at the time). Through the lens of double-entry accounting, such a transaction has two sides. The first side is that the business acquired a chariot, a productive asset that cost five shat. The second side is that the lender obtained a claim on the business and the business acquired a debt obligation, a liability worth five shat. The two sides are linked since the chariot was financed by the loan. Double-entry accounting ensures that both sides of the transaction are recorded: following the accounting equation, the assets of the business increase by five shat with the addition of the piece of equipment, and the liabilities of the business increase by five shat with the addition of the debt obligation.

The accounting equation includes a term called *equity* on the right-hand side. Equity represents the amount of money that the owners (equity holders) have put into the business through cash payments or reinvested profits. In any year, the change in equity is equal to the profits for the year minus the net cash payments the owners have received (dividends):

$$\Delta \text{ equity} = \text{profits} - \text{dividends,}$$

where Δ stands for the change in the account (for example, Δ assets this year is equal to the value of the assets this year minus the value of the assets last year). Since *profits* is the amount of money that the business made and *dividends* is the amount of money that the business is distributing to the owners (equity holders), the difference represents the amount of profits that are being reinvested in the business (also called the *retained earnings*). Combining both equations, one can express the following important alternative expression of the accounting equation, which describes how the accounting equation changes over time:

$$\Delta \text{ assets} = \Delta \text{ liabilities} + \text{profits} - \text{dividends.}$$

These equations are at the heart of financial accounting, and they are used as the basis for building two primary records or *financial statements* of the status of the business. The first record is called the *balance sheet*. The balance sheet is a record of the financial position of the business at a point in time. The balance sheet details all the assets, liabilities, and equity at a specific point in time, say the end of the year. Because it is at a specific point in time, a balance sheet is like a snapshot of the business at that moment. The balance sheet records the value of each account (assets, liabilities, and equity) at that time by showing how much money has been invested in business assets and how those assets were financed. Following the accounting equation, the total assets listed on the left-hand side of the balance sheet must always balance with the total liabilities and equity of the business on the right-hand side of the balance sheet. This financial statement is called a balance sheet because both sides must balance (meaning the left-hand side and right-hand side always add up to the same amount).

The second type of financial statement is called the *income statement* or *profit and loss statement* (*P&L*). The income statement is a record of the financial performance of the business over a period of time. While the balance sheet is a snapshot of the business assets and financing, the income statement shows the flows of money in and out of the business over a certain period, say the course of a year. The income statement focuses on the profits element of the accounting equation by reporting the total amount of revenue the business has generated over the period minus the total amount of business costs incurred over the same period.

Together, the balance sheet and income statement provide the foundation for understanding the financial performance and financial position of a business. These two statements are at the heart of understanding business performance.

TERMINOLOGY

Income statement. When businesses sell stuff, they create sales or revenue, but creating that revenue entails business costs. The income statement is a financial statement that indicates, over a period of time, the magnitude of the business sales relative to the magnitude of the business costs. The net difference in sales and costs over a certain period is the profit of the business. The costs listed on the income statement are commonly divided in several categories. *Cost of goods sold (COGS)* are the direct costs associated with making or buying the products or services that the business sells. *Selling, general, and administrative (SG&A)* costs are the indirect costs associated with operating the business, such as water and energy costs, management salary, and advertising expenses. COGS and SG&A costs are considered operating costs in that they are directly associated with the operations of the business. Other costs, such as interest expense or income taxes, are not operating costs and tend to be listed lower in the income statement. A typical period for an income statement is a year, but a month or a quarter are also common. Finance people have other terms for the income statement, including *profit and loss statement*, or P&L.

Balance sheet. Businesses need physical things such as cash, inventory, and equipment to carry out their operations. The balance sheet is a financial statement that indicates all the assets and liabilities of the business at a point in time (e.g., at the end of the year). The assets and liabilities are commonly listed on the balance sheet at their cost (i.e., what it cost to acquire the asset). The balance sheet provides a tabulation of all the business's assets (e.g., cash, inventory, and equipment) on the left-hand side, and a tabulation of how those assets were financed (e.g., trade credit, debt claims, or equity claims) on the right-hand side. By the rules of accounting, the balance sheet balances, meaning the tabulation on the left-hand side always equals the tabulation on the right-hand side. This balancing of the balance sheet isn't magic—it's the result of standard double-entry accounting that matches the cost of the assets acquired to how the business paid for them.

Cash. *Cash* is a term used to indicate the amount of currency that the business has, including the cash currency and the liquid currency in bank accounts and other financial securities. The term *liquidity* refers to the ease with which an asset can be turned into currency. For example, money held in bank accounts is considered liquid because businesses can typically turn bank account holdings into cash currency very quickly and at low cost.

Receivables. The term receivables is used to refer to bills that the company is owed. Companies often sell their goods and services to customers on *credit*. For example, they deliver a load of goods and leave an invoice stating that the customer has 30 days to pay for the goods. This invoice is a receivable for the seller. The seller expects that the receivable will eventually be turned into cash when the invoice is paid, but for the time being, the company tabulates the asset as a receivable. Suppose a hospital treats a patient for a broken arm. Once the broken arm is repaired, the hospital issues a bill to the patient's health insurance carrier for payment for its services. Until this payment is received, the hospital will list the expected payment among its assets as a receivable. In issuing the receivable, the hospital is extending credit to the patient and insurance company by waiting for a later payment.

Payables. The opposite of receivables, payables is used to refer to bills that the company owes. When an invoice creates a receivable for the seller, it also creates a payable for the buyer. In the hospital example, the hospital's receivable is a payable for the insurance company. The term *accounts payable* refers to bills the business has received for goods it has purchased but not paid for. Payables also includes other operating liabilities that the business may have incurred but not paid for. For example, suppose a business pays its employees once per month. In this case, the business accrues *wages payable* throughout the month for all the work its employees have completed and that it will pay them for at the end of the month. Payables can be an important form of financing for businesses.

Inventory. Businesses commonly produce goods for sale. In order to have material to sell, businesses typically hold a stock or supply of these goods. This stock of goods is referred to as inventory. Since the business typically pays for the inventory prior to selling it, inventory can be a sizable investment asset for a business. Inventory does not refer to the assets used to make those goods, like equipment; it refers only to items that are made for sale.

Property, plant, and equipment (PP&E). A business's PP&E refers to the cost of all the long-term tangible assets the business owns. These assets include the cost of the land the company owns, the cost of the buildings the company owns, and the cost of all the long-term equipment the company owns. All these long-term assets are considered *tangible assets* (i.e., there is a physical thing one can handle). By the conventions of accounting, PP&E is listed at cost (how much it historically cost to acquire it) and not at its prevailing market value. The verb *capitalize* means to put an asset on the balance sheet. For example, if a business needed to repair a piece of equipment, the manager would either capitalize the repair costs by adding the costs to the equipment and then expensing (depreciating) that capitalized cost over several years, or the manager would *expense* the cost by running it immediately through the income statement as a repair charge. If the cost is expensed, it might appear on the income statement as an SG&A expense.

Intangible assets. Businesses also make investments in assets that are not tangible—meaning that there isn't much one can handle or take a picture of. Such intangible assets include the benefits of productive research and development. If a company has been able to generate an asset with commercial value (e.g., a new drug, a promising patent, or a valuable copyright or trademark), the cost of developing that asset is considered an intangible asset.

Profit. A company's profit is a measure of the difference over a period of time in the magnitude of revenue bringing money into the business relative to the magnitude of costs taking money out of the business. The term *profit* is synonymous with *income* or *earnings*. When profit is positive, revenue exceeds costs. When profit is negative (commonly called a loss), costs for the period exceed revenue. The net between the revenue and costs is the profit of the business over a certain period—say, a year. There are different definitions of profit based on what category of costs is included. *Gross profit* refers to profit that includes only the direct costs of producing the products sold. For example, gross profit is equal to the revenue less the direct cost of goods sold (COGS). The terms *operating profit* and *operating income* refer to profit defined by including all the operating costs of the business (including the indirect costs associated with the overall business operations). The terms *net profit, net income,* and *net earnings* refer to profit defined by including all the costs of the business, including the financing costs such as interest expense and income taxes paid to the government. Since interest expense has been deducted, net profit is a measure of profit that goes only to equity holders. In contrast, operating profit is a concept of profit that is available to both debt holders and equity holders, since interest expense is not yet subtracted out. To provide some help in keeping track of all of these profit definitions, here are some mathematical profit definitions:

$$\text{Gross profit} = \text{revenue} - \text{COGS}.$$

$$\text{Operating profit} = \text{revenue} - \text{operating costs}.$$

$$\text{Net profit} = \text{revenue} - \text{all costs}.$$

Depreciation and amortization. Businesses often make investments in long-term assets, such as buying a building or investing in a patent. Since the productive life of these assets may be many years, finance people spread the cost of those long-term investments over the investment's life. This cost-spreading technique is called depreciation and amortization. The annual charge for depreciation and amortization is put on the income statement and reduces profit by capturing the costs associated with use of the fixed assets. *Depreciation* refers to the annual charge of tangible assets like property, plant, or equipment. *Amortization* refers to the annual charge of intangible assets like patents. It is important to note that depreciation and amortization expenses aren't ever really paid, since they are just accounting allocations of investment expenditures made previously. As an example, suppose Jumbo Airlines spent USD1 million on a new building it expected to use for 10 years: How should it charge that USD1 million against profits? One way to account for that expenditure would be to incur the expense in the year it occurs. In that case, Jumbo would have a big USD1 million building expense on the income statement in the year of the expenditure, which would make business profits in that year low and profits in future years high (since there would be no charge in subsequent years). An alternative way to account for the expenditure would be to spread the USD1 million charge over all 10 years, by allocating a USD100,000 building depreciation charge each year over the 10 years of the building's life. This allocation of the investment expenditure smooths out profits by matching the expenditure not to when it is made but instead to when it benefits the business. This approach to smoothing profits is at the heart of depreciation and amortization charges.

THE DAWN OF CKD

Narin Kang grew up in a small village in the mountains in the south of the Korean Peninsula. Her family farmed the rugged land during the day and made traditional Korean music at night. As Kang grew up, she fully embraced her family's love of music. But she also had a personal passion—a passion for accounting. From an early age, Kang went everywhere with a wol-geum[12] in one hand and a financial newspaper in the other. By the time she was in high school, Kang was well known in her local community as a solo singer-songwriter with a unique orientation in her music. Kang believed that musicians wasted far too much energy on songs focused on romantic love. Such songs were far less interesting or meaningful than songs with lyrics focused in the much more nuanced, dramatic, and relevant world of accounting and finance. Following her beliefs, she had written a host of songs that explored a variety of such yearnings of the soul, including some local favorites like "Your Assets Are Intangible, Baby!," "He's Got One Strong Balance Sheet," and her personal theme song, "We're All Both Payables and Receivables." With a growing following, she was going by the catchy artist name Chabyon Kwa Daebyon, or CKD.

In February of her last year of high school, Kang launched her professional music career by depositing KRW8 million[13] in a bank account under the name Chabyon Kwa Daebyon. The KRW8 million was hard-earned cash she had accumulated over years of work. Having established a bank account for her business operations, she knew that she needed to finance some new sound equipment. To do this, she took out a KRW10 million loan from the bank to purchase KRW10 million in sound equipment.

---

[12] A traditional Korean musical instrument somewhat like an American banjo.
[13] KRW = Korean won.

A contact of hers agreed to be her booking agent, and within a few weeks the agent had booked five concerts for CKD—four in July at various venues across Kang's local region and one in December in the big city of Busan. She was excited to have a tour schedule and paid the agent KRW2 million for her booking services.

In preparation for her first tour, Kang spent KRW2 million on CKD merchandise. Once July arrived, Kang and a friend, Bora Bak, loaded up her family's Kia minitruck with the sound equipment, merchandise, and a suitcase, and, using Kang's new driver's license, they hit the road. Bak was excited and Kang was ecstatic. The eight-day tour went well. Kang and Bak learned a lot from the experience, and they were really happy with how well the concerts turned out. People seemed to really connect with accounting and enjoy CKD's unique brand of music. When the summer concerts were over, Kang's share of the concert proceeds was KRW7 million. This amount was electronically transferred to her bank account in September.

In August, Kang left home again, this time to start her university studies in Jinju. Kang's music quickly gained a following at the university. Fans included an economics professor who allowed Kang to put all her assignments to music and submit them for extra credit as recorded songs. By the end of the semester, she felt like school had mostly been a success. In mid-December, Kang performed a final concert of the year to her largest crowd yet, again in Busan, further growing her fan base. The booking agent informed Kang that she should expect a payment of KRW3 million for the concert sometime in January.

With her first financial year of operation wrapping up on New Year's Eve, Kang realized that her music wasn't just an amusement. She was running a business, and she was excited to know how well that business was doing financially. It was finally time to build some financial statements and nail down her financial position and performance.

Kang invited Bak over for some evening fun as they celebrated the new year. As they talked about what they might do, Kang suggested some accounting recreation.

"You want to do what, Narin?" Bak asked in disbelief. "Can't we watch a movie or something?"

"Ah, come on, Bora," replied Kang. "We got to do something better than that to celebrate being back together. Look, I've got this list of transactions for the year." (See **Table 8.1.**) "You're going to love this. Believe me. It's like doing a puzzle."

"You know I don't do puzzles for fun either. I'm not buying it. This looks like schoolwork to celebrate New Year's Eve," Bak complained.

"I promise this will be fun. We can turn up the song "He's Got One Strong Balance Sheet." I think it'll be pretty exciting if we can figure it out. We'll just do one transaction at a time," Kang coaxed.

"Okay. Okay, if that's really what you want," conceded Bak. "But I get a dalgona drink if the band is making money."

"Fine! I'll take that bet," Kang agreed, victorious. "I don't think it'll take long." She pulled out a pen and pad and turned to the list of transactions. "To build the financial statements, we'll need to keep track of individual accounts by adding or subtracting from these accounts as the transactions are recorded."

TABLE 8.1. Financial transactions for CKD.

Transaction
1 Deposited KRW8 million in a bank account under the name Chabyon Kwa Daebyon.
2 Took out a KRW10 million loan from the bank to purchase KRW10 million in sound equipment.
3 Paid booking agent KRW2 million in cash for her booking services to be recorded as a general expense.
4 Spent KRW2 million in cash on merchandise inventory.
5 Received KRW7 million in cash for concert proceeds to be recorded as revenue.
6 Received promise of KRW3 million for Busan concert proceeds to be recorded as revenue and accounts receivable.
7 Received KRW2 million in cash on merchandise inventory to be recorded as revenue of KRW2 million. Since the markup on the inventory was 100%, this transaction also requires a recognition of a decrease in KRW1 million in inventory and an expensing of KRW1 million in COGS.
8 Spent KRW2 million in cash on travel expenses for the year to be recorded as general expense.
9 Spent KRW0.3 million in cash on interest expenses on the loan.
10 Spent KRW1.7 million in cash on tax expense.

"Whatever." Bak rolled her eyes. "I cannot believe that of all the people I could have as my friend, I picked you."

Smiling gratefully, Kang continued on as if she were reciting a line from a song, "Following the principles of double-entry accounting, each transaction will give two entries for posting."

"Yes, accounting girl. That's a lyric with promise," acknowledged Bak with feigned enthusiasm. "You do the first one."

Transaction 1. Deposited KRW8 million in a bank account under the name Chabyon Kwa Daebyon.

"This transaction is my original equity investment in the business," explained Kang. "For this transaction, the two accounts being impacted are the cash account and the equity account. Specifically,

Cash: +8
Equity: +8

TABLE 8.2. CKD balance sheet with Transaction 1 recorded (in millions of Korean won).

Assets		Liabilities and equity	
Cash	8	Equity	8
Total assets	8	Total liabilities and equity	8

"After this transaction, my balance sheet looks very simple." (See **Table 8.2.**) "You see that there is only one asset in the business: KRW8 million in cash. That asset was financed with an equity investment of KRW8 million. That's how the business started."

"Got it. One down," said Bak. "Let me take on Transaction 2."

Transaction 2. Took out a KRW10 million loan from the bank to purchase KRW10 million in sound equipment.

"This transaction is the loan you used to buy the sound equipment. For this transaction, the two accounts being impacted are the equipment account and the debt account. Specifically,

Equipment: +10
Debt: +10

"Is that right?"

"Is that right? Do you eat kimchi? Yes, of course it's right," Kang said. "Nicely done. Now, can you update the balance sheet?"

"I think so." Bak took a few minutes to write out what she believed to be the updated balance sheet (see **Table 8.3**). "After Transaction 2, the balance sheet looks like this. See that now the business has KRW18 million in assets, including KRW8 million in cash and KRW10 million in equipment. These assets are financed with debt of KRW10 million and equity of KRW8 million."

TABLE 8.3. CKD balance sheet with Transaction 2 recorded (in millions of Korean won).

Assets		Liabilities and equity	
Cash	8	Debt	10
Equipment	10	Equity	8
Total assets	18	Total liabilities and equity	18

"Nice work! That's a pretty good-looking balance sheet. I'll take Transaction 3," volunteered Kang.

Transaction 3. Paid booking agent KRW2 million in cash for her booking services to be recorded as a general expense.

"This transaction is the cash I paid to the booking agent. For this transaction, the two accounts being impacted are the cash account and the general expense account. Specifically,

Cash: −2
General expense: +2

"This transaction is a little tricky because operating expense goes up while cash goes down. This is because general expense is an equity account, and expenses affect profits or equity in a negative way. Because of that negative relationship, cash goes down when expenses go up." Kang sketched out the evolving financial statements, including what she called "the beginnings of our income statement" (see **Table 8.4**).

TABLE 8.4. CKD balance sheet and income statement with Transaction 3 recorded (in millions of Korean won).

Balance Sheet				
Assets			Liabilities and equity	
Cash	6		Debt	10
Equipment	10		Equity	6
Total assets	16		Total liabilities and equity	16
Income Statement				
Revenue	0			
General expense	2			
Net profit	−2			

Kang explained how profit in the income statement was calculated as revenue less expenses. She demonstrated how the cash account had declined from KRW8 million to KRW6 million due to recording the booking agent payment, and how the equity account had declined by KRW2 million due to the negative net profit of −KRW2 million. Bak offered to take Transaction 4.

Transaction 4. Spent KRW2 million in cash on merchandise inventory.

"This transaction is the cash you paid for the merchandise inventory," explained Bak. "Inventory is what businesses produce for sale. For this transaction, the two accounts being impacted are the cash account and the inventory account."

Cash: −2

Inventory: +2

"For this transaction, only the balance sheet is affected, not the income statement, so I'll only include the updated balance sheet." (See **Table 8.5.**) "Since both accounts affected are on the asset side of the balance sheet, there will be a swap of assets happening there. The cash account goes down by 2 million and the inventory account goes up by 2 million, but there is no change to the overall assets of total liabilities and equity. They both stay at 16 million. There's again no change in the income statement."

TABLE 8.5. CKD balance sheet with Transaction 4 recorded (in millions of Korean won).

Balance Sheet

Assets		Liabilities and equity	
Cash	4	Debt	10
Inventory	2	Equity	6
Equipment	10		
Total assets	16	Total liabilities and equity	16

"You've got accounting fever!" wailed Kang, raising an imaginary microphone to her mouth and singing the last word at full power, holding the note for a very long time. "Okay, I'm back. I just needed to acknowledge the obvious. I'll take Transaction 5."

Transaction 5. Received KRW7 million in cash for concert proceeds to be recorded as revenue.

"This transaction is the cash I received from the concert proceeds. For this transaction, the two accounts being impacted are the cash account and the revenue account. Specifically,

Cash: +7

Revenue: +7

"With this revenue, our income statement will look a little more normal. Now we have profit of . . . KRW5 million!" (See **Table 8.6.**)

TABLE 8.6. CKD balance sheet and income statement with Transaction 5 recorded (in millions of Korean won).

Balance Sheet

Assets		Liabilities and equity	
Cash	11	Debt	10
Inventory	2	Equity	13
Equipment	10		
Total assets	23	Total liabilities and equity	23

Income Statement

Revenue	7
General expense	2
Net profit	5

"The cash account has increased by KRW7 million to KRW11 million, due to the cash inflow; and the revenue account has increased by KRW7 million. With the new revenue raising profits by KRW7 million, the equity account increases by KRW7 million, from KRW6 million to KRW13 million. "

"Halfway done!" hollered Bak. "Let's do this job. I've got T6."

Transaction 6. Received promise of KRW3 million for Busan concert proceeds to be recorded as revenue and accounts receivable.

"This transaction is like the last one. It is revenue from a concert performance, but in this case, the cash has yet to be received. We received a promise of a future payment, also called an account receivable." Bak paused to let Kang congratulate her for her ability to remember what Kang had taught her about receivables in primary school. "Companies often sell their goods and services to customers on credit. For example, they deliver a load of goods and leave an invoice stating that the customer has 30 days to pay for the goods. This invoice is a receivable for the seller. The seller expects that the receivable will eventually be turned into cash when the invoice is paid, but for the time being, the company tabulates the asset as a receivable," recited Bak with a speed and comprehension that even she was surprised by.

"The two accounts being impacted are the revenue account and a new line item, the account receivable account. Specifically,

Account receivable (acc. rec.):   +3
Revenue: +3

"But I'm not done yet! The revised financial statements include this additional revenue and receivable," Bak said, scribbling out the revised financial statements in short order (see **Table 8.7**). She continued, "The accounts receivable account has increased by KRW3 million, and the revenue account has increased by KRW3 million, such that the profits are now KRW3 million higher, at KRW8 million. With the increased profit, the equity account has increased by KRW3 million to KRW16 million."

TABLE 8.7. CKD balance sheet and income statement with Transaction 6 recorded (in millions of Korean won).

Balance Sheet

Assets		Liabilities and equity	
Cash	11	Debt	10
Acc. rec.	3	Equity	16
Inventory	2		
Equipment	10		
Total assets	26	Total liabilities and equity	26

Income Statement

Revenue	10
General expense	2
Net profit	8

"Oh yeah!" exulted Kang, and both women lifted a hand for a high five. "I've got Transaction 7."

Transaction 7. Received KRW2 million in cash on merchandise inventory, to be recorded as revenue of KRW2 million. Since the markup on the inventory

was 100%, this transaction also requires a recognition of a decrease in KRW1 million in inventory and an expensing of KRW1 million in COGS.

Kang explained, "This transaction is another revenue effect like Transactions 5 and 6, but this one also includes COGS for the merchandise sold. For this transaction, there are four accounts affected. The first two accounts record the revenue generated. This is done exactly like Transaction 5, since it is a cash transaction. Specifically,

Cash: +2
Revenue: +2

"The second two accounts record the KRW1 million reduction of the inventory that has been sold. Specifically,

Inventory: −1
COGS: −1

"Including these four account adjustments in the financial statements gives us the following revised statements." (See **Table 8.8.**)

TABLE 8.8. CKD balance sheet and income statement with Transaction 7 recorded (in millions of Korean won).

Balance Sheet

Assets		Liabilities and equity	
Cash	13	Debt	10
Acc. rec.	3	Equity	17
Inventory	1		
Equipment	10		
Total assets	27	Total liabilities and equity	27

Income Statement

Revenue	12
COGS	1
General expense	2
Net profit	9

Kang explained, "The cash account has increased by KRW2 million and the inventory account has decreased by KRW1 million, such that the revenue is up KRW2 million, the costs are up KRW1 million, and the profits are up KRW1 million higher, to KRW9 million. With the increased profit, the equity account has increased by KRW1 million to KRW17 million."

"Good work," Bak acknowledged, then continued to Transaction 8 without skipping a beat.

Transaction 8. Spent KRW2 million in cash on travel expenses for the year to be recorded as general expense.

"This transaction is a cost effect like Transaction 3. For this transaction, there are two accounts affected—cash and general expense. And just like Transaction 3, one account goes down while the other goes up."

Cash: −2
General expense: +2

Bak worked furiously on paper to update the financial statements (see **Table 8.9**).

TABLE 8.9. CKD balance sheet and income statement with Transaction 8 recorded (in millions of Korean won).

Balance Sheet

Assets		Liabilities and equity	
Cash	11	Debt	10
Acc. rec.	3	Equity	15
Inventory	1		
Equipment	10		
Total assets	25	Total liabilities and equity	25

Income Statement

Revenue	12
COGS	1
General expense	4
Net profit	7

Bak continued, "The cash account has decreased by KRW2 million, such that the total assets are now down to KRW25 million. The general expense has increased by KRW2 million such that the profits are down KRW2 million. This reduction in profits reduces the equity account by KRW2 million to a new balance of KRW15 million. Adding the KRW10 million in debt to the KRW15 million in equity gives KRW25 million for the right-hand side of the balance sheet. The KRW25 million on the right-hand side matches the KRW25 million on the left-hand side."

"All seems to be in order with the accounting equation!" celebrated Kang, her fist in the air. "Let's see what Transaction 9 gives us."

Transaction 9. Spent KRW0.3 million in cash on interest expense on the loan.

"This transaction is another cost effect like the last transaction. For this transaction, there are two accounts affected—cash and the interest expense account. In this case, interest expense goes up and cash goes down.

Cash: −0.3
Interest expense: +0.3

"Here are the adjustments to the financial statements." (See **Table 8.10.**)

"The cash account has decreased by KRW0.3 million, such that the total assets are now down to KRW24.7 million. The interest expense has increased by KRW0.3 million, such that the profits are down KRW0.3 million from KRW7 million. This reduction in profits reduces the equity account by KRW0.3 million to a new balance of KRW14.7 million. Adding the KRW10 million in debt to the KRW14.7 million in equity gives KRW24.7 million for the right-hand side of the balance sheet. Again, the right-hand side matches the KRW24.7 million on the left-hand side. All continues to be in order with the accounting equation," Kang said.

"One thing I added to this income statement is a line for operating profit," she continued. "I use operating profit to classify the business expenses in two ways: operating expenses and non-operating expenses. I

TABLE 8.10. CKD balance sheet and income statement with Transaction 9 recorded (in millions of Korean won).

Balance Sheet

Assets		Liabilities and equity	
Cash	10.7	Debt	10
Acc. rec.	3	Equity	14.7
Inventory	1		
Equipment	10		
Total assets	24.7	Total liabilities and equity	24.7

Income Statement

Revenue	12
COGS	1
General expense	4
Operating profit	7
Interest expense	0.3
Net profit	6.7

think about operating expenses as those expenses that occur as the business is pursuing its business operations. Expenses like COGS and general expenses like booking fees and travel expenses are what I consider operating expenses. Non-operating expenses are those, like interest expense, that are separate from the business operations. Interest expense is an expense not due to business operations but instead to how I choose to finance the business assets. Interest expense occurs because I made the decision to use debt financing to acquire the sound equipment. If instead I had financed that acquisition with equity (e.g., my own money), there would be no interest expense incurred. Because people often find it helpful to distinguish these two types of expenses, it is common to organize income statements in this manner, with two measures of profits—the operating profits that are net of all operating expenses, and net profit that is net of all expenses, including non-operating expenses."

"Nice work, champ," acknowledged Bak as she prepared to end the event. "Let me finish up with the last transaction."

Transaction 10. Spent KRW1.7 million in cash on tax expense.

"This transaction is again a non-operating cost effect like Transaction 9. For this transaction, there are two accounts affected—the cash account and the tax expenses account. The transaction is recorded as

Cash: −1.7
Tax expenses: +1.7

"The adjustment to the financial statements is very similar to what you just did with interest expense—I simply added a line for tax expense at the bottom of the income statement and then the adjusted equity account so it was in line with the revised profits." (See **Table 8.11**.)

"In summary, the cash account has decreased by KRW1.7 million such that the total assets are now down to KRW23 million. The tax expenses have increased by KRW1.7 million such that the net income is down KRW1.7 million. Note that the operating profit is unaffected as tax expenses are not included as operating expenses. The reduction in net profit reduces the equity account by KRW1.7 million to a new balance of KRW13 million. Adding the KRW10 million in debt with the KRW13 million in equity

TABLE 8.11. CKD balance sheet and income statement with Transaction 10 recorded (in millions of Korean won).

Balance Sheet

Assets		Liabilities and equity	
Cash	9	Debt	10
Acc. rec.	3	Equity	13
Inventory	1		
Equipment	10		
Total assets	23	Total liabilities and equity	23

Income Statement

Revenue	12
COGS	1
General expense	4
Operating profit	7
Interest expenses	0.3
Tax expenses	1.7
Net income	5

gives KRW23 million for the right-hand side of the balance sheet. Again, the right-hand side matches the KRW23 million on the left-hand side. All continues to be in order with the accounting equation. And who gets the dalgona drink?" Bak inquired.

"It looks like you do, Bora. I did indeed generate a positive profit of 5 million."

"Yes, pretty good for your first year."

"But we should recognize that there is so much more information contained in these statements than just knowing the profit number. For example, if we made KRW5 million, how come neither of us feels any richer?"

"That's a great question. Where did the money go?" asked Bak.

"A good way to see that is to compare the financial statements after Transaction 10 (**Table 8.11**) with the one after we set up the business after Transaction 2 (**Table 8.3**). If we compare those two balance sheets, we'll notice that total assets increased from KRW18 million when we set up the business to KRW23 million now. What is that difference?"

"Uhh, KRW5 million—the same amount as the profit."

"That's right. Our assets increased by KRW5 million because we did not take out any of the profit; we put it all back into the assets of the business. If we go down the different asset accounts, we can see what we did with the profits. First, the cash account went up by KRW1 million [KRW8 million to KRW9 million], which means our profits increased cash by KRW1 million. The accounts receivable went up by KRW3 million [KRW0 to KRW3 million]. Once we collect that receivable, hopefully next month, our cash balance will go up by another KRW3 million, but for now KRW3 million of our profit is sitting as a receivable. Lastly, our inventory went up by KRW1 million [KRW0 to KRW1 million]. This means that KRW1 million of the profit went into making the KRW1 million of merchandise we still have waiting to sell. The financial statements show where the profits ended up."

"I agree, that is pretty interesting," Bak said. "I notice that the right-hand side of the balance sheet also went up by KRW5 million. Since debt remained the same at KRW10 million, all of the increase in assets was due to an increase in equity."

"Excellent observation! Yes, the equity account increased because all the asset financing came from the profits. That retained earnings increases the equity account. If we had cashed out those profits for ourselves as dividends, then the equity account would not have increased and the increases in assets would have had to be financed some other way. Hey, Bora, if you are not taking any of the profits, I think it is time for a New Year's Eve dalgona. Agreed?"

"Agreed! And congratulations on a great first year."

CONCEPT WRAP-UP

This chapter introduced financial statements as an important tool for measuring a business's financial performance and financial position. The balance sheet provides a record of the financial position of the business at a certain time. It details all the assets, liabilities, and equity at a specific point in time, like a snapshot of the business at that moment. Following the accounting equation, the value of all the assets listed on the left-hand side of the balance sheet must always balance with the total liabilities and equity of the business listed on the right-hand side. The income statement provides a record of the financial performance of the business over a period of time. The income statement focuses on the profits of the business by reporting the total amount of revenue the business has generated over the period minus the total amount of business costs incurred over the same period. These two financial statements, the balance sheet and the income statement, provide the foundation for understanding the financial performance and financial position of a business.

Double-entry accounting is the process by which financial statements are built. It provides a record of the effects of transactions for the assets, liabilities, equity, and profits of the business in a way that single-entry accounting does not. Single-entry accounting keeps track of the simple inflows and outflows of cash, like a bank account statement. While it is not essential to understand all the nuances associated with building financial statements the way accountants do, it is essential to understand how to interpret financial statements. This chapter is so important because of this ability to interpret financial statements.

REVIEW QUESTIONS

Although Bora Bak was active in supporting Narin Kang's musical endeavors, she had also developed a venture of her own, making traditional Korean musical instruments. She called her business BAK EUMAG. Her experience with Kang motivated her to spend some of the following day recording the transactions she had experienced with her own business over the past year (see **Table 8.12**).

Question 1. Go through each of the eight transactions in **Table 8.12** and record the accounting transactions by identifying the pairs of accounts affected and the precise financial effect.

Question 2. Using your responses to question 1, build out the financial statements for BAK EUMAG, including both a balance sheet and an income statement.

Question 3. What can you tell about Bak's business based on the financial statements you prepared?

TABLE 8.12. Financial transactions for BAK EUMAG.

Transaction 1. Deposited KRW15 million in a bank account under the name BAK EUMAG.

Transaction 2. Paid KRW1 million in cash to rent woodshop space for year.

Transaction 3. Paid KRW5 million in cash to purchase KRW5 million in woodshop equipment.

Transaction 4. Paid KRW2 million in cash to purchase high-quality wood and hardware for woodshop inventory.

Transaction 5. Paid KRW1 million in wages for neighbor to help in shop.

Transaction 6. Received KRW4 million in cash to be recorded as revenue for selling 10 instruments. The inventory sold was on the books at KRW2 million.

Transaction 7. Bought KRW2 million of high-quality wood and hardware for woodshop inventory. Agreed to pay suppliers in January.

Transaction 8. Spent KRW1 million in cash on tax expense.

9

Financial Analysis and the Diagnosis of AZUL

DR. MALADIE'S QUESTION

It was the first class of the first day of medical school. The new students filed into the large lecture hall, anxiously took their seats, and waited. Suddenly, their professor, Dr. Maladie, burst in, striding across the floor with seriousness in every step. She stopped abruptly at the center of the room, turned to the class, and scanned the students slowly with a gaze that caused each one to question their future in medicine.

Finally, drawing a breath, Maladie asked, "What is a doctor's most important tool?"

Gideon McAllen, an outdoorsman from Tennessee, was the first to raise his hand. "A scalpel," he offered. "A doctor's got to get inside and see what's going on."

"Back of the class!" screeched Maladie. "Exploratory operations are always a last resort—and someone take the buck knife away from that boy."

Next, Ling Li, an engineer from southern China, raised her hand. "New technology," she said. "Good doctors stay up to date with the latest tools."

"Back of the class!" hissed Maladie. "New equipment is secondary. Basic tools are vastly more critical."

Next, Tomas Garcia, an Argentine urbanite, raised his hand. "Drugs," he suggested. "A prescription pad is a doctor's most important tool."

"Back of the class!" sneered Maladie. "Diagnosis always supersedes intervention."

Finally, Esperta Silva, the owner of a Portuguese ornamental tile empire and the youngest member of the class, spoke up. Silva was dressed in her new white coat, with a polished stethoscope and blood pressure cuff draped around her neck and a clinical thermometer tucked behind her ear. "Dr. Maladie, a doctor's most important tool is an observant mind and the basic tools of our trade," she said, pointing to the stethoscope, cuff, and thermometer.

A smile swept over Maladie's face. She leaped onto the surface of the classroom lab desk and danced with joy in front of the astonished group of students. "Brava!" Maladie cried. "Brava! Yes, my dear, it all starts with a keen mind and an appreciation of the power of vital signs."

CONCEPT

In medicine, the four primary health indicators are body temperature, heart rate, blood pressure, and respiratory rate. These vital signs are the basic quantitative indicators of the state of the body's life-sustaining function. A value of any one of the signs outside a range considered normal for the person's characteristics indicates that some body function is not working normally. For example, the normal respiratory rate (number of breaths per minute) is 12 to 16 for an adult at rest. A respiratory rate outside of that range for an adult at rest calls for further analysis. In a medical examination, a physician commonly begins by examining the patient's vital signs. She then pursues additional exploratory diagnostic testing only if it is suggested by abnormalities in vital signs. The standard approach in medicine is to assess broad physical function first and then drill into more specific testing if the broad tests indicate a cause for concern.

Business enterprises vary in their health just like people do—but for a business, health is financial rather than physical. Some businesses are vibrant, with an overabundance of the resources needed to thrive. Other businesses struggle with various forms of financial dysfunction that arise from a myriad of sources. Because of the importance of financial health to the performance of any venture, finance people, like medical people, spend a lot of time examining and evaluating the financial health of business enterprises. Their evaluation approach is similar in that a financial examination usually involves first assessing a business's broad financial function, then further evaluating specific areas of financial function based on observed need. Financial vital signs are the first thing to turn to when evaluating the health of any business.

In this chapter, young Portuguese medical student Esperta Silva will demonstrate the basics of financial analysis by examining the financial statements of her business. Finance people use financial statements to assess the financial health of a business; this is also called financial analysis. Silva's approach will be similar to that of a physician, were a business enterprise to be wheeled into their examination room. She will review the vital signs associated with broad business function, compare those to adjusted norms, and identify opportunities for more specific diagnostic tests to further investigate and establish the financial condition of the enterprise. Once a full diagnosis is achieved, appropriate interventions can be recommended for the business to regain financial health.

The crash course that Silva and her neighborhood friends provide in the chapter illustrates the basics of financial analysis. The chapter builds on what was introduced in chapter 8 and provides plenty of review of those concepts. In this chapter, a group of neighborhood kids pick up the skills relatively quickly. The ease with which they master the basics of financial analysis is not meant to suggest that this material is trivial, but rather to provide a straightforward, non-intimidating setting that keeps the material approachable. The hope is that you will follow along in their effort to diagnose the problem and identify appropriate recommendations.

TERMINOLOGY

Profit margin. Profit margin measures the amount of profit generated as a percentage of the sales price. Its magnitude is determined by the relation of business costs to sales. If the sales price is high relative to the per-unit cost, then the profit margin is high. If total revenue is low relative to total costs, then profit margin is low. Profit margins may differ widely across businesses. For example, some businesses may operate at a high margin by pricing their goods or services at 50% above their costs, whereas other businesses may operate at a low margin by pricing their goods or services at 10% above their costs. The profit margin can be thought of as the percentage of the sales price that represents profit to the business. Profit margin can be determined based on various definitions of profit as in the above description. As such, profit margin can be defined based on *gross margin* (using gross profit), *operating margin* (using operating profit), or *net profit margin* (using net profit).

Asset turnover. Asset turnover measures the productivity or efficiency of the business assets. It is defined as a measure of flow (i.e., sales) divided by investment (i.e., total assets). Productive or efficient assets are able to generate a lot of sales proportionally. A business that can generate two dollars of revenue for every one dollar of assets is more productive or efficient than a business that can only generate one dollar of revenue for every one dollar of assets. Turnover measures the times the assets are turning over with revenue.

Return on investment (ROI). Finance language includes a lot of terms to describe the returns that are expected or realized on investments made. In general, ROI is defined as the gain investors receive divided by the investment money they put up. Finance people use lots of terms for this concept because it is so important. ROI is important because it measures the annual gain investors get on the investment they have made. There are many different definitions of ROI, based on the definition of the annual gain and the definition of the investment. For example, *return on equity (ROE)* measures the gain that equity holders receive through their equity investment; it is defined as net profit divided by the amount of investment that equity investors have made through owner's equity.

THE DIAGNOSIS OF AZUL

Azulejos, an important feature of Portuguese culture, are distinctive ornamental ceramic tiles that traditionally cover the exterior and interior of buildings all over the country. Prior to becoming the wonder student of Dr. Maladie's classroom, Esperta Silva loved three things: medicine, financial analysis, and azulejos. Silva was best known in her hometown as the child who had turned a small collection of poorly run azulejo shops into a multinational operation that was now the pride of the city. The name of the business was AZUL.

AZUL had previously been run by Silva's stepbrother, Victor Falador. Falador was a 20-something regular on the Algarve beach scene, and he had a history of talking big but delivering little. In those days, Silva, a mere youngster, had a medical office on her front porch from which she provided care for neighborhood stuffed animals and dolls, action figures, and occasionally a beloved pet.

Silva remembered the day when her father interrupted an appendectomy she had been performing on a toy crocodile. "Esperta," he had said, "I've long noticed the careful attention you give to restoring health to all in the neighborhood. I have a patient I'd like to commit to your care. It's a very sick patient, but I think you have what it takes to bring it back to health." And just like that, Falador had been relieved of his duties, and AZUL had become the formative focus of Silva's adolescence.

On her first day on the job, Silva gathered her playmates around her makeshift outdoor operating table and spread out AZUL's recent financial statements for all to see (see **Table 9.1**). With a manner belying her years, she rallied her friends and exclaimed that it was time to evaluate the health of this new patient.

"Naturally, we will begin our examination with the financial statements," she explained, "including both the balance sheet and the income statement. The balance sheet is a snapshot of the amount of money that has been invested in the existing business assets at the end of the year and how

TABLE 9.1. Financial statements for AZUL (figures in thousands of euros).

	Last year	Two years ago
Balance Sheet		
Cash	10	45
Receivables	200	180
Inventory	550	435
Property and equipment	400	455
Total assets	1,160	1,115
Accounts payable	40	42
Wages payable	30	32
Debt	575	561
Equity	515	480
Total liabilities and equity	1,160	1,115
Income Statement		
Sales	900	925
Cost of goods sold (COGS)	345	439
Gross profit	555	486
Selling, general, and administrative (SG&A) expenses	480	375
Operating profit	75	111
Interest expenses	25	25
Taxes	15	30
Net profit	35	56

those assets were financed. As you can see here," she said, pointing to the total assets figure, "at the end of last year AZUL had spent EUR1.16 million on the assets in the business. This EUR1.16 million was composed of EUR10,000 in cash, EUR200,000 in receivables, EUR550,000 in inventory, and EUR400,000 in property and equipment."

"I understand that inventory is all the tiles that the business keeps in stock, but what are receivables, Esperta?" called out young Pedro, the four-year-old brother of Silva's friend Maria. Because of his age, Pedro wasn't normally allowed near Silva's operating room.

"Good question, Pedro. Receivables represent the amount of sales that AZUL made on credit to AZUL customers but whose payment has not yet been collected. For any sale, we usually deliver an order of tile and leave an invoice for the customer to pay us in 60 days. That invoiced payment due is an account receivable," explained Silva. There was some discussion about why AZUL sold things on credit, but Silva quickly explained that sales credit was an important tool that AZUL and other businesses used to accommodate customer needs and stimulate sales. Most of the children present were simply amazed that their friend was in charge of a mountain of tile inventory worth a whopping EUR550,000.

"Now, let's look at the other side of the balance sheet, below the total assets line, which tells us how that EUR1.16 million of assets was financed," Silva said. "The total amount of financing must equal the total amount of assets. There are four sources of financing that add up to EUR1,160,000: accounts payable (EUR40,000), wages payable (EUR30,000), debt (EUR575,000), and equity (EUR515,000). How does all that financing work? The accounts payable are purchases of tile or raw materials that AZUL hasn't yet paid for. In effect, AZUL's suppliers give AZUL credit so that we'll buy more product from them. This credit helps us finance some of our inventory. The wages payable are employee wages that employees have earned but not yet received. This combined amount of EUR70,000 [EUR40,000 plus EUR30,000] in payables financing is valuable asset financing for us because it doesn't cost us much. In effect, EUR70,000 of our assets are financed by our suppliers and employees. This trade credit keeps us from having to borrow more."

Silva continued, "Debt is the financing we get from banks or other debt holders. Debt holders provide financing but expect specific fixed interest payments until the end of the debt contract. In AZUL's case, the debt holders are getting EUR25,000 every year in interest on the EUR575,000 they have put up in debt financing. Equity holders provide financing but without a fixed payment—instead, they can claim whatever money is left over after everyone else is paid. A primary source of these equity payments is business profits. The total equity financing amount of EUR515,000 is the amount that my family, the owners, has put into AZUL since its beginning, including the initial investment made to start the business and all additional direct or indirect investments we made by reinvesting some of AZUL's profits back into the business."

"Let me make sure I've got this right," interjected Ana, a friend who was normally more interested in neighborhood football games than Silva's medical practice. "So, your company has been able to acquire over a million euros of azulejos stuff because you have a little bit financed by the suppliers and employees, and a large amount financed by your family and the bank. Is that right?"

"Perfeita!" exclaimed Silva. "Note that by definition, the total assets of a business always balances with—meaning, is equal to—the total liabilities and equity of the business. It is called a balance sheet because both sides balance (meaning they add up to the same amount). I think you have got the balance sheet down and are ready to move on to the income statement. While the balance sheet is a snapshot of the business assets and financing, the income statement shows the flows of money in and out of the business over the course of the year. Last year, AZUL had EUR900,000 in total sales flowing in—that's a lot of azulejos we sold! To generate all those sales, AZUL incurred a large amount of costs. The amount required to purchase or produce the tile inventory was EUR345,000—that is called the *cost of goods sold*, or COGS for short. Subtracting the COGS from sales gives what is called *gross profit*. Gross profit is the net inflow of money AZUL makes above and beyond the cost of the inventory. Last year's gross profit was EUR555,000."

"What is gross profit again, Esperta?" asked Pedro.

"Gross profit represents the money we make on the tile we sell after we subtract the direct costs of those tiles," responded Silva. "It's the gross profit before we consider any indirect type of costs."

"Got it." Pedro considered what gross profit he could make by chipping the azulejos off his bedroom wall and hawking them at the local market.

Silva continued, "Other operating costs, including the costs of maintaining the warehouse and most of the employee salaries, totaled EUR480,000. Those costs are called *selling, general, and administrative* (SG&A) expenses. Netting out the SG&A expenses from gross profit gives us an important figure called *operating profit*. Operating profit is the net inflow of money after all operating costs are considered. Last year, the SG&A expenses totaled EUR480,000. Subtracting EUR480,000 from the gross profit of EUR555,000 gives an operating profit of just EUR75,000."

"But EUR75,000 is still a lot of profit!" shouted Ines, whose family owned a neighborhood bakery and who was fairly financially astute.

"Yes, I guess so, but note that we haven't yet factored in the non-operating costs—such as interest expenses, which are financing costs, and taxes, which are paid to the government," Silva said. "AZUL paid EUR25,000 in interest on its EUR575,000 in debt—that's an interest rate of about 4.5%. We also paid EUR15,000 in income taxes to the government. Removing both the tax and the interest expenses gives a net income of EUR35,000."

Silva continued, "To review the income statement, the costs are divided into three major components: (1) the direct costs associated with making the tiles—COGS; (2) the indirect business costs associated with running the business—SG&A costs; and (3) the non-operating costs such as interest expense—a financing cost that is not directly associated with business operations but rather is due to how the business assets are financed—and taxes. Starting with business revenue, it is helpful to compute three levels of profits by sequentially subtracting these three types of costs. The three levels of profits are gross profit (which subtracts COGS), operating profit (which subtracts COGS and SG&A), and net profit (which subtracts all three types of costs)."

Silva looked at each of her friends in turn. "Now, what do you think of the EUR35,000 in net profit at AZUL? Is it a good number?"

"Well, AZUL's net profit isn't negative," offered Ana. "Doesn't that mean it's healthy?"

"Not so quick, menina!" countered Silva. "Our examination is just beginning. Now that you have a broad understanding of the balance sheet and income statement, it's time to take the vital signs!" As her audience gathered closer, she whispered the names of her two key business health indicators, or vital signs, of business performance: business growth and return on investment (ROI).

VITAL SIGN 1. BUSINESS GROWTH

"Let's start with business growth," Silva said. "In the Silva family, we like to see businesses that are growing. Growth isn't always critical for a good business, but a lack of growth raises questions. In reviewing a business, I often start by looking at the growth rate in sales. In the case of AZUL, I am immediately struck by the decline in sales over the past year. Two years ago, AZUL generated EUR925,000 in revenue, but this past year it was just EUR900,000. To calculate the growth rate, we take the difference between the two—that's −EUR25,000—and divide by the previous value. That gives an annual growth rate of . . ."

"Negative 2.7%!" shouted Pedro, working the calculator on his sister's phone.[14] "Total sales at AZUL have declined by 2.7% since last year."

"That's right, Pedro," said Silva. "AZUL's sales dropped almost 3% last year. That decline in revenue seems odd, since last year was a pretty good one for the building and construction industry. Sales growth is driven by one of two things: price increases or volume increases. I got a sales report from my stepbrother and discovered that the total units of tiles sold last year was 565,000, which was down from 647,000 the year before. Pedro, what does that mean for the unit volume growth rate?"

"Unit volume growth is down 12.7% year on year," Pedro said, in a tone that suggested he was suddenly feeling better about starting school. "This means that AZUL sold 12.7% fewer tiles than it did last year. The unit volume means the number of tiles sold, not the dollar amount of tiles sold."[15]

"Obrigada," Silva said. "Does everyone understand the implications of those two growth rates? How can revenue growth be −2.7% while unit volume growth is −12.7%?"

"It means that your stepbrother raised AZUL's tile prices by 10%!" declared Sandra, who was known in the group for her talents in dramatic arts and fistfighting.

---

[14] The value −2.7% is equal to (EUR900,000 − EUR925,000)/EUR925,000.
[15] The value −12.7% is equal to (565,000 − 647,000)/647,000.

"That's right, the price increases of 10% conceal the unit growth of −12.7%. The total sales growth of −2.7% is a sum of the two." (See **Table 9.2.**)

Total sales growth = unit growth + price growth.[16]

"A 10% price increase is large," Silva remarked. "I wonder why Victor did that. It seems that it sure slowed down unit growth. Lots of customers must have been turned off by the big price increase."

TABLE 9.2. Growth rate for AZUL (figures in thousands of euros).

	Last year	Two years ago
Sales	900	925
Revenue growth	−2.7%	
Unit sales	565	647
Unit growth	−12.7%	

VITAL SIGN 2. RETURN ON INVESTMENT

"Let's now go to my second vital sign," Silva continued. "Investors don't fund businesses just for the fun of it." Pedro looked at her with wide eyes and increasing admiration. "By putting up investment capital in the business, they anticipate a return on that investment. Investors put up investment money so they can earn a return on their investment, or ROI. Since ROI is the lifeblood of businesses, this indicator is a critical vital sign of business health.

"Return is defined as the annual gain to the investor divided by the amounted invested. A favorite measure I like for ROI is called return on equity, or ROE. This is a measure of ROI for equity holders. Equity holders are the owners of the business; they share the business profits and losses. ROE is defined as net profit divided by equity. This measure of returns is relevant for equity investors, like my family, since net profit is

---

[16] Note the additive relationship of price increases and unit growth is only approximately true.

the amount of profit available to the equity investor, and equity is the amount the equity holders have invested. For AZUL, this ratio is equal to 6.8%—that's the net profit of EUR35,000 divided by the equity of EUR515,000. My family, of course, has other investment opportunities, so when we consider whether to leave our money in AZUL, we need to know whether the 6.8% ROE we are getting with AZUL is good enough. What do you think?" Silva asked the group (see **Table 9.3**).

"No way," Pedro murmured, now using his sister's phone to look up typical investment returns for public tile retailers in Portugal. "I calculated ROE measures using the financial statements at some other public tile retailers in Portugal. I found that you could be getting 10% ROE investing in these other Portuguese azulejo retailers. Not only is 6.8% below the returns of comparable companies, it is way below the ROE of 11.7% that AZUL was generating two years ago."

Most of the friends eyed Pedro with dumbfounded respect. "That's right, Pedro," Silva said, her voice laden with concern. "AZUL's current ROE is below benchmark rates for both AZUL historically and for comparable firms. That's exactly why the situation at AZUL is so dire, my friends. AZUL is suffering from low returns and low growth. We've got a sick patient on our hands. No wonder my father turned to me. AZUL needs serious medical intervention." Silva knew that her financial vital signs were measures of the business's overall health, just as broad medical vital signs were for a body. And in the case of her current patient, she knew those signs indicated trouble. It was now time to start looking more closely, to find the root cause of the poor return.

TABLE 9.3. ROE for AZUL (figures in thousands of euros).

	Last year	Two years ago
Equity	515	480
Net profit	35	56
ROE	6.8%	11.7%

Silva knew a trick to identifying what was going on inside ROE. Her trick, as she explained to her friends, was to decompose ROE into three component measures: *margin, turnover,* and *leverage.* She showed the group this decomposition, using a bit of algebraic magic. "See," she explained, "ROE, which is profit divided by equity, can be expanded into three terms: profit over sales, which is margin; sales over assets, which measures turnover; and assets over equity, which captures leverage:

$$\text{ROE} = \frac{\text{profit}}{\text{equity}} = \frac{\text{profit}}{\text{sales}} \times \frac{\text{sales}}{\text{assets}} \times \frac{\text{assets}}{\text{equity}}.$$

"Since sales and assets are included in both the numerator and denominator of the ROE expansion, they algebraically drop out such that the three terms collapse down to profit/equity, or ROE."

$$\text{ROE} = \frac{\text{profit}}{\text{equity}} = \frac{\text{profit}}{\cancel{\text{sales}}} \times \frac{\cancel{\text{sales}}}{\cancel{\text{assets}}} \times \frac{\cancel{\text{assets}}}{\text{equity}}.$$

Although none of the rest of the friends had much of an idea what Silva had just shown them algebraically, they took it on trust and nodded enthusiastically.

"Because of this algebraic trick," Silva said, "when I think about ROE, I think about three component levers of ROE: first, margin, meaning profit/sales; turnover, meaning sales/assets; and finally, leverage, meaning assets/equity. Because of this relation, we are assured that all changes in ROE are due to the combined effect of changes in margin, turnover, and leverage. If AZUL's ROE is low, it must be due to low margin, low turnover, or low leverage. Let's dig into these three components and see what they tell us about what is going on with AZUL's drop in ROE."

"This is getting so exciting!" enthused Mafalda, who was nearly 11 and known widely as the neighborhood expert on bike and scooter repair. "I think we're going to figure this out and save this business!"

COMPONENT 1: MARGIN

"Yes of course we are," Silva replied with an air of confidence, "but we're not there yet. The first component of return is profit margin, profit/sales. Profit margin measures the amount of profit generated as a percentage of the sales price. High margins contribute to high returns, and low margins contribute to low returns. The magnitude of margin is determined by the relation of business costs to sales. If the sales price is high relative to the per-unit cost, then the profit margin is high. If total revenue is low relative to total costs, then profit margin is low."

Silva had Pedro calculate AZUL's net profit margin. He divided the EUR35,000 in net profit from last year by the EUR900,000 in sales and told them it was 3.9%. He knew the tile business tended to be a low-margin business—tapping furiously on his sister's phone, he had used the financial statements of the comparable tile firms to verify that net profit margins of about 4% had been common last year—so AZUL's net profit margin seemed completely normal to him. Taking her phone back, Pedro's sister Maria noted that the net profit margin the previous year had been higher, at 6.1% [EUR56,000 in net profit/EUR925,000 in sales]. See **Table 9.4.**

TABLE 9.4. Margin for AZUL (in thousands of euros).

	Last year	Two years ago
Sales	900	925
Gross profit	555	486
SG&A expenses	480	375
Operating profit	75	111
Net profit	35	56
Net profit margin	4%	6%
Operating margin	8%	12%
Gross margin	62%	53%
SG&A percentage	53%	41%

"That's a good point," confirmed Silva, "and what seems even more odd is that prices increased last year by 10%. One would think that the profit margin would go up with such a price increase."

To further investigate the net profit margin, Silva invited her friends to explore margins more deeply. She asked Pedro to calculate two other measures of margin: gross margin and operating margin. Gross margin was gross profit divided by sales, and operating margin was operating profit divided by sales. These measures of margin provided alternative ways to consider various types of cost relative to total revenue. It seemed clear to the group that margin calculations were always some measure of profit divided by sales. Pedro quickly did the math in his head and alerted the group that gross margin had increased from 53% to 62% over the past year, while operating margin had decreased from 12% to 8%.

"Isn't that interesting?" mused Silva. "While gross margin shot up by 9 percentage points with the price increase, the operating margin actually declined. Why would that be?"

"SG&A!" shouted three of Silva's friends in unison. "We think that your brother was spending money on stuff. Haven't you noticed all the surfboards he has and the new cars he's been driving?"

"I can't say I have," acknowledged Silva, "but with SG&A expense jumping from EUR375,000 to EUR480,000, it is obvious that he's spending money on something that isn't generating more sales!"

COMPONENT 2: TURNOVER

"Excellent work everybody. I think we're learning stuff," Silva said with a smile. "Shall we keep examining our patient?" The wild roar from the growing crowd of neighborhood children confirmed they were fully into it.

"The second component of return is asset turnover, sales/assets," Silva continued. "Asset turnover measures the productivity or efficiency of the business assets. Assets that are productive or efficient are able to generate proportionally high sales. A business that can generate two euros of revenue for every one euro of assets is more productive or efficient than a

TABLE 9.5. Operating turnover for AZUL (monetary figures in thousands of euros).

	Last year	Two years ago
Inventory	550	435
Total assets	1,160	1,115
Sales	900	925
Cost of goods sold	345	439
Total asset turnover	0.78	0.83
Inventory turnover	0.63	1.01

business that can only generate one euro of revenue for every one euro of assets. Turnover measures the number of times that the assets are turning over with revenue. Got it?"

"Yeah, but in AZUL's case it isn't good," Pedro asserted. "AZUL's asset turnover is low and getting worse. Last year's asset turnover was just 0.78—considering sales of EUR900/total assets EUR1,160—and that's down from 0.83 the previous year. This is pathetic asset turnover for an azulejo retailer. My research tells me that a typical asset turnover level for this type of business is above two times." (See **Table 9.5.**) With his new-found financial agility, Pedro was now considering testing out of primary school and heading directly to a graduate business school.

"As I expected," Silva agreed. "I don't think Victor was sufficiently concerned about asset productivity. He was thinking only about margin. That's a common issue among business managers. It is common for managers to forget about asset turnover . . . but we won't! We recognize that turnover is just as important as margin. If you multiply profit margin by asset turnover, you get return on assets (ROA), which is profit divided by assets. This follows the same logic that we used for the ROE decomposition. In this case, ROA can be decomposed into two components: margin, profit/sales, and turnover, sales/assets."

$$\text{ROA} = \frac{\text{profit}}{\text{assets}} = \frac{\text{profit}}{\text{sales}} \times \frac{\text{sales}}{\text{assets}}.$$

"As we can see from this relation, there are two ways to generate high ROA. You can get a high ROA from a high margin and moderate turnover, or you can get a high ROA from a high turnover and moderate margin. The high-margin, moderate-turnover approach is like a luxury retailer that marks up inventory with high prices and thus high margins and expects the inventory to move out of the store at a moderate pace. Alternatively, the high-turnover, moderate-margin approach is like a discount retailer that maintains low margins through a very shallow price markup but the inventory flies out of the store with high inventory turnover. Either approach can result in high ROA."

Silva continued, "Let's look more deeply at the various assets to identify the problem. We can investigate turnover across the various types of corporate assets. Let's start with receivables turnover. Recall that receivables are the bills that AZUL hasn't collected on sales it has made to customers on credit. Receivables turnover measures how quickly those bills are collected and is calculated as revenue divided by receivables. For AZUL last year, the receivables turnover was 4.5 times. That means that AZUL was collecting payments from its customers about 4.5 times per year. This is pretty normal for this business. That's good to see."

"I think inventory turnover is the real problem," offered Ines. "That pile of inventory I was so excited about is maybe not so good."

"Brilliant!" exclaimed Silva. "Yes, let's calculate inventory turnover as COGS/inventory. We use COGS in the numerator since inventory is priced at cost, not the retail price. We can calculate inventory turnover by dividing COGS (EUR345,000) by inventory (EUR550,000), which gives us about 0.6 times. You are absolutely right, Ines. AZUL is simply sitting on a massive stack of tile and doing nothing with it. That's not good for anybody. Victor's purchasing tile but few people are buying it . . . maybe because the price is so high. All that inventory is really affecting our ROE. Imagine if we could generate the same sales with only half that inventory (EUR225,000 rather than EUR550,000). The equity financing my family requires might drop by EUR225,000 to EUR290,000, and the ROE would rise from 6.8% to a whopping 12.1%.[17] Holding all that inventory is costly to AZUL's investors."

Ines bellowed, "What a waste of investment! Reducing it to a more productive level is an easy way to boost returns!"

COMPONENT 3: LEVERAGE

"Are you ready for the last component of ROE?" Silva asked.

The group screamed for more, and many of the children present vowed to one day become investment bankers.

"Okay. Well, this last component will definitely help you in your banking careers—it is called leverage," Silva said. "As we noted before, there are many ways to finance the assets of the business. We can use suppliers and employees through holding payables. We can use debt. And we can use equity. Our leverage component is defined in my equation as assets/equity. In other words, the less the business is financed by equity, the higher the ROE. Let's do an example. Suppose that Mafalda has a cycling business that is generating ROA (profit/assets) of 5% but is completely financed by equity. In this case, the level of assets is the same as the level of equity, so ROE would also be equal to 5%. Mafalda is making a return on her equity investment of 5%. In contrast, Ana has a business that is identical, with just one difference: her business is financed with only 10% equity, meaning that the asset/equity ratio is equal to 10. The remaining 90% of assets are funded a little by business payables and mostly by debt. With such a financing arrangement, what is Ana's ROE? Since the asset/equity ratio is 10, we multiply the 5% ROA by 10 and get 50%. That's right, poor Mafalda is earning a measly 5%, while Ana, an owner of nearly the same business, is raking it in with 50% annual returns."

"That doesn't seem fair!" Mafalda yelled.

---

[17] ROE of 12.1% is calculated as net profit of EUR35,000 divided by equity of EUR290,000 [EUR290,000 is equal to the original EUR515,000 in equity less the EUR225,000 reduction caused by the lower inventory level].

"Sure it's fair!" Ana retorted. "Don't you see I'm taking on much more risk? What if the business has a bad year with ROA of −5%? In your case, you would lose only 5%, but in my case I would lose 50% of my investment. That's how leverage works. It magnifies your operating returns—both good and bad."

"I think that the same thing is going on at AZUL," Maria observed.

"Yes, that's right," Pedro chimed in. "The company is being largely financed with debt. As such, your family should require a higher ROE since you are bearing some additional financial risk. Maybe it should be a little higher than my original estimate."

"Well done, friends," Silva said with a smile. "I think we have diagnosed what's going on with our patient. What do you all recommend we do to get our patient to better financial health?"

"Cut SG&A!" Maria called out.

"Stimulate sales by reducing prices!" Ana shouted. "We can give up some gross margin, but we have to get better asset turnover."

"Reduce inventory investment!" Ines insisted. "I don't think we need to buy more tile for at least a year."

"With the reduction in inventory, we could reduce our debt financing," Mafalda suggested.

"You know, you all are right," acknowledged Silva. "I think our financial analysis is over. Let's go fix a business!"

A roar of support went up as Silva and all her friends—well, all but Pedro, who had already begun working on his business school applications—rushed off to AZUL's small office, financial statements in hand, to deliver their prognosis.

CONCEPT WRAP-UP

Like a medical examination, financial analysis commonly starts with broad tests of financial performance followed by deep drills to identify sources of abnormality. In this chapter, Esperta Silva demonstrated her prowess at assessing financial health. The process of understanding what was going on at AZUL was intriguing and informative. As we saw, a lot can be learned from a careful study of financial statements and ratios. The analysis resulted in a number of action items that the managers could use to make significant gains in improving the financial health of the business.

In this chapter, it was also evident once more that finance people use a lot of unique terms. Since finance people use financial statements so often, it is critical to become comfortable with the words associated with the income statement and balance sheet. And since the financial ratios featured in this chapter are also very common, it is important to become comfortable with the general definition and usage of these ratios. You'll see many of these concepts and terminology in future chapters.

REVIEW QUESTIONS

Following the session at the operating table, Mafalda returned home to organize the financials for her bike and scooter repair business. The number of bikes and scooters she had repaired was 20 last year (Year 1) and 23 this year (Year 2). The repairs had resulted in revenue of EUR120 last year and EUR138 this year. The direct costs of the repairs (COGS) was EUR70 last year and EUR103 this year. The fixed cost (general and administrative [G&A] expenses) had been EUR5 each year, paid to her grandmother in exchange for using her patio as the shop. Mafalda paid no taxes or interest expense. The assets for her business included EUR30 in tools and EUR20 in repair inventory. These amounts had not changed year over year. Her cash balance had increased from EUR50 last year to EUR70 this year. She had never before extended credit to her customers, but Ana hadn't been able to pay recently, so she still owed Mafalda EUR10 for a recent repair. Mafalda had used her own money to finance all the assets of the business.

Question 1. Use the given information to build an income statement for Mafalda's repair business. This should include the number of bikes and scooters repaired for each of the two years and the resulting revenue for the two years. Subtracting the COGS from revenue gives the gross profit for the two years. Subtracting the G&A expenses from gross profit gives the operating profit. See the template in **Table 9.6**. What does the income statement tell Mafalda about her business?

TABLE 9.6. Template for Mafalda's repair business income statement.

Income Statement	Year 1	Year 2
Bikes and scooters repaired (number)		
Revenue		
COGS		
Gross profit		
G&A expenses		
Operating profit		

Question 2. Use the given information to build a balance sheet for Mafalda's repair business. This should include the cash balance, the receivables (invoices that haven't yet been paid), and the inventory for each of the two years. Adding these three items up gives the current assets for both years. The tools Mafalda owns are the business's equipment. Summing the current assets and the equipment gives the total assets she owns. Since she doesn't owe anything to anyone, the right-hand side of her balance sheet contains only one account—equity. The amount of equity must equal the total assets amount so that the balance sheet balances. See the template in **Table 9.7**. What does the balance sheet tell Mafalda about her business?

TABLE 9.7. Template for Mafalda's repair business balance sheet.

Balance Sheet	Year 1	Year 2
Cash		
Receivables		
Inventory		
Current assets		
Equipment		
Total assets		
Equity		

Question 3. Based on the financial statements you created in questions 1 and 2, perform a financial analysis of the business. In your analysis, calculate the following financial ratios: the unit and revenue growth rate, return on equity (ROE), gross and operating margin, asset turnover, and financial leverage.

Question 4. What do you observe about Mafalda's business? Is the unit growth and revenue growth the same? What does that suggest? Is the ROE increasing or decreasing? What is the cause? How do the other ratios help you identify the cause of changes in ROE?

Question 5. What would you say to Mafalda about the financial health of her business?

10

Financial Modeling and Operation NO MORE CORN

TRAGEDY AT THE CROSSROADS

As the sun rose, two solitary figures could be seen wandering the remains of the horror that once had been a verdant field. Just hours before, this had been the scene of a brutal hand-to-hand conflict that had ended in the complete annihilation of the military force these two men had commanded. General Echec, the senior officer for the campaign, was with his aide, Sergeant Maquette, in the early morning hours, trying to make sense of the tragedy.

"My instinct assured me that we would prevail if our forces were concentrated at the crossroads," began Echec, "but that instinct betrayed me. The battle plan was terribly flawed. Our forces are destroyed. Hundreds of lives are lost. The blame for this terrible tragedy rests completely on my shoulders."

"Easy, General," Maquette responded. "How could you have known how hard it was going to be to hold our line? How could you have known the size of their force? How could you have known how things were going to play out?"

"How could I have known?" Echec echoed. "I could have considered alternative scenarios. I foolishly trusted my instincts when more thorough analysis was so easily available. My uncle used to say, 'The School of Hard

Knocks demands the costliest tuition.' I agree—there is nothing costlier than terribly unnecessary mistakes. Paper learning beats blind life learning every day."

"I see, General," said Maquette. "It is too easy to have confidence in your gut."

"It is, Maquette," agreed Echec. "I should have gone through this battle on paper from every angle, over and over, before I ever had the confidence to run it in real life." He hefted the sword of a fallen soldier and added, "It is infinitely better to gain military insight from a model than to do it in battle."

CONCEPT

Finance people like building financial models that allow them to test out the implications of their decisions. Financial models commonly consist of electronic spreadsheets with lots of assumptions that drive all sorts of implied financial outcomes—like profit, cash flow, and net present value (NPV). Finance people are rarely satisfied with just one version of a financial model; instead, they work their models hard by scrutinizing the variation in outcome across all sorts of potential scenarios and assumptions, asking questions like, "What is our outcome if competition intensifies?"; "What about if demand is soft?"; "What about if demand is strong?"; and "What if our costs are greater than expected?"

What is the point in modeling all these scenarios? Since finance decisions are rooted in large amounts of uncertainty about the future, it is important to appreciate the implications of various outcomes. Finance people—like General Echec—have learned that it is more prudent to quantify and understand the implications of all that uncertainty than to simply close their eyes and trust their gut.

In this chapter, we meet two women who learn the value of financial modeling as they examine the implications of pricing and product choice on the operating profit for their new venture, which they designed to save their community from the ravages of creamed corn.

TERMINOLOGY

Financial model. A financial model is a financial forecast of a business outcome based on various assumptions. Financial models are commonly built using electronic spreadsheet software. A financial model is like a prototype of a product—it allows the analyst to examine and test a "mocked-up" business scenario without actually pursuing the project in real life. Good models allow the analyst to adjust assumptions and easily see how the outcomes vary. Financial models are powerful tools for financial decision-making.

AGNES AND ZINA'S LAST STAND

It was lunchtime at Goodtimes Senior Living Center. Longtime tablemates Agnes Adams and Zina Zamboni sat chatting together while their meal arrived. At ages 87 and 92, respectively, they counted their combined experience at the nursing home facility as close to five years. The pair enjoyed most aspects of living at Goodtimes, which offered modern amenities and an engaging community. The food was the one thing with which they and many of their fellow residents were often disgruntled. It seemed that few considered mealtime at Goodtimes a good time.

Their plates were placed on the table, and as she looked at the meal, Zamboni felt she'd had enough. "Another lunch of mediocre Salisbury steak, mashed potatoes, and creamed corn. How much longer are we going to put up with this, Agnes?"

Adams bellowed, "I'm not going to put up with it another day! Watch this, Zina!" Adams looked both ways and then, with a quick fling of her wrists, launched the entire contents of her plate into the air. Zamboni shielded her head, concerned that the falling food might damage her new permed hairdo. But there was no need; the entire meal was stuck perfectly, artfully, and entirely to the dining room ceiling. Adams raised both arms in victory.

Looking up, Zamboni paused to admire her friend's table manners. She then declared, "Agnes, it is time for a revolution. It is time for Operation NO MORE CORN."

Operation NO MORE CORN was a radical plot the tablemates had been concocting for years. They wanted to start their own food truck business to bring high-quality meals to the residents at Goodtimes. The pair had already negotiated a parking spot on a property adjacent to the senior center and had spoken to two of their teenage grandsons about working the truck during the summer. Perusing online marketplaces, the two women had found a food truck owner who had offered to rent them a truck for a reasonable monthly fee. The business would be marketed as Granny Truck.

"Let the operation begin! If we don't get that truck launched soon, I'm going to really start causing trouble in here," Adams threatened. Leaning on her walker, she stood up. Then, steadying herself, Adams got a foot up and slowly managed to climb to a full standing position on her chair at the dining table.

"Residents of Goodtimes!" she announced at the top of her 87-year-old lungs. "Are you oppressed by cafeteria tyranny? Is your GI tract revolting? It is time to unite. It is time for a revolution!" With the full attention of the residents in the cafeteria, Adams led everyone in a fervent chant: "No more corn! No more corn! No more corn!"

Suddenly, a swarm of Goodtimes staff members rushed to Adams's table, quieted the chant, and helped Adams down from the chair and back into her seat. After some scolding from Jackie, a favorite staff member, and a warning to all that disruptive residents could be banned from the center's regular competitive bingo games, calm was restored to the cafeteria.

"What were you thinking, sister?" scolded Zamboni. "That's not the way we're going to win this war. You've got to think more with your head and less with your stomach."

"Huh?"

"That's right," agreed Mary Marino, who had shuffled over to their table. "I know what you are up to, and I want you to hear me out. In the business world, suckers do and winners model."

"Huh?" Adams and Zamboni said in unison.

Ignoring their confusion, Marino continued, "If a revolution is what you want, there's one skill you both need more than knitting, puzzles, or food slinging. You need to be modelers—*financial* modelers."

OPERATION NO MORE CORN

To survive the Goodtimes cafeteria fare for the past year, Adams and Zamboni had encouraged their teenage grandsons to make midnight deliveries of homemade sandwiches through the nursing home windows. Not only had the system maintained the women's emotional and physical health, the sandwich deliveries had also given them a good understanding of what food was both tasty and easy on their geriatric digestive systems.

The success had led to late-night discussions of how to scale up the operation to benefit the other Goodtimes residents, as well as provide jobs for their grandsons. In their deliberations, the women had narrowed the business plan to two concepts—Zamboni advocated for a submarine sandwich outlet and Adams wanted to serve Greek gyros—but they didn't know which one to pursue. Either way, they agreed to keep the menu simple and offer just two options: a discount sandwich priced at either USD5.00 or USD7.00 and a premium sandwich priced at either USD7.00 or USD9.00.

Their history of midnight deliveries had given them a good sense of the production costs associated with their sandwiches. Based on the costs and selected prices, the friends had created a schedule of gross profit on each sandwich sold (see **Table 10.1**). Their per-unit gross profit was equal to the price of the sandwich minus the costs of the ingredients.

Based on this schedule, they learned that if they priced the discount sandwich at USD5.00, the gross profit would be USD1.00 per sandwich on the Greek offering and USD1.50 per sandwich on the submarine offering. Alternatively, if they priced the discount sandwich at USD7.00, their

TABLE 10.1. Estimates of per-sandwich gross profit by offering and price point (in US dollars).

	Price	Gross profit (per-unit price less per-unit cost)	
		Greek	Subs
Low-price scenario			
Discount sandwich	5.00	1.00	1.50
Premium sandwich	7.00	2.00	2.50
High-price scenario			
Discount sandwich	7.00	3.00	3.50
Premium sandwich	9.00	4.00	4.50

gross profit would be USD3.00 on the Greek offering and USD3.50 on the submarine offering. Higher gross profits were expected on the premium sandwich. As they scanned the schedule, Adams was first to observe that the gross profit was consistently better on the submarine offering than on the Greek offering. "It looks to me that due to their lower costs, the submarine sandwich line is the way to go," she admitted. "There is consistently more profit in subs."

"Not so fast, sister," countered Zamboni. "While you are right on a per-sandwich basis, total profits may tell a different story. We know nothing about demand—what people want to eat. In order to figure out which concept and price points give us better overall profit, we need to do some market research."

To keep the nursing home administration off their tail, the pair had reached out to Tom O'Brien, an 88-year-old friend who lived on Hallway B and happened to be a former partner at a metropolitan market research firm. He agreed to run some focus groups in the facility to measure demand for the food truck concept. After a week of randomized small-group meetings in the TV room, O'Brien returned with his results. **Table 10.2** provides his estimates of weekly sandwich demand for both offerings at the two proposed price points. As compensation, O'Brien asked for a month's worth of line-cutting privileges at the sandwich truck.

TABLE 10.2. Weekly sandwich demand estimates by offering and price point (in US dollars).

	Price	Demand			
		Greek		Subs	
Discount sandwich	5.00	415	(400)	350	(300)
Premium sandwich	7.00	300	(280)	250	(200)
Discount sandwich	7.00	275	(250)	175	(150)
Premium sandwich	9.00	200	(180)	125	(100)

Note: For the demand values, the expected demand figure is listed first, with the low-side demand figure in parentheses.

Both women were delighted to see confirmation that there was robust demand for their sandwiches. But Adams was particularly pleased to see that the market had an obvious preference for the Greek offering. At any price point, Greek sandwiches were preferred, with higher sandwich demand over the sub offering. With the demand favoring Greek and unit profits favoring subs, it wasn't clear which offering was best for the business.

While they had done considerable planning, Adams and Zamboni knew they had more to do. Granny Truck was still a dream, not a reality.

THE WONDER: A FINANCIAL MODEL

Back at the cafeteria, where the contents of Adams's plate were still stuck to the ceiling, Marino sat down with the would-be entrepreneurs and repeated her caution: "If a revolution is what you want, there's one skill you both need more than knitting, puzzles, or even food slinging. You need to be financial modelers."

Zamboni leaned forward and asked, "Financial what?"

"Financial modelers, girls," Marino repeated. "A financial model is an electronic spreadsheet that allows you to forecast a business's outcome and performance based on various basic assumptions. It allows you to test various assumptions for importance on business outcomes. By modeling the performance of the business beforehand, you can learn a lot about the business and drivers of performance well before going to market. It is kind of like building a prototype of a product prior to going to market. You'd never launch a product without building a prototype! Financial models are powerful tools for any financial decision-making."

"Mary, I thought you used to be a librarian," Zamboni said wonderingly.

"That's right. I was head of research at Morgan Stanley," Marino said.

"Got it," Zamboni said, with raised eyebrows. "So how do we go about building a financial model?"

"I'm happy to help," offered Marino with a smile, "and I'll promise to keep my billing rate modest."

Marino pulled a laptop out of the basket on her walker, fired up the machine, and opened a blank spreadsheet. "A financial model will help you put together the demand, pricing, and cost data to identify which scenarios are best."

Sitting at the cafeteria table, the three went to work. As a base-case model, they decided to go with the low-price scenario and price their sandwiches at USD5.00 for the discount sandwich and USD7.00 for the premium sandwich. They intended to make their truck a "food for the people" kind of business and didn't want to charge too much. They added in the corresponding demand estimates from O'Brien and various cost estimates they had been collecting. This allowed them to build a hypothetical income statement, or what Marino called a *P&L* (profit and loss statement), for the business. Adams and Zamboni added the weekly wage rate at which they planned to compensate their grandsons, as well as the weekly rental of the truck and other miscellaneous expenses they anticipated. **Table 10.3** provides the initial base-case financial model that Adams and Zamboni put together, with substantial help from Marino.

Multiplying the price by the expected weekly units sold for each sandwich gave the expected weekly revenue: USD4,175 for the Greek concept and USD3,500 for the sub concept. So far, so good for the Greek. Then they added a line for the expected gross profit, by multiplying the estimated amount of gross profit per sandwich by the expected weekly sandwiches sold to get the expected weekly gross profit: USD1,015 for the

TABLE 10.3. Financial model of weekly profits (low-price scenario; monetary values in US dollars).

	Granny's Greek	Granny's Subs	
Plate 1 price	5.00	5.00	
Units 1	415	350	
Gross profit 1	1.00	1.50	
Plate 2 price	7.00	7.00	
Units 2	300	250	
Gross profit 2	2.00	2.50	
Total revenue	4,175	3,500	P1price × units1 + P2price × units2
Total gross profit	1,015	1,150	GP1 × units1 + GP2 × units2
Wages	928	800	Weekly hours × 16/hour
Rent (equipment and parking)	400	350	Rental rate for trailer + 100 for lot
Other fixed costs	100	100	
Operating profit	−413	−100	Total gross profit − other expenses

Greek concept and USD1,150 for the sub concept. Because of the lower per-sandwich production costs, the sub concept looked better on a gross-profit basis.

Then they added estimates for fixed costs. For the submarine offering, they expected that their grandsons would work 25 hours per week. Since the Greek offering required cooked meat, the grandsons' work hours would be slightly longer, at 29 hours per week. At a wage of USD16 per hour, the wages would run USD800 per week for the submarine offering and USD928 per week for the Greek offering. They had a firm quote on the rental cost for the trailer. The base rate was USD250 per week. This would be fine for the sub trailer, but the Greek trailer would need additional equipment to cook the meat, which would increase the rental cost to USD300 per week. The ladies added these figures, along with the USD100 weekly rental cost for the parking area, into their model to give a rental expense of USD400 for the Greek offering and USD350 for the sub offering. Finally, they estimated a number of additional fixed costs, including power and propane costs at USD100 per week.

Once the fixed costs were added in, the news was not good. The sub concept was expected to lose USD100 per week and the Greek concept was expected to lose USD413 per week. This wasn't going to work. The ladies didn't have the appetite or means to subsidize the business every week. It was clear that they needed to model some alternative assumptions.

Marino agreed. Confident that Adams and Zamboni now knew what they were doing, she congratulated them on their modeling prowess and encouraged them to borrow her laptop to run additional scenarios. Handing it to them, she shuffled off. The two women retired to Adams's room for more analysis.

"We need to look at the effect of raising our prices, Zina," Adams said. "I know we'll lose demand, but maybe the higher gross profit is enough to offset that loss—hopefully USD7.00 and USD9.00 sandwiches can still be sandwiches for the people."

They replaced the unit prices in their model with the prices and gross profits of the high-price scenario. Next, they adjusted the units demanded: if the sandwiches were going to be priced higher, they needed to change the units demanded as suggested by O'Brien. The fixed-cost assumptions were unaffected. The revised model is provided in **Table 10.4**.

The revised model suggested that the increased gross profits created by the higher prices more than offset the reduction in volume demanded. And in the new model, the overall profits were increased. For the sub concept, the weekly loss was now just USD75. However, the model suggested that the Greek concept could be profitable with a weekly operating profit estimated at nearly USD200.

Climbing on her bed and bouncing high enough to get over a second of hang time, Adams hollered, "It looks like we're going Greek, Grandma! I love financial modeling!"

Zamboni quieted Adams's enthusiasm by reminding her that those estimates had been completed using the expected demand. "Aren't you worried about our outcome if our concept generates the low-side demand

TABLE 10.4. Financial model of weekly profits (high-price scenario; monetary values in US dollars).

	Granny's Greek	Granny's Subs
Plate 1 price	7.00	7.00
Units 1	275	175
Gross profit 1	3.00	3.50
Plate 2 price	9.00	9.00
Units 2	200	125
Gross profit 2	4.00	4.50
Total revenue	3,725	2,350
Total gross profit	1,625	1,175
Wages	928	800
Rent (equipment and parking)	400	350
Other fixed costs	100	100
Operating profit	197	−75

figures O'Brien estimated?" Adams looked unfazed, but Zamboni went ahead and altered the demand figures to reflect the low-side demand forecast. The result of the change is provided in **Table 10.5**: the Greek concept still made positive operating profit, even with the low-side demand.

TABLE 10.5. Financial model of weekly profits (high-price and low-side demand scenario; monetary values in US dollars).

	Granny's Greek	Granny's Subs
Plate 1 price	7.00	7.00
Units 1	250	150
Gross profit 1	3.00	3.50
Plate 2 price	9.00	9.00
Units 2	180	100
Gross profit 2	4.00	4.50
Total revenue	3,370	1,950
Total gross profit	1,470	975
Wages	928	800
Rent (equipment and parking)	400	350
Other fixed costs	100	100
Operating profit	42	−275

Zamboni acknowledged that the high-priced Greek sandwich offering did indeed seem to be the most viable way to go, and then she joined Adams for a celebratory bounce on the bed.

CONCEPT WRAP-UP

This chapter has showcased the value of a simple financial model in deciding on the rollout of Adams and Zamboni's new venture. The model helped them examine the implications of pricing and product choice on the operating profit before they started the business in real life.

Finance people like to build models. They have learned that it is more prudent to quantify and understand the implications of all the uncertainty faced by their business than to simply close their eyes and trust their gut. Finance people are rarely satisfied with just one model, instead working their models hard by scrutinizing the variations in outcome across every scenario they can imagine. They model all these scenarios because they appreciate that finance decisions are rooted in large amounts of uncertainty about the future. By using a financial model to analyze the outcomes from every possible angle, finance people are able to generate insights that greatly aid their decision-making.

REVIEW QUESTIONS

Question 1. Using the template in **Table 10.6**, replicate Agnes Adams and Zina Zamboni's financial model for the high-price scenario detailed in **Table 10.4**. Your replicated model should use assumption input values for all of the cells colored gray, including plate 1 gross profit, unit 1 demand, plate 2 gross profit, unit 2 demand, wages, rent, and other fixed costs as specified in the table. All other values in the template (those not colored gray) should be calculated based on these assumption input values. The end result should be a

TABLE 10.6. Template.

	Granny's Greek	Granny's Subs
Plate 1 price	7.00	7.00
Units 1		
Gross profit 1		
Plate 2 price	9.00	9.00
Units 2		
Gross profit 2		
Total revenue		
Total gross profit		
Wages		
Rent (equipment and parking)		
Other fixed costs		
Operating profit		

model that matches **Table 10.4.** Consider doing this using electronic spreadsheet software.

Question 2. Imagine an even-higher-price scenario. Suppose Tom O'Brien tested a demand scenario for even higher prices and found the estimated demand values outlined in **Table 10.7.** Adjust the financial model you created in response to question 1 to include these new assumptions. Would you recommend that Adams and Zamboni consider pricing their sandwiches even higher?

Question 3. For the last several years, O'Brien and Mary Marino have lived off WOW Sauce, a hot sauce that their granddaughters concocted to help their grandparents mask the bland taste of the Goodtimes food. O'Brien and Marino chatted about starting a business to market bottles of WOW Sauce to the other Goodtimes residents. Their granddaughters' production costs were USD5 per bottle of WOW Sauce. The weekly hours were low, such that the wage costs were expected to be just USD160 per week for both granddaughters. The other

TABLE 10.7. Even-higher-price scenario per-unit gross profit and weekly sandwich demand estimates by offering and price point (monetary values in US dollars).

	Granny's Greek	Granny's Subs
Plate 1 price	9.00	9.00
Units 1	155	140
Gross profit 1	5.00	5.50
Plate 2 price	11.00	11.00
Units 2	110	75
Gross profit 2	6.00	6.50

fixed costs were USD100 per week. Weekly demand was estimated at 100 bottles per week, if priced at USD8 per bottle, and 75 bottles per week, if priced at USD10 per bottle.

Build a financial model that indicates the business profits under the following two scenarios: a price of USD8 per bottle and a price of USD10 per bottle.

11

Cash Flow and
El Rancho de las Vacas Bailando

EL PROBLEMA PANTANOS

With arguably the world's richest soil and most reliable sunshine, the Pantanos Valley was South America's most productive agricultural region for salad greens. But what was commonly known as the "Latin salad bowl" did not look so inviting today.

With a dry, wilted head of lettuce in his hand, Pablo Ganancia looked out over the 50-acre tract of lettuce fields his family had tended for generations. The ground was scorched and thirsty. With just one mile separating his fields from one of the country's great rivers, irrigation had long been used to provide water to the fields of the Pantanos Valley. Faraway glacial snowpack, high in the Andes Mountains, had long been a reliable water source for the river.

With deep concern, Pablo looked to his wife Sofia, who had joined him in the field. "Where is the water, Sofia?" he asked. "This has not been a drought year. There was plenty of snowfall. There should be plenty of water, but look at our dying crop. Where is the water?"

Sofia was quick to respond, "This is tragic, mi esposo, but I think you could benefit from a better understanding of river hydrology. There is a lot going on in any hydrological system—more than meets the eye.

Precipitation is only one factor that drives downstream river flow. Other factors include infiltration, which is precipitation that seeps into the ground; interflow, which is water that moves underground; evapotranspiration, which is water that evaporates back into the air; and diversion, which is water that is diverted away from the waterway for consumption or other purposes. Because of the complexity in any river system, an assessment of reasonable snowfall in the headwaters is wholly insufficient to predict healthy downstream river flow, my dear Pablo."

"But we've been to the river," Pablo said. "We know that our great river is now just mud and a trickle of water. I don't understand it. There was plenty of snow last winter and good rain all spring!"

"Yes, mi esposo. But maybe your understanding would be helped if you listened to what I've been saying about river hydrology. I don't believe that there has been much change to the infiltration rates, interflow rates, or evapotranspiration rates in our watershed. If we can both accept that assumption, the only explanation is a change in diversion rates," explained Sofia.

"Yes, of course, dear," responded Pablo, still holding aloft his dry head of lettuce.

"Good. I'm so glad you understand," Sofia said. "Using an archive of satellite imagery for our watershed that I found online, I examined evidence of changes in water diversion from the river."

"You did? What did you find?" asked Pablo with renewed eagerness and respect.

"Plenty," Sofia replied. "The images I observed indicated the presence of 26 new upstream diversion canals on the river. These canals are feeding new housing construction and increased agricultural activity upstream."

"¡Dime que no es cierto!" exclaimed Pablo in indignation, holding high the wilted lettuce, which was drooping even more as he held it in the sun.

"I'm afraid it is true," confirmed Sofia. "The problem appears to be upstream usage. There are simply too many straws in the river above the Pantanos Valley. With all the water being diverted to other activities upstream, the river doesn't have enough water to continue a healthy flow by the time it gets to us."

"So what you are telling me, Sofia, is that with all those straws in the river upstream, normal snowfall isn't enough to ensure irrigation to our valley. The downstream farmer gets nothing if the upstream folks divert everything for their purposes. With all the diversion, our only hope for irrigating our land is heavy snowfall seasons in the headwaters. Is that it?" Pablo asked, increasingly agitated. "Then what are we supposed to do, Sofia? Sabotage the upstream canals by pouring concrete into their headgates in the middle of the night?" Pablo hurled the head of wilted lettuce into the air.

"No, my dear. I don't see sabotage as the appropriate solution," Sofia answered tenderly. "I think we have three alternatives: (1) hope for regular heavy snowfall that will provide enough precipitation to overwhelm the upstream diversion; (2) use the political process to get the upstream people to use less water; or (3) switch crops from lettuce to sorghum. I understand that sorghum doesn't need much water."

"Hmm. What's sorghum?"

CONCEPT

Finance people care about the gains investors get from their investments. One measure of those gains is business profit, but like snowfall in mountain headwaters, profit doesn't account for all the diversion that happens to company profit. The main source of diversion is business investment. When managers reinvest profits into the business by acquiring new equipment or increasing inventory, investors don't pocket their immediate business gains. Businesses that plow most of the profit into business investment leave little cash flow for the downstream investors. Profits never make it to investors if the company always reinvests those profits back into the business. Confusing mountain snowfall and downstream irrigation water is like confusing profits and cash flow—profits never make it to cash flow if they are diverted through business investment. What really matters to investors is cash flow—the cash that is returned to investors and "waters their fields."

While it is true that investors can always get cash by cashing out their investment—meaning selling it to another investor (e.g., selling their shares of stock)—the cash value of the investment should correlate with the business's expected cash flow. For example, the stock of a company with healthy cash flow will sell for substantially more than the stock of a company with weak cash flow. Thus there is no way for investors to avoid the meaningful implications of business cash flow.

In this chapter, we will look into cash flow and show how elusive it is, particularly in the context of business growth. We will establish why cash flow, not profit, is the true lifeblood of any business and critical for business success. To examine this issue, the chapter uses the example of el Rancho de las Vacas Bailando, a cattle ranch in Uruguay, where everything seems to be going well.

TERMINOLOGY

Working capital (net working capital). Working capital—or, equivalently, net working capital—refers to the net difference between a business's current operating assets and its current operating liabilities. It can be calculated by adding up the operating cash, receivables, and inventory, then subtracting the operating accounts payable and wages payable. This difference is a measure of the net amount of the current assets the business has less the current liabilities it owes. Because we generally think of having lots of stuff as a good thing, it is common to think that businesses want lots of working capital. But finance people recognize that lots of working capital is costly because investors have to finance it all, and so they tend to prefer low, efficient amounts of working capital (i.e., inventory that moves quickly and accounts receivable that get collected quickly). Since working capital is a measure of the amount of funding required to finance the business's net current assets, that funding requirement should be minimized as much as possible. For example, if working capital is equal to zero (e.g., accounts payable offsets accounts receivable and inventory), investors don't have to come up with the money to fund the company's current operating assets; the generosity of suppliers and employees of the company (by not demanding immediate payment) is large enough that it completely funds all the cash, customer credit, and inventory. If working capital is greater than zero, then investors finance the working-capital balance.

Fixed assets (net fixed assets). The total investment in both long-term assets, such as property, plant, and equipment (PP&E), and intangible assets is called fixed assets. Fixed assets are different from working capital because fixed assets are long-term assets while working capital exists in the short term.

Cash flow. Cash flow is the net amount of money a business generates for its investors. Cash flow represents the financial effect on investors in the business or business project. Positive cash flow means a current positive payout to investors. Negative cash flow means a current negative cash effect to investors (i.e., investors pay money into the business). Investors care about how businesses consume or produce cash, because the only way they get compensated for investing in the business is through business cash flow or selling their investment to someone else. Investors recognize that measures of profit have a number of distortions that can make business profit differ substantially from business cash flow. One of these distortions is noncash expenses like depreciation and amortization. Another distortion occurs when management doesn't distribute profits but instead plows them back into the business by buying additional assets. Technically, a standard definition of cash flow is equal to net operating profit after tax (NOPAT), adding back depreciation and amortization, subtracting capital expenditures in fixed assets, and subtracting net investment in working capital. The intuition behind this formula is that cash flow starts with the operating profits of the business and adds back any depreciation or amortization expenses since those expenses don't really require cash payment—they are only allocations included to reduce taxes. Finally, the business investment, which is equal to changes in net working capital and capital expenditures, is subtracted.

THE WISDOM OF AN ABUELO

The sunset was spectacular over the wide-open pampas, its glow reflected in the Yí River winding through Uruguay's heartland. This was a land where cattle outnumbered people 10 to 1 and rugged gauchos were the norm.

Eight-year-old Marta Acosta and her abuelo—her grandfather—sat on the backs of two Uruguayan Criollo horses, soaking in the view at the end of a long day on the ranch. It was times like this that Marta extracted the best wisdom from her usually tight-lipped, ranch-worn abuelo.

"Abuelo," asked young Marta, "is anywhere more beautiful than Uruguay?"

Marta's grandfather smiled. "No, my granddaughter, this land is beautiful. I know of nowhere that compares."

The two sat in silence for nearly 10 minutes before Marta spoke again. "Abuelo, why is it that we are gauchos?"

Marta's abuelo smiled again. "My granddaughter, as cattle were made for Uruguay, so too were Uruguayans made for cattle. We were made to be gauchos."

The two sat for another 10 minutes, until Marta's grandfather observed that darkness was settling in, and he stirred to begin making their way home.

"Before we go, Abuelo, I have one last question," Marta said. Her grandfather nodded, so she continued, "I know that the ranch we work is very successful, while other ranches always seem to have troubles. Why is that? Some say it is because of the cattle we breed and the way that you treat them. Is that so?"

Her grandfather's eyes narrowed. "It is right that we do have fine cattle and I do treat them well, but that is not why our ranch does well, mi nieta." He leaned toward Marta and in a voice both quiet and commanding, he said, "The secret is not necessarily the cattle or the land. What keeps this ranch strong, my dear, is flujo de fondos—cash flow."

He continued, "Many things are important to the success of an organization—the mission, the people, the assets, the customers, the strategy, the competition, the industry dynamics. But ultimately, one thing distinguishes financially healthy organizations from those that are unhealthy, and that characteristic is cash flow. Just as a ranch doesn't work if the cattle eat more than they produce, so it doesn't work if the ranch itself eats more than it produces. This cash flow problem is particularly acute with a ranch like ours that is trying to put on weight, or grow, quickly. I've found that slowing the weight gain can do a lot to improve the cash flow."

TROUBLE AT EL RANCHO DE LAS VACAS BAILANDO

It was a surprise to no one that decades later, Marta Acosta was living a gaucho life on the cattle ranches of Uruguay. She was working as cattle manager at el Rancho de las Vacas Bailando. It had been a good year. Fernando Fernandez, the ranch owner, had grown the cattle herd substantially. Silvia Suarez, the ranch manager, kept the ranch's army of gauchos busy and productive. Arturo Lopez, the ranch financial manager, was bragging about the year's record profits. Yet despite all the swagger by the most senior people at the ranch, there was a deep sense that something was not right.

Antonio Marchado, the ranch cook, had said to himself more than once, "Why is it that fideos con tuco is the only thing I have to feed our gauchos for their breakfast, lunch, and dinner?"

Acosta, who was particularly proud of the size of the herd, had overheard a conversation in which another ranch worker mentioned that the ranch's bank had refused to extend further credit. Acosta was alarmed at the effect that might have on her herd.

Rodrigo Fernandez, Fernando's seven-year-old son, had watched his mother take pictures of his bed; when he asked her why, she said the pictures were to help sell it. He wondered what would motivate a mother to sell her own son's bed.

One day, while Marchado was setting a large pot of noodles on the stove to cook, Rodrigo Fernandez and Acosta entered the kitchen together.

They were discussing what was amiss at el Rancho de las Vacas Bailando, and Marchado invited them to stay for lunch. Acosta passed the communal maté cup to Marchado as Fernandez spread out a copy of the ranch financial statements that he had somehow gotten hold of (see **Table 11.1**). Acosta and Marchado eagerly leaned over to look.

With his finger on the income statement, Fernandez was first to highlight the important increase in sales and profits. "Both sales and profits are up 38%. From everything I can tell, this past year has been the ranch's best year ever."

Acosta studied the balance sheet and noticed the sizable increase in debt. "But look, che, the ranch debt has gone up even more. Look at

TABLE 11.1. Financial statements for Rancho de las Vacas Bailando (figures in millions of Uruguayan pesos).

	2022	2021
Balance Sheet		
Cash	0.2	1.4
Receivables	1.2	0.8
Inventory	8.8	5.5
Property and equipment	3.3	2.1
Total assets	13.5	9.8
Payables	1.8	2.5
Debt	4.8	2.5
Equity	6.9	4.8
Total liabilities and equity	13.5	9.8
Income Statement		
Net sales	12.5	9
Cost of goods sold	7.8	5.6
Gross profit	4.7	3.4
General expenses	2.0	1.5
Operating profit	2.7	1.9
Interest expenses	0.2	0.1
Taxes	0.4	0.3
Net profit	2.1	1.5

that—from UYU2.5 million to UYU4.8 million.[18] Why would a ranch that is doing this well be adding so much debt? No wonder the bank didn't want to offer more credit."

Fernandez noted the substantial decline in the cash account, from UYU1.4 million to UYU0.2 million.

Acosta reflected on her childhood conversations with her grandfather. She was certain he would fully appreciate the problems at Vacas Bailando, and she was confident that her abuelo's wisdom would help her and her friends get to the root of what was going on.

"Let's start by simplifying the balance sheet into the four main components," she suggested, remembering a trick her grandfather used to do. "We can aggregate the balance sheet items into two categories of assets—fixed assets and net working capital—and two categories of financing—debt and equity." She then drew a diagram with four boxes (see **Figure 11.1**).

"Fixed assets includes the value of all the long-term assets of the ranch, including the land, buildings, and equipment. In financial accounting, these are reported at their historical cost, after depreciation has been deducted. In our case, this amount is the same as the property and equipment, which is listed on the balance sheet as UYU3.3 million."

Acosta went on, "The value of net working capital—or just working capital—is a little more difficult. We begin with the ranch's current assets, which includes all the short-term assets such as cash, receivables that the ranch has yet to collect, and inventory—which in our case is the amount of money we've put into our cattle herd. Adding up all the current assets from the balance sheet gives UYU10.2 million—that's cash of UYU0.2 million + receivables of UYU1.2 million + inventory of UYU8.8 million. As with the fixed assets, someone needs to finance all of that UYU10.2 million in current assets. Since it is common for suppliers to give a business some time before paying for their goods or services, these suppliers provide partial funding for the current assets. Because of this common arrangement,

[18] UYU = Uruguayan pesos.

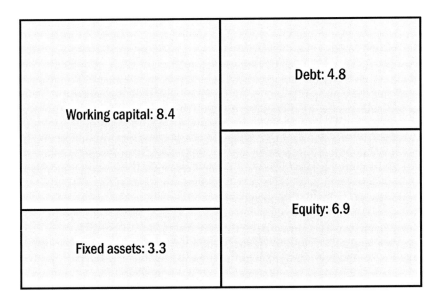

Working capital + fixed assets = 11.7 = debt + equity
= total capital of UYU11.7 million.

FIGURE 11.1. Managerial balance sheet for 2022 (figures in millions of Uruguayan pesos).

investors don't need to fund all the current assets—they just need to fund the amount of current assets not financed by the suppliers. This 'net' amount of current assets is what gives rise to the concept of net working capital. Again, working capital captures the important concept that the investment in current assets is partially financed by our suppliers, because they do not require immediate payment. For that reason, we subtract the amount of the payables, UYU1.8 million, from the UYU10.2 million in current assets, to give a working-capital, or net-working-capital, balance of UYU8.4 million."

Writing hurriedly, Acosta continued, "Summing the UYU8.4 million with the UYU3.3 million in fixed assets gives the total capital balance of UYU11.7 million. Total capital represents the total amount of money that investors have invested in the business—how much money investors have put up to acquire the buildings and equipment associated with fixed assets and the inventory and receivables associated with working capital. Total capital differs from total assets in that total assets represent all the assets of the business, whereas total capital represents all the assets that are financed by investors. Accounts payable, for example, represents a source of financing provided by the business suppliers. The portion of the total assets that is financed by the suppliers is included in total capital. In the case of el Rancho de las Vacas Bailando, UYU11.8 million is the amount of total capital. The total capital is how much of the ranch's total assets that are financed by investors—or in other words, how much investors have tied up in the business."

Acosta explained, "The ranch finances the UYU11.7 million capital with UYU4.8 million in debt and UYU6.9 million in equity, so this diagram shows the structure of the main categories of investments and how they are financed. Let's do the same thing for the year before, and you'll see how things have changed."

Acosta then added another box for the preceding year (see **Figure 11.2**). "You can see that the balance sheet has gotten much bigger. Working capital has increased by UYU3.2 million, because of all the money that has been put into the larger herd.[19] Fixed assets have increased by UYU1.2 million because of the additional equipment needed to manage the larger herd."[20]

Marchado appreciated the balance sheet tutorial, but he was still somewhat baffled. What did any of this have to do with the austerity the ranch was feeling? He quietly asked, "Isn't that good, Marta? The ranch has substantially more valuable assets that can make more money for the ranch."

Fernandez thought he saw where Acosta was going. "The problem is that all that increase in investment requires money. Isn't that right, Marta?"

"Correct!" responded Acosta. "Many years ago, I asked my grandfather about the source of ranch success. The secret, he told me, is flujo de fondos—cash flow."

"The secret is a cash cow?" asked Fernandez.

---

[19] This UYU3.3 million increase comes from working capital going from UYU5.2 million to UYU8.5 million.

[20] This UYU1.2 million increase comes from fixed assets going from UYU2.1 million to UYU3.3 million.

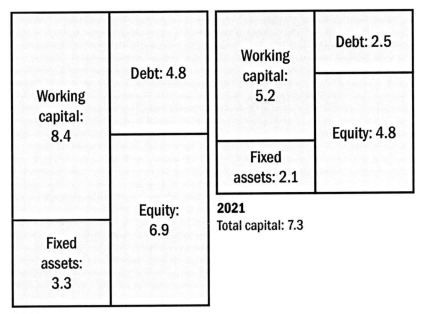

2022
Total capital: 11.8

FIGURE 11.2. Managerial balance sheet for both 2022 and 2021 (figures in millions of Uruguayan pesos).

"No, not cash cow!" Marchado clarified. "She said cash *flow*."

"That's right," Acosta said. "I wondered the same thing, Rodrigo! Mi abuelo said that cash flow is the amount of money that flows out of the business to the investors. This amount can be very different from profits if the business requires lots of investment. For our ranch, we have a lot of investment. Last year, the ranch invested UYU1.2 million in fixed assets. I know this by taking the difference between last year's fixed-asset balance and the fixed-asset balance from the year before: UYU3.3 million – UYU2.1 million." She wrote down her fixed-asset calculations so her friends could see the figures for themselves:

Fixed-asset investment:

UYU1.2 million = UYU3.3 million – UYU2.1 million.

"Even more importantly," she continued, "last year, the ranch invested UYU3.2 million in working capital—last year's UYU8.4 million minus the year before's UYU5.2 million." She added to her paper:

Working-capital investment:

$$\text{UYU3.2 million} = \text{UYU8.4 million} - \text{UYU5.2 million.}$$

"When we sum those two amounts—UYU1.2 million investment in fixed assets with UYU3.2 million in investment in working capital—we get UYU4.4 million. Did you two get that? UYU4.4 million in investment!" Acosta scribbled another few lines of calculations for Fernandez and Marchado to ponder:

Total investment:

$$\text{UYU4.4 million} = \text{UYU1.2 million in fixed-asset investment}$$
$$+ \text{ UYU3.2 million in working-capital investment.}$$

"Where did the ranch come up with UYU4.4 million?" asked Fernandez.

"The first thing was using all the ranch profits," replied Acosta. "The ranch made UYU2.1 million in profit last year, and every Uruguayan peso of profit was plowed back into the ranch. To reflect that retained profit, the equity rose by UYU2.1 million.[21] The rest of the investment money came from new debt, which rose by UYU2.3 million."[22]

"So what did your abuelo mean by cash flow?" asked Marchado.

"Cash flow is the amount of money flowing to the investors in the business," Acosta said. "It is the amount by which they are better off for having invested in the business. If we look at the ranch example, we can tell that the ranch cash flow is negative and large. The cash flow to the equity

---

[21] This UYU2.1 million increase comes from equity going from UYU4.8 million to UYU6.9 million.
[22] This UYU2.3 million increase in debt comes from debt going from UYU2.5 million to UYU4.8 million.

holders is zero, since they don't keep any of the profits. All the profits are being put back into the business. The cash flow to the debt holders is −UYU2.3 million, since the debt holders are putting UYU2.3 million in rather than getting money out.[23] So the ranch cash flow for last year was −UYU2.3 million. The investors—the debt holders and the equity holders—didn't get compensated for their investment. Instead, they paid in an additional UYU2.3 million."

Acosta continued, "To summarize, this cash flow amount is often calculated as the business profits minus the total investment for the year. For the ranch last year, this amount would be a profit of UYU2.1 million minus the total investment of UYU4.4 million, which is equal to −UYU2.3 million." Acosta added the following general equation to her paper, emphasizing it by capitalizing every letter:

$$\text{CASH FLOW} = \text{PROFIT} - \text{INVESTMENT.}$$

"So why are we always eating fideos con tuco?" asked Fernandez. "And why are my parents hocking my bed?"

"I think it is because the ranch is 'eating' more than it is producing. The eating is the investment. The producing is the profits. It is a cash flow problem," answered Marchado.

"That is right!" Acosta cheered. "The ranch needs to generate positive cash flow. One way it can do that is by increasing profits. Reducing costs, such as the money spent on feeding the gauchos, can increase profits in the near term—as long as the gauchos stay around and are not too weak to work hard."

"How does my bed produce cash flow?" Fernandez asked.

"Selling your bed reduces investment," responded Marchado. "By selling some of the fixed assets, such as your bed, the ranch generates cash flow that can be used pay down debt."

---

[23] Note that this doesn't include the UYU0.2 million in interest payments. For simplicity, we are not considering the interest payments in this example.

Acosta looked impressed with Marchado's response. "Do you think there are better ways for the ranch to generate cash flow?" she asked.

"Maybe we don't need such a big herd," offered Marchado. "It seems to me that we grew the herd too quickly. We could generate at least UYU0.88 million of cash flow by trimming the herd by 10%—if we look at 10% times the investment of UYU8.8 million."

"I agree," said Fernandez. "I think the ranch managers have been celebrating the wrong stuff. It seems that the ranch would be better off if it celebrated cash flow rather than focusing so much on growth."

"Yes," agreed Acosta, "the ranch seems to be growing too fast. All that growth is creating cash flow problems because our investment requirement far exceeds our profits."

"Nice work, my friends," Fernandez acknowledged. "Let's get my father in here to have some fideos con tuco with us."

And just like that, the great mystery of el Rancho de las Vacas Bailando was solved. That evening, when all was understood, Acosta played her Urugayan guitar, Fernandez sang, and all the gauchos danced.

CONCEPT WRAP-UP

This chapter illustrates the distinction between business profit and business cash flow, with an emphasis on how business growth can create cash flow problems for businesses. Cash flow is the amount of money flowing to the investors in the business. It is the amount by which they are better off for having invested in the business.

Finance people appreciate this distinction between cash flow and profit because they recognize that business profit, like snowfall in the headwaters, doesn't account for the diversion that happens to company profits. Business investment is the main source of diversion. As managers reinvest profits into the business by acquiring new equipment or increasing inventory, investors don't pocket the immediate business gains. Businesses in which reinvestment captures most of the profits leave little cash flow for the downstream investors.

This equation demonstrates how investment distinguishes profit from cash flow. One can appreciate that if all the business profit is being reinvested by buying all sorts of things, there will be little left over to distribute to investors.

$$\text{Cash flow} = \text{profit} - \text{investment}.$$

It is cash flow, not profits, that is the lifeblood of any business. As such, finance people evaluate the costs and benefits of business investment in terms of cash flow, not profit. Finance people look into the cash flow implications of any business decision.

REVIEW QUESTIONS

Rodrigo Fernandez had the opportunity to examine the financial statements for a neighboring ranch, el Rancho de las Vacas Cantoras. The financial statements for this ranch are provided in **Table 11.2**.

Use these financial statements in **Table 11.2** to calculate the following figures for 2022:

Question 1. Working capital

Question 2. Total capital

Question 3. The year's investment (change) in working capital

Question 4. The year's investment (change) in fixed assets

Question 5. Total cash flow

Question 6. How do you interpret the total cash flow figure that you calculated? How are investors affected financially by their investment in el Rancho de las Vacas Cantoras?

TABLE 11.2. Financial statements for Rancho de las Vacas Cantoras (figures in millions of Uruguayan pesos).

	2022	2021
Balance Sheet		
Cash	5.0	5.0
Receivables	3.0	5.0
Inventory	20.0	30.0
Property and equipment	17.0	17.0
Total assets	45.0	57.0
Payables	3.0	5.0
Debt	5.5	16.0
Equity	36.5	36.0
Total liabilities and equity	45.0	57.0
Income Statement		
Net sales	43.0	43.0
Cost of goods sold	26.0	25.5
Gross profit	17.0	17.5
General expenses	4.0	3.5
Operating profit	13.0	14.0
Interest expenses	1.0	1.0
Taxes	3.0	3.0
Net profit	9.0	10.0

SECTION IV
VALUATION

Finance people like to trade stuff. They trade stocks; they trade bonds; they trade businesses and corporations. They trade car loans, student loans, and home loans. They trade ideas and technology. They trade contracts that depend on oil prices, bean prices, and orange juice prices.

With all that trading, it's important to know what stuff is worth. Finance people call this *valuation*. Because many a fortune has been won or lost over the valuation of a thing, finance people care deeply about understanding the valuation of things. Getting familiar with the tools of valuation is foundational to finance.

The material in the earlier chapters is highly relevant to the tools of valuation. Valuation requires two activities: (1) modeling expected cash flow and (2) estimating a discount rate (the risk-adjusted benchmark rate). Both of these concepts have been introduced in the earlier chapters.

At the heart of the concept of valuation is the idea of "home cooking." Home cooking means that the value of a thing can be measured by how much it costs you in basic ingredients to create the same effect. If you can make your mother's prize-winning salad for USD5 of basic ingredients, the home-cooked value of the salad is USD5. For finance people, the home-cooked value is the amount of cash you need to invest today to create the future financial payout. As a simple example, let's suppose that someone offers to sell you a promise (or an IOU) of USD110 in one year. What is the value of the promise if prevailing interest rates are 10%?

Using the principle of home cooking, a finance person would answer that question by asking, "How much money do I need today to home cook the USD110 payment in one year?" The answer would be USD100. Why? Because if someone took USD100 and "put it in a pot" that earned 10% for one year, by the end of the year they would have USD110. Because you can home cook the promised USD110 future payment with USD100 today, the value today of the USD110 promise is USD100.

If that basic intuition makes sense, you are well on your way to understanding the basics of valuation. If not, don't despair! There will be lots of examples in the coming chapters. The next two chapters will give you a good tour of the world of valuation. Chapter 12 begins with a primer on the principle of home cooking and an opportunity to compete alongside Rupert Rudolfinquist in the Farout Investment Challenge—a series of investment challenges with a milkshake on the line.

This chapter showcases the fundamental concept of *present value* and the technique of *discounting*, which together allow finance people to transform future promised payments into values today. This transformation process is at the heart of valuation in finance. Chapter 13 builds on the basic present-value concepts from chapter 12 by introducing three valuation formulas. These formulas enable you to value three types of payment profiles: a fixed perpetual stream of payments called a *perpetuity*, a fixed finite stream of payments called an *annuity*, and a growing perpetual stream of payments called a *growing perpetuity*. These three present-value formulas may at first seem academic and useless, but you will learn to appreciate why finance people use them all the time to value stuff. If, for example, you needed to put a value on a business, you'd find the perpetuity formula helpful because the cash flow generated by the businesses may go on forever. The perpetuity formula helps put a value on an expected payment that goes on forever. If you are borrowing money to buy a car, you'll find that the annuity formula is really helpful to calculate the payments you'll make on the loan, as they'll be a fixed stream of payments that goes on for a finite period of time.

Be warned that there is lots of math in this section. All the calculations can easily seem intimidating and overwhelming, but know that many a math-phobic person has walked this path before you. While this section won't overwhelm so much with new terms, it does contain a lot of number crunching. With practice, time, and effort, you, like so many before you, will soon become comfortable figuring out the home-cooked value of anything.

12

Valuation and
Rupert's Home Cooking

RUPERT AND THE QUICK-HEAT BOX

Brothers Rupert and Rudger Rudolfinquist lived on a lake near the small Canadian town of Farout, Saskatchewan. Rupert was into inventing and walleye fishing derbies, while Rudger was into eating and economic theory.

One day, after a long week of inventing, Rupert emerged from the garage with a cry of "Eureka!" Holding a large metal box, he excitedly showed off what he called the "Quick-Heat Box," explaining that he had discovered a new way to quickly warm up things like food. He demonstrated his technology to Rudger by putting a piece of cold pizza into the Quick-Heat Box, pressing some buttons, and waiting for 15 seconds. Rupert then opened the door of the Quick-Heat Box and showed Rudger that the pizza was perfectly warm.

"Isn't that amazing?" he enthused. "I'll bet people would be willing to pay at least CAN1,000 for one of my boxes!"[24]

Rudger smiled, took a big bite of the pizza, and offered, "Rupert, this really is remarkable, but why would people pay CAN1,000 for your box when they can do the same thing with a CAN100 microwave oven? The

[24] CAN = Canadian dollars.

sad reality is that despite the remarkable nature of your invention, market prices tend to be determined by relative values. If a customer like me can achieve the same outcome as the Quick-Heat Box with a CAN100 microwave oven, the market price for your invention is unlikely to be higher than CAN100."

"Wait," Rupert said. "I don't think you appreciate how amazed people are going to be with my heat box. You better eat some more pizza."

"No, I get it, Rupert," responded Rudger. "But since the heating effects of your heat box and a microwave oven are identical, it is only reasonable that in a competitive market both products should have the same value and the same price. If someone can 'home cook' the same outcome as the Quick-Heat Box by buying a CAN100 microwave oven, the implied value and market price of the Quick-Heat Box is CAN100. Market prices are not arbitrary—they're competitively determined based on the relative prices of similar goods and services."

Rupert scratched his head, took back what remained of the pizza slice, and returned to the garage, muttering about the injustice of CAN100 for a Quick-Heat Box.

CONCEPT

Financial markets are filled with financial promises—payment terms of all sorts and shapes. A government promises to pay USD1,000 in 10 years. A homeowner promises to pay USD2,000 per month for 30 years. A company promises to pay 5% on USD10 million for 5 years. Finance people refer to promises of the sort promised by the government, homeowner, or company (a series of specified future cash payments) as loans, bonds, or debt contracts. By contrast, consider a contract with unspecified payouts, such as the residual contract between a business and its owners, in which the owners receive uncertain business profits. Finance people refer to these contracts on profits as *stock* or *equity*. Every day, across the world, people trade thousands and thousands of different bonds and stocks in financial markets. With so many stocks, bonds, and other promises trading all the time, how do finance people settle on fair prices for all these different contracts?

The foundational idea is the principle of home cooking. Home cooking means that the value of a thing can be measured by how much it costs you in basic ingredients (and in finance, basic ingredients are cash) to create the same effect. The home-cooked value of any financial contract is the amount of cash you need to invest today to create the future financial payout. If one can arrive at the same financial outcome with existing products, the required cash value provides the implied competitive market value for the outcome and hence the contract. Like Rupert's Quick-Heat Box, market values are determined by the cash required to home cook the same outcome with basic ingredients, such as a common microwave oven. In Rupert's case, CAN100 is the implied market value of the Quick-Heat Box, since with CAN100 in cash one can allegedly deliver—or home cook—the same outcome by purchasing a microwave oven.

A related principle of finance is that things that pay identical amounts have identical values. This is the *law of one price*. The law of one price implies that one can value one financial contract by observing the value of another financial contract with similar expected payments and risk. Finance people determine the value of a financial contract by computing the value of contracts in the market that can be used to cook up similar payoffs.

One values financial securities by examining how much money it takes to arrive at the same payoffs by combining existing financial products to create a home-cooked version of the securities. As such, finance people expect a security to trade at the same price as the cost of the assembled home-cooked version.

With this brief introduction, it is now time for you to get out your pots, pans, and apron and try your hand at home cooking. In this chapter, we will work through valuing five financial contracts, beginning with simple, single cash payment contracts and moving to contracts with multiple cash payments, such as a car loan with a monthly payment. To simplify the examples, we will assume that there is no default risk, meaning we don't need to be concerned that the promised payment will not be made.

TERMINOLOGY

Financial securities. Debt and equity holders have claims on the profits and governance of the business. Sometimes investors will find it advantageous to be able to trade these claims. The ability to trade gives owners flexibility to buy into or sell out of claims in the business at a lower cost. To facilitate trading, financial securities are created; these formalize the claim into a uniform contract. For equity holders, the uniform contracts are called *shares* or *stocks*. Suppose the total equity holdings in Jumbo Airlines are divided into 1 million shares. The shares or stocks delineate the portion of equity that is traded, such that one share of stock in Jumbo is a claim on one-millionth of the voting privilege and the profit payouts of the equity. A similar thing can be done for debt, where claims on a debt contract are divided into financial securities called *bonds*. If Jumbo issues 1,000 bonds in a USD1 million bond offering, then each bond has a claim on USD1,000 of the debt raised. To facilitate the trading of financial securities, financial markets are created for investors to buy and sell financial securities. Shares of stock are commonly bought and sold on *stock exchanges* such as the London Stock Exchange, Euronext, or NASDAQ. These exchanges provide gathering places for buyers and sellers of stock to trade with each other. Stock exchanges maintain listing requirements— companies or investors must comply with these listing requirements in order for shares of their stock to be traded on the exchange. Bonds are commonly bought and sold on *over-the-counter exchanges*—informal networks of traders who buy and sell bonds. *Security brokers* are organizations (e.g., Interactive Brokers, TD Ameritrade) that help investors with securities trading by providing access to *securities markets* (formal exchanges or informal networks) and managing all the logistic details that the investor doesn't want to deal with. When investors buy or sell their stocks or bonds, they typically do so with the help of a security broker.

Present value. The present value is the amount of cash needed today to generate a specified payment in the future at the prevailing risk-adjusted market return. Because of the ability to self-generate the future payment with the current cash, one is said to be indifferent between a future value and a present value. The formula that calculates the present value is

$$V = \frac{C}{(1+R)^T},$$

where V is the present value, C is the future cash payment, R is the prevailing periodic risk-adjusted return, and T is the number of periods until the cash payment is expected. This formula is the bedrock tool for financial valuation. Finance people call it the *present-value* or *discounting* formula. Such calculations are called *present-value calculations* because they reduce the value of an expected future payment stream to a current present value.

Internal rate of return (IRR). The IRR is the annual rate of return implied by an investment of a certain amount of cash today with a potential to generate a specified payment in the future. It is an annual rate that can be compared to the benchmark return to establish whether the investment is worthwhile. As an example, suppose that an investment of USD1,000 is expected to generate a payoff of USD2,000 in five years. The increase from USD1,000 to USD2,000 is a 100% increase, but the increase occurs over five years. The IRR is calculated by solving for R in the equation,

$$\text{USD1,000 investment} \times (1+R)^5 = \text{USD2,000 expected payoff.}$$

The exponent 5 refers to the five years of delay in realizing the USD2,000 payment. Solving for R gives an IRR of 15%. This means that 15% is the annual percentage return that transforms USD1,000 into USD2,000 in five years.

NAVIGATING THE FAROUT INVESTMENT CHALLENGE

Inspired by a milkshake bet with his brother, Rupert committed to train for and compete in the Farout Investment Challenge—the nearest thing to financial Olympic stardom north of the 53rd parallel. The Farout Investment Challenge involved answering five surprise investment challenge questions—Alpha, Beta, Gamma, Delta, and Epsilon—within 60 minutes.

Over several weeks, he trained diligently with Rudger. When the big day came, Rupert arrived at the competition wearing an apron and chef's hat, both emblazoned on the front with the words HOME COOKING. Rupert felt confident with his preparation. He was to face 31 other competitors—one from as far away as St. Cloud, Minnesota. Each had come to compete for financial glory. The participants were each assigned a smallish desk in the gymnasium of Farout Junior High School. At the top of each desk loomed a stack of five sealed envelopes. Rupert found his assigned desk and squeezed into it.

When the starting horn sounded, Rupert reached for the first envelope and tore it open as if he were a child with a present on Christmas morning. He rapidly read the first question.

Investment Challenge Alpha

Contract Alpha is a risk-free promise of CAN1,000 cash in one year. What are you willing to pay for Contract Alpha if other similar risk-free bonds are yielding 5% per year?

Rupert knew the naive answer was CAN1,000. Rookies, ignorant of home cooking, might pay CAN1,000 today for a risk-free promise of CAN1,000 in a year. But Rupert looked down at his apron and recognized that if there were other similar bonds out there returning 5%, he had the know-how to home cook the Alpha Contract today for some amount less than CAN1,000.

To identify the home-cooked cost, he needed to know how much cash he needed today to get the CAN1,000 cash outcome in a year. Since the challenge said that other no-risk investments were yielding (meaning returning) 5% per year, he wrote down, "How much money do I need to invest today at 5% to create a payoff of CAN1,000 in one year?" He then wrote down the following elegant mathematical equation:

$$P(1+5\%)=1,000.$$

He mumbled to himself, "If I buy P amount of the one-year bonds earning 5% per year, I will have CAN1,000 in cash in one year. P is the key home-cooked amount. To know how much money I need to invest today at 5% per year, I need to solve for P." A smile stole over his face as he rearranged the expression to find the precise amount:

$$P=1,000/(1+5\%)=\text{CAN}952.38.$$

Feeling pleased as a fat walleye feasting on yellow perch in a deep, cool northern lake, Rupert wrote on his paper, "If I take exactly CAN952.38 in cash today and buy the similar risk-free bonds, the value of my investment will increase in value by 5% over the year such that in one year, I will have exactly CAN1,000 in cash. Since I can home cook the CAN1,000 promised risk-free payoff in one year with CAN952.38 in cash, I'm not willing to pay more than CAN952.38 for the promise. Since everyone else in the market faces the same prevailing 5% rate, the CAN952.38 value is not unique to me but is shared by others in the market. The price of Contract Alpha should rationally be exactly CAN952.38."

Then for additional flourish, he wrote "RECIPE ALPHA: The home-cooking recipe for a CAN1,000 cash payment in one year is to take CAN952.38 in cash, put it in a pot at 5% heat and let simmer for one year. Anyone should be indifferent between CAN952.38 in cash today and a promise of CAN1,000 in one year if the prevailing yield on similar bonds is 5%."

Rupert had burned barely 10 minutes. He set the first challenge aside and slashed open the second envelope.

Investment Challenge Beta

Contract Beta is a risk-free promise of CAN1,000 cash in 10 years. What are you willing to pay for Beta if other similar risk-free bonds are yielding 5% per year?

Rupert quickly recognized that this challenge was similar to the previous one, but he noted that the outcome of this contract was a CAN1,000 cash payment in not 1 but 10 years, while the returns on other similar bonds was again 5% per year. The home cooking was the same except that the cash needed to stay on the heat for a longer amount of time.

Before going further, he reflected on an important convention in finance—all rates of return are expressed on an annual basis. Even though the bond under consideration in this example had a horizon of 10 years, the associated 5% rate of return was an annual figure. To capture the compounding nature of investing, the 5% annual rate had to be compounded 10 times. Pressing hard with his number 2 pencil, Rupert wrote out a pricing equation for the 10-year investment, where he added the power of 10 to capture the 10 years of compounding:

$$P\left(1 + 5\%\right)^{10} = 1,000.$$

As other 10-year risk-free promises were returning 5%, the value of the promise was the amount of money Rupert needed to invest today at 5% per year to create a CAN1,000 cash payoff in 10 years. Since the cash had substantially more time to grow in value, he recognized that the amount of cash he needed today was going to be much less. To find the precise amount, he solved the equation he'd written for P:

$$P = 1,000/\left(1 + 5\%\right)^{10} = CAN613.91.$$

Working the exponent feature on his calculator, Rupert saw the figure CAN613.91 shining back at him in glorious LED luminescence. The value of CAN613.91 felt right. He recognized that if he had CAN613.91 in cash today, he could home cook the CAN1,000 cash payment by investing the CAN613.91 at 5% for 10 years. He checked his calculations by running the home cooking:

$$CAN613.91(1 + 5\%)^{10} = CAN1,000.$$

With the sort of swagger usually displayed by national cooking show winners, Rupert wrote: "RECIPE BETA: The home-cooking recipe for a CAN1,000 cash payment in 10 years is to put CAN613.91 of cash in a pot at 5% heat and leave it simmering for 10 years. Because everyone faces the same interest rates, anyone should be indifferent between CAN613.91 in cash today and a promise of CAN1,000 in 10 years if the prevailing yield on similar 10-year bonds is 5%."

Reflecting on his instinctive financial competency, Rupert adjusted his chef's hat so its appearance modeled the professional that he was, then stylishly slid his pencil into the next envelope and confidently popped its flap.

Investment Challenge Gamma

Going back to Investment Challenge Alpha, how would your willingness to pay for that contract change if the prevailing annual yield on similar bonds is 6% rather than 5%?

"Those sly dogs," chuckled Rupert. He appreciated that his rookie competitors would suspect that at the higher prevailing rate, the bonds would be worth more. He took off his hat and kissed his HOME COOKING logo.

Rupert deftly recognized that if prevailing yields were higher, he would actually need less, not more, money to home cook the same CAN1,000 payout. Finance people know that market yields and market prices move inversely—if the market yield increases, then the implied value of financial contracts decreases. Rupert snickered aloud as he wrote the expressions below to show that the implied value declined from CAN952.38 with the Alpha Challenge to CAN943.40 with the Gamma Challenge:

$$\text{Alpha } (R = 5\%): P = \text{CAN}1,000/(1 + 5\%) = \text{CAN}952.38;$$

$$\text{Gamma } (R = 6\%): P = \text{CAN}1,000/(1 + 6\%) = \text{CAN}943.40.$$

He added explanation: "If prevailing yields are 6%, I am no longer willing to pay CAN952.38, since that price yields only 5%. With yields at 6%, the cash required to home cook the contract is lower, as I only need CAN943.40 today to generate CAN1,000 in one year. With the rise in yields, the value of the contracts declines. This example illustrates a well-known relation in bond markets—bond prices and bond yields are inversely related. When bond yields rise, then bond prices fall; and when prices rise, yields fall."

Rupert sprang away from his desk and did the sort of victory routine he had seen practiced in the end zones of American professional football games. Ignoring a flurry of annoyed looks by neighboring competitors, he pounced on the fourth envelope and ripped it open with his teeth, making the sound of a snarling wolf in combat.

Investment Challenge Delta

What are you willing to pay today for a risk-free promise of three cash payments of CAN1,000 at the end of each of the next three years, if similar promises are returning 5% per year?

Calling on a mental competitive technique he had perfected, Rupert pictured himself in a clean, well-stocked kitchen. There, he thought through the details of what appeared to be a pretty complicated culinary challenge—cooking up a promise of not one but three payments of

CAN1,000. Then with sudden clarity, he realized that the way to cook up this stream of payments was identical to that of the earlier challenges—identifying how much was needed today to home cook the same payment stream. He recognized that he could consider each of the three payments individually.

He already knew the value of the first CAN1,000 payment because he had calculated it earlier in Challenge Alpha at CAN952.38. The second payment could be considered in a similar way, where the home-cooked value was equal to P in the following equation:

$$P(1+5\%)^2 = CAN1,000,$$

which he rearranged to

$$P = CAN1,000/(1+5\%)^2 = CAN907.03.$$

With CAN907.03 today, he could home cook the second CAN1,000 payment in two years. The third payment followed the same pattern, where the home-cooked value was equal to P in the following equation:

$$P(1+5\%)^3 = CAN1,000,$$

which he rearranged to

$$P = CAN1,000/(1+5\%)^3 = CAN863.84.$$

Adding the three values—952.38 + 907.03 + 863.84—Rupert came up with a total cash need of CAN2,723.25. With a lucidity of thought that elevated him, he explained in written form how, by investing CAN2,723.25 today, he could generate the three CAN1,000 payments. He followed that with a full recipe to again demonstrate his wide-ranging mastery of financial valuation, including the concept of the internal rate of return, or IRR.

"RECIPE DELTA: The home-cooking recipe for a CAN1,000 cash payment for each of the next three years is to put CAN2,723.25 cash in a pot at 5% heat and leave it simmering for a year. At the end of the year, the cash will have grown to CAN2,859.41 [CAN2,723.25 (1 + 5%)]. Remove CAN1,000 in cash for yourself, and leave the remaining CAN1,859.41 in the pot for another year at 5%. At the end of the second year, the cash will have grown to CAN1,952.38. Remove CAN1,000 in cash for yourself and leave the remaining CAN952.38 in the pot for another year. At the end of the third year, the cash will have grown to exactly CAN1,000. Remove the CAN1,000 in cash for yourself. In summary, by investing CAN2,723.25 today at 5%, one can perfectly home cook the three CAN1,000 cash payments. Because of the home-cooking principle, an investor should be indifferent between CAN2,723.25 in cash today and a contract for three payments of CAN1,000 for each of three years if the prevailing yield is 5% per year."

To further demonstrate his mastery, Rupert added an additional piece on the IRR of the investment by writing, "Suppose that I could buy the DELTA contract for CAN2,600 today, the internal rate of return I obtain is 7.5%. This is obtained by solving for R in the following present-value equation:

$$CAN2,600 = CAN1,000/(1 + R)^1 + CAN1,000/(1 + R)^2 + CAN1,000/(1 + R)^3.$$

"The R of 7.5% is the annual rate of return that is implied by the price and the payments. Another way to understand the IRR is to note that 7.5% is the discount rate on the project that makes the present value of the payments equivalent to the amount you are paying. The rate of 7.5% is the amount upon which you are indifferent."

Rupert looked at the clock. He now had less than nine minutes remaining. With technique that can only come from endless hours of envelope-opening practice, Rupert expertly split open the last envelope with a simple flick of the wrist.

Investment Challenge Epsilon

What are you willing to pay today for a promise of 36 cash payments of CAN100 at the end of each month for the next three years, if similar promises are returning 6%?

Rupert sat staring at the paper for a full minute, sweat beading his forehead. Then, experiencing what felt like a heaven-sent revelation, Rupert recognized that this contract was actually a lot like the Delta Challenge, only now the payments were every month instead of every year. The approach for valuing this stream of payments was, of course, similar to that of the earlier examples—identifying how much was needed to home cook the same payment stream. With Delta, the amount needed to home cook the payment streams could be defined as a series of cash payments (C):

$$\frac{C}{(1+R)}+\frac{C}{(1+R)^2}+\frac{C}{(1+R)^3}.$$

The monthly setting of Challenge Epsilon required Rupert to use a monthly return of $1/12$ of the annual rate of 6%, so his R was 0.5% $[0.5\% = 6.0\%/12]$.[25] Except for that change, the setup was the same, but with 36 payments. This gave him the following pricing equation:

$$\text{Value}=\frac{\text{CAN100}}{(1+0.5\%)}+\frac{\text{CAN100}}{(1+0.5\%)^2}+\cdots+\frac{\text{CAN100}}{(1+0.5\%)^{35}}+\frac{\text{CAN100}}{(1+0.5\%)^{36}},$$

where for simplicity of presentation only the first two and last two terms are presented. With the dexterity of a Saskatoon stoat, Rupert cranked

---

[25] A common convention among finance people is to quote interest rates in a form called the annual percentage rate (APR). This form means that annual rates are simple additions of periodic rates. If a monthly loan has a monthly rate of 0.5%, the convention is to express that rate as an annual rate by simply multiplying the monthly rate of 0.5% by the number of periods in a year, or 12 months in a year. By multiplying 0.5% by 12, we get the 6.0% annual rate. It is because of this APR convention that Rupert knows he can get to the monthly rate by simply dividing the annual rate by 12.

out the math. In an equation with 36 terms, he ended up with the value of CAN3,287.

"What does that mean?" he wrote, at a speed that risked lighting his pencil on fire. "It means that I am indifferent between cash of CAN3,287 now or a promise of CAN100 at the end of each month for 36 months if the prevailing annual yield on similar contracts is 6% per year. Why? Because with CAN3,287 in cash now, I can generate the promised monthly cash payments by investing it at 6% and taking out the monthly cash payments."

As the ending horn blasted, Rupert closed with his signature: "Home cooked by Rupert."

Rupert stood from his desk to await the judges' verdict. His head was high, his clothing was moist, and in his heart was an abiding trust that a milkshake prize was in his future.

CONCEPT WRAP-UP

This chapter has introduced home cooking as a foundational principle of financial valuation. Home cooking is everywhere in finance: it is implicit in such principles as the law of one price, relative value pricing, and the no-arbitrage rule. Finance people are completely into home cooking. The principles of moving the value of money from one period to another with home cooking is fundamental to valuation in any context. Such calculations are called *present-value calculations* because they reduce the value of an expected future payment stream to a current present value.

The thing that allows money in the future to be valued today is the discount rate. We spent a lot of time in earlier chapters exploring the discount rate, or required rate of return. Since the discount rate is adjusted for expected inflation and a risk premium, the present-value calculations allow finance people to include all those important effects in their valuations. It makes sense to include inflation and risk, since an investor needs to be compensated for the effects of inflation and risk. As such, it is natural that the home-cooked values are adjusted for inflation and risk through the appropriate discount rate.

To review some of the fundamental principles of home cooking, consider the following basic principles:

1. A financial contract is worth the amount of money required to replicate or home cook the promised payoffs at the rate of return prevailing for similar contracts.

2. The home-cooking equation for identifying the present value V of a contract for future payments is

$$V = \frac{X_1}{(1+R)} + \frac{X_2}{(1+R)^2} + \cdots + \frac{X_{T-1}}{(1+R)^{T-1}} + \frac{X_T}{(1+R)^T},$$

where X_t represents the expected cash payment at period t and R is the prevailing risk-adjusted periodic rate of return.

3. All rates of return are quoted on an annual basis. A 5% return on a 10-year contract is expected to earn 5% *per year* over 10 years.

REVIEW QUESTIONS

Question 1. Take on Rupert Rudolfinquist's investment challenge yourself by solving the same five problems, Alpha through Epsilon. For some of the questions (particularly Delta and Epsilon), it will be easier to use an electronic spreadsheet to automate the calculation of all the terms.

Question 2. Having gone through investment challenges Alpha through Epsilon, you should be able to value many financial contracts. Here's another one: Suppose that Rupert is considering buying a fishing boat and has the budget to afford a monthly payment of CAN100 over the next three years. How large a loan should he be willing to take, with no down payment, if prevailing interest rates are 6% per year for a similar loan?

Question 3. If the amount in question 2 is not enough to get Rupert the boat of his dreams, how large a loan should Rupert be willing to take if he were able to double the payment and the interest rate declined to just 3%?

13

Perpetuities and the Champagne of Table Water

MONEY FOR ETERNITY

It was a hot, dry summer day in the South of France. John Harmsworth, a wealthy British gentleman, was saying goodbye to the friends he had made during his stay at Les Bouillens Spa before boarding a coach going north.[26] The good weather and the opportunity to perfect his French had drawn Harmsworth to the area for an extended visit in the summer of 1897. But as he stood there, waterside, with spa proprietor and local doctor Louis Perrier, he recognized that there might be another purpose at work.

Perrier approached a brass spigot at the bar that dispensed distinctive mineral water directly from the famous Les Bouillens spring. Filling a fresh glass with the spring water, he exclaimed, "À votre santé," and offered Harmsworth another glass of the water that was the focus of the therapeutic treatments at his spa.

Harmsworth found the taste of the water to again be exquisite and exclaimed, "Merci bien, Monsieur Perrier. This truly is the champagne of table water."

---

[26] In this chapter, the history of the actual sale of the Les Bouillens spring from French doctor Louis Perrier to British businessman John Harmsworth is highly stylized to further demonstrate how finance people think.

Two things had become obvious to Harmsworth: first, Perrier was sitting on a valuable asset in the spring, and second, Perrier lacked the capital or know-how to realize its potential. Surrounded by Perrier's patients lounging about the spa, Harmsworth continued, "Thank you for your generous hospitality during my stay." He then seized the opportunity he'd identified and asked, "Monsieur Perrier, I hope I'm not being indiscreet, but I can't help but notice how much work this spa requires of you. I wonder, Monsieur, is there a price at which you might consider selling Les Bouillens?"

Perrier turned back slowly to face Harmsworth and responded in a way that intrigued Harmsworth: "Ah oui, mon ami, I would consider selling it. But you must understand that this spring is difficult to value. It has been producing water in the same way for thousands of years. Do you realize that in 200 BC, Hannibal and his army stopped right here at Les Bouillens to refresh themselves? This place is special and unlike other assets that deplete. You see, Monsieur Harmsworth, Les Bouillens is eternal."

"Yes, well said, my friend. This truly is a remarkable place," agreed Harmsworth.

"Oui, Monsieur, and its infinite life makes it very hard to value," added Perrier. "I might imagine that a buyer like you could make millions of little green bottles, say, fill them with this spring water, and sell them all over the world as 'the champagne of table water.'"

"Very perceptive of you," expressed Harmsworth.

"But when you consider value," continued Perrier, "what is most distinctive is that you'll be able to continue to sell those green bottles for ever and ever. How can one put a value on something that produces money infinitely? Isn't that exactly the definition of priceless?"

"Excuse me, Monsieur Perrier," responded Harmsworth. "Are you looking to value something that produces money for eternity? That's easy."

"Easy?" replied Perrier dubiously.

"Yes, easy, Monsieur Perrier," added Harmsworth respectfully. "The value is simply C divided by R."

CONCEPT

The previous chapter introduced the concept of present value, which means that the value of future cash payments is equal to the amount of cash you need today to home cook the implied future payments. The home-cooking formula that calculates the present value is

$$\text{Present value of a future payment} = \frac{C}{(1+R)^{T}},$$

where C is equal to the future cash payment, R is equal to the prevailing periodic risk-adjusted return, and T is the number of periods until the cash payment is expected. This formula is the bedrock tool for financial valuation. It is called the *present-value* or *discounting* formula.

We saw in the last chapter that the calculations quickly get annoying when there are lots of cash payments that need discounting. For example, suppose that you are calculating the present value of a standard 30-year mortgage where someone has promised to make a specific monthly mortgage payment over 30 years. Since such a contract produces 360 monthly future payments, the work required to do the 360 present-value calculations can be intimidating. This chapter showcases some algebraic tricks to make such discounting easier. These tricks are common among finance people and are worth getting comfortable with.

TERMINOLOGY

Perpetuity. A perpetuity is a promised payment of expected cash flow that repeats at a regular interval forever. An example of a perpetuity is a promise of a USD100 payment every year forever. The formula for calculating the present value of a perpetuity is

$$V = \frac{C}{R},$$

where V is the present value, C is the promised payment or expected cash flow, and R is the risk-adjusted discount rate. As an example, suppose that Jumbo Airlines is considering offering new flight service between San Jose and Santo Domingo. Jumbo expects that the service will generate USD1 million of cash flow per year. Since Jumbo has no expectation for ending the service, investors might expect the USD1 million cash flow to go on forever and value this business opportunity as a perpetuity. If the relevant discount rate is 10%, the formula for calculating the present value of the San Jose–Santo Domingo business is

$$V = \frac{\text{USD1 million}}{10\%} = \text{USD10 million}.$$

If you think about it, a value of USD10 million seems reasonable, since if an investor had USD10 million and invested it at an expected rate of return of 10%, the investor would earn USD1 million each year forever. In effect, a sum of USD10 million allows one to home cook an annual USD1 million payment forever. Finance people also commonly use an *alternative present-value formula* that accommodates cash flow that is expected to grow at a constant rate (instead of remaining constant without growing). The present-value formula for this growing perpetuity is

$$V = \frac{C_1}{R - g},$$

where V is the present value of the growing perpetuity, C_1 is the first promised payment, R is the risk-adjusted discount rate, and g is the expected growth rate for the cash flow.

Annuity. An annuity is a promised payment of expected cash flow that repeats at a regular interval and then ends at some defined point. A common example of an annuity is a loan where the borrower agrees to make a specific payment every month for a specified number of months. The formula for calculating the present value of an annuity is

$$V = \frac{C}{R} - \frac{C}{R(1+R)^T},$$

where V is the present value of the annuity, C is the regular promised payment, R is the risk-adjusted periodic discount rate, and T is the expected number of periods until maturity. As an example, suppose that Ingrid has agreed to make payments of USD290 per month to her bank for five years to finance USD15,000 of the classic antique car she is buying. If the prevailing annual interest rate for car loans of this type is 6%, is the loan fair for both Ingrid and the bank? To figure this out, we first note that Ingrid has agreed to pay a monthly annuity to the bank. If the annual relevant risk-adjusted rate is 6%, then the monthly periodic rate is 0.5% (which comes from 0.5% = 6.0%/12 months in a year). The number of periods to maturity is 60 months (which comes from 60 months = 5 years × 12 months per year). Inputting the appropriate values into the annuity present-value formula, we get a present value of USD15,000:

$$V = \frac{USD290}{0.5\%} - \frac{USD290}{0.5\%(1+0.5\%)^{60}} = USD15,000.$$

Since the present value of the annuity is equal to USD15,000, the bank's willingness to offer Ingrid USD15,000 seems appropriate. The terms of the loan seem fair for both parties.

VALUING LA SOURCE PERRIER

The conversation between Harmsworth and Perrier had piqued the interest of all who were gathered at the large spa pool that morning. After Harmsworth made his proposal to Perrier, a balding older gentleman, James Thornberry, who was sitting in a near corner of the pool, was quick to interject. "Spot on, old boy, it all starts with present value," he offered.

"Yes, because of home cooking, a franc today is worth more than a franc tomorrow!" Now seeking hair-restoration therapy from the spa, Thornberry had spent his professional career at the Bank of England, where business valuations had been his bread and butter.

"Yes, that's right of course, a franc invested today allows one to home cook more francs tomorrow," agreed Arthur Birdwhistle, a gentleman whose expansive girth was far greater than his towel could cover. Birdwhistle had come to Les Bouillens hoping that the spa therapy could reduce his physical circumference. "The present value of a promise of FRF100 in a year is worth that FRF100 divided by $(1 + R)$."[27]

"What is this nonsense?" asked Perrier.

"Doctor, if you have FRF95.24 today that can be invested at 5%, that's financially equivalent to having a promise of FRF100 in a year. Note that FRF95.24 $\times (1 + 5\%) =$ FRF100," continued Birdwhistle. Then, grabbing his belly, he proclaimed with a chuckle, "Home cooking is what built me into the man I am, and it's no different with valuation."

Margaret Berrycloth, known to be the wealthiest patient at the spa, had come to cure a case of gout so bad that she now relied on a wheelchair to get around. From her chair, Berrycloth smiled at Birdwhistle and then encouraged, in her characteristic noble tone, "But do let's talk through the value of this lovely water." Meanwhile, Perrier hurried to pour another glass for Berrycloth as he thought through this bewildering present-value math.

"All right," agreed Harmsworth. "Let's say this spring produces enough water to fill 10 bottles a minute. That means a production rate of 600 bottles an hour, or 10,800 bottles a day, assuming an 18-hour work day. At 10,800 bottles a day, and assuming a 250-day work year, this spring could turn out . . . let's see . . ." He tried to do the math in his head.

"A good 2.7 million bottles a year," barked Thornberry.

---

[27] FRF = French francs.

"Yes," acknowledged Harmsworth slowly. "Every year, 2.7 million bottles."

"And you think people will buy that many bottles a year of this lovely water?" questioned Jane Carmichael, who had recently arrived from Manchester for a three-week stay at the spa in hopes of curing the painful boils and cysts that covered large portions of her skin.

"Easy," argued Harmsworth. "The Queen will buy half the lot."

"Fine. So let's talk cash flow," invited Birdwhistle. "Let's say that you sell each bottle for a franc apiece—that's FRF2.7 million per year in revenue. If annual operating expenses are reasonably expected to run FRF1.7 million, you'd expect to net FRF1 million per year."

"Ah, that truly is a lovely spring," sighed Berrycloth. "A spring that prints a lovely FRF1 million a year from now to eternity."

"Oui, c'est ça," cut in Perrier. "That is why I call it a truly priceless spring. Isn't it obvious that an infinite stream of FRF1 million disbursements . . . sums to an infinite value?"

"Hold on, Perrier," cautioned Birdwhistle. "Let's remember the principle of home cooking. The value of something doesn't come from just summing up the projected payments. No, the value is in appreciating how much money Harmsworth needs today to home cook that same stream of lovely payments. Given that the prevailing risk-adjusted return on similar risk investments is 5%, we can calculate how much money he needs today to do the home cooking."

The question of exactly how to calculate that figure caused a heavy quiet to roll across the variously attired group gathered at the spa.

"We can do this," Thornberry said encouragingly. "At a rate of 5%, how much money does Harmsworth need today to generate proceeds of FRF1 million a year?"

"All of FRF20 million," quietly offered Alice Ainsworth, a tear running down her cheek. Ainsworth sported a large, fashionable hat and ordinarily kept to herself due to a condition that caused her to tear up and cry profusely at the most ordinary of situations. She had dealt with this condition since childhood and was desperate for relief.

"You would be correct," confirmed Harmsworth. "How did you get that?"

"Well think about it!" sobbed Ainsworth, wiping her cheeks. "At 5% for one year, a FRF20 million investment earns exactly FRF1 million a year, since 20 million times 5% produces interest of 1 million a year."

"Can you repeat that?" asked Carmichael.

"Yes!" agreed Ainsworth, slightly louder and with a surprising improvement in composure. "Five percent of 20 million is the expected annual increase of the investment. Since that amount is FRF1 million, I should expect my FRF20 million investment to increase by 5%, or FRF1 million per year."

"Brilliant!" exclaimed Thornberry. "So let me verify how you got 20 million. You divided the annual payment of FRF1 million by 5% to get FRF20 million. In general terms, that's the cash flow C divided by the risk-adjusted return R, or C divided by R."

"C divided by R. Yes, that is Harmsworth's perpetuity formula!" exclaimed Birdwhistle.

Thornberry gave Birdwhistle a hearty fist bump, some peach fuzz on his head catching the sunlight. He then asked, "Now, what happens if Ms. Ainsworth keeps her FRF20 million invested at 5% for another year?"

"It will generate another FRF1 million," offered Berrycloth.

"And how about another year?" asked Thornberry.

"Another FRF1 million," continued Berrycloth. "In fact, if you leave that FRF20 million invested forever, you'll generate a stream of FRF1 million payments every year for . . . forever."

A smile bloomed on every face in the spa.

"Do you recognize what you've done?" asked Thornberry.

"Yes," Berrycloth said. "I've used FRF20 million to home cook the expected payment stream of this lovely spring. With FRF20 million invested forever, I can generate a stream of FRF1 million payments every year . . . in perpetuity." And with that, Berrycloth jumped to her feet and, to everyone's astonishment, did some energetic steps of a classic mazurka dance.

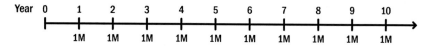

FIGURE 13.1. Graphical representation of perpetuity and its valuation.

A realization had been dawning on Perrier. He moved into the center of the group and asked, with an air of acceptance, "Are you saying that my spring is not priceless? Are you saying it's only worth FRF20 million?"

"Yes, that is exactly what we're saying—as long as we all agree with the assumptions," emphasized Harmsworth. "A perpetual stream of cash flows is appropriately valued as C (the value of the expected perpetual cash flow) divided by R (the risk-adjusted return), because that's what one needs today to home cook the perpetual stream of payments. C divided by R is the present value of a perpetuity. If we draw it," and here Harmsworth took from his pocket a coach ticket and pencil and began to draw what looked like a timeline, "a perpetuity looks graphically like a stream of payments from Years 0 to 10 that then continues on forever. The present value at Time 0 for the perpetuity is equal to C divided by R." (See **Figure 13.1**.)

$$PV_0 = 1 \text{ million}/5\%;$$

$$PV_0 = \text{FRF20 million.}$$

"But Mr. Harmsworth," interrupted Carmichael, who had noticed that the heated discussion of present-value math seemed to be soothing her boils and cysts. "What if it doesn't turn out that well? How does the value change if we expect the spring to dry up in 50 years?"

"Ah, good question, Ms. Carmichael," granted Harmsworth. "In that case, we'd be looking at valuing an annuity rather than a perpetuity. An annuity is a finite rather than infinite stream of identical cash flows. What you are describing is a 50-year annuity. Does anyone know how we could value Ms. Carmichael's annuity scenario where the spring dries up in 50 years?"

"You could always do it the brute-force way, by summing up the discounted value of each of the 50 future payments," suggested Birdwhistle.

"Yes, you could," confirmed Harmsworth. "But how about something more elegant?"

"Well, how about this?" suggested Perrier, who was horrified at the thought of the spring drying up, but also seemed to be gaining in understanding. "The value of the 50-year spring is the same as the value of a perpetual spring now, minus the value today of another perpetual spring that begins in 50 years."

"Très bien, monsieur! You are a French mathematical genius!" Harmsworth exclaimed. "Yes, that is correct. Let me show this graphically." He drew more figures on the paper ticket (see **Figure 13.2**). "Let me draw a second perpetuity that I'll call Perpetuity 2. Perpetuity 2 is a perpetuity of FRF1 million that starts in Year 51. As you see, it is still a perpetuity that pays FRF1 million every year forever, but the payments don't start for 50 years. Graphically, if we take those two figures and subtract the values in each year, we'll end up with Ms. Ainsworth's 50-year annuity. This is because all the payments made after Year 50 will be canceled out by subtracting Perpetuity 2 from Perpetuity 1. The perpetuity payments cancel out after Year 50 because they are the same after Year 50."

"I don't understand," Carmichael admitted. "How does that help?"

"It provides tremendous help," emphasized Ainsworth with a cheery grin and dry eyes. "Now we know that the present value of the 50-year annuity can be valued as the present value of Perpetuity 1 minus the present value of Perpetuity 2."

"You are making my head hurt," said Carmichael.

"No, my dear lady, you have got this," Perrier encouraged. "Look at Harmsworth's picture. We all understand that the present value of

Perpetuity 1. A perpetuity of FRF1 million, paid starting in Year 1.

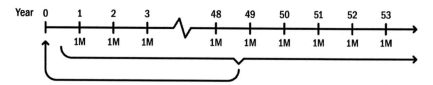

$$PV_{time0}^{perp1} = \frac{C}{R} = \frac{FRF1M}{5\%} = FRF20M$$

Perpetuity 2. A perpetuity of FRF1 million, paid starting in Year 51.

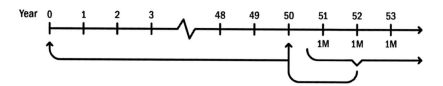

$$PV_{time50}^{50Y\,annuity} = \frac{C}{R} = \frac{FRF1M}{5\%} = FRF20M$$

$$PV_{time0}^{perp2} = \frac{C}{R(1+R)^{50}} = \frac{FRF1M}{5\%(1+5\%)^{50}} = FRF1.7M$$

50-year annuity of FRF1 million.

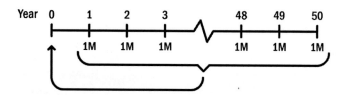

$$PV_{time0}^{50Y\,annuity} = PV_{time0}^{perp1} - PV_{time0}^{perp2} = \frac{C}{R} - \frac{C}{R(1+R)^{50}}$$

$$= FRF20M - FRF1.7M = FRF18.3M$$

FIGURE 13.2. Graphical representation of perpetuity and its valuation. The trick is that the present value of the 50-year annuity is equal to the present value of Perpetuity 1 less the present value of Perpetuity 2.

Perpetuity 1 is equal to C/R, which comes to FRF20 million. The present value of Perpetuity 2 is a little trickier, but the first part is easy. The present value of Perpetuity 2 in Year 50 is the same old C/R, or FRF20 million. This is because the present value of an infinite stream of cash flows is always equal to C/R, no matter when it starts."

"Yes," Carmichael agreed, albeit hesitantly.

Perrier continued. "However, we need to find the present value of Perpetuity 2 in Year 0. This means we need to discount the Year 50 value of 20 million to a Year 0 value by dividing the value by $(1 + 5\%)^{50}$. This is the present-value formula for home cooking a FRF20 million payment in Year 50. With 50 years of compounding, that value turns out to be small: just FRF1.7 million. Because of home cooking, the value of FRF1.7 million is equivalent to FRF20 million in 50 years at a discount rate of 5%. So the value of Perpetuity 1 at Year 0 is FRF20 million and the value of Perpetuity 2 at Year 0 is FRF1.7 million. We can compute the value of the 50-year annuity by taking the difference, which is FRF18.3 million."

Carmichael took a deep breath and, deciding she did understand, ventured to confirm the explanation. "So the value of a spring that pumps out water for 50 years is not that much different from the value of a spring that pumps out water forever. Why is that, you ask? It is because the payments that start in 50 years aren't worth that much, because we have 50 years to home cook them. Those payments are so far in the future that we can leave the money simmering for a very long time, so that the home-cooked value is small."

"What progress!" Ainsworth exclaimed, recognizing Carmichael's mastery of the concept but referring—and pointing—to her skin.

Looking down at herself, Carmichael cried, "Wow, it is a miracle! My cysts and boils are healing. What a therapeutic effect this present-value math has on me."

"Very well," said Birdwhistle, finding to his surprise that his towel was providing dramatically more coverage. "As shown on the paper ticket, the present value for an annuity is equal to the following." Borrowing Harmsworth's pencil, he wrote out:

$$\text{Present value of a } T \text{ period annuity} = \frac{C}{R} - \frac{C}{R(1+R)^T}.$$

"This is where C is the periodic payment, R is the appropriate periodic discount rate, and T is the number of periods to maturity," Birdwhistle said. "This formula can be used for both annual periods and shorter periods like months. This formula is used all over the place. For example, to see how much money you could borrow to buy a house with a 30-year monthly mortgage, you would use the following formula." He continued writing:

$$\text{Present value of a 30-year annuity} = \frac{C}{R} - \frac{C}{R(1+R)^{360}}.$$

"Here, C is the monthly payment, R is the appropriate monthly discount rate (i.e., the annual interest rate divided by 12 months), and 360 is the number of months in 30 years."

"So I guess we don't need to worry all that much about the petering-out part," mused Carmichael.

"Yes, I think that is mostly true," agreed Perrier. "But what about the flip side? What are the value implications if Harmsworth can increase prices over time, such that profits rise 2% per year over time?"

"Let's do this!" hollered Berrycloth, as she waltzed around the pool, clutching Thornberry, whose new bangs kept blowing into his eyes.

Ainsworth assertively announced, "It is time to home cook a growing perpetuity!" With a confident laugh, she plucked away Harmsworth's paper ticket and pencil from Birdwhistle. She then drew a diagram representing the FRF1 million payment growing each year by 2% (see **Figure 13.3**).

FIGURE 13.3. Graphical representation of a growing perpetuity and its valuation.

She then presented to the others, who all hung on her words in rapture, the present-value formula for a growing perpetuity:

$$\text{Present value of a perpetuity with growth } g = \frac{C_1}{R-g}.$$

"Just as the formula C over R captures the present value of a perpetuity, the formula C over R minus g captures the present value of a growing perpetuity—that is, a perpetual cash payment that grows at a constant rate per period," Ainsworth said. Working out the math, she noted that the present value in Year 0 of the FRF1 million payments growing forever at a rate of 2% was FRF33 million.

$$PV_0 = \frac{C_1}{R-g}.$$

$$PV_0 = \frac{\text{FRF1M}}{5\% - 2\%}.$$

$$PV_0 = \text{FRF33M}.$$

"How about that?" commented a lean Birdwhistle. "So growth in the cash flow matters. The 2% growth rate raises the value 67%, from FRF20 million to FRF33 million."

"That growing perpetuity formula is sensational, Alice," granted Carmichael, her clear skin glowing.

Harmsworth stopped the discussion and offered each member of the group a tall, cold glass of the spring's mineral water. "Monsieur Perrier," he began. "I am ready to offer you FRF20 million for your lovely spring. Will you take it?"

"Oui, monsieur," responded Perrier without hesitation. "It is clear to me that I need the money to open the world's first spa de valeur actuelle—present-value spa. There is obviously nothing better for the ailments of the world than working present-value problems."

The group cheered and drank mineral water with abandon for the next 30 minutes.

Harmsworth closed the festive gathering by announcing to Perrier that he would see to it that Perrier's lovely water would be treasured throughout the world as the champagne of table water. Handing Perrier a large check, Harmsworth asked, "Does anyone know how to make green glass?"

CONCEPT WRAP-UP

This chapter extended our understanding of approaches to estimating the present value of a future cash flow by examining perpetuities and annuities. A perpetuity means a repeated cash flow that is expected to continue on forever. The formula for calculating the present value for a constant-growth perpetuity is

$$V = \frac{C_1}{R - g},$$

where C_1 is the first promised payment or expected cash flow, R is equal to the risk-adjusted periodic discount rate, and g is the expected growth rate. An annuity means a repeated cash flow that is expected to continue on for a defined number of periods. The present value of an annuity is defined as

$$V = \frac{C}{R} - \frac{C}{R(1+R)^T},$$

where C is the promised payment or expected cash flow, R is equal to the risk-adjusted periodic discount rate, and T is the expected number of periods until maturity. Finance people use these two expressions all the time as shortcuts for calculating the present value for commonly observed financial forecasts.

REVIEW QUESTIONS

Question 1. James Thornberry opens a barber shop in the Midlands that generates profits of GBP40,000 per year.[28] Thornberry expects that the shop can operate forever. What is the value of the barber shop if the relevant risk-adjusted benchmark return on hair cutting profits is 5%?

Question 2. Jane Carmichael offers to pay Arthur Birdwhistle GBP200 a year for 10 years on a loan to finance the construction of a mineral water cellar at her house. How much of a loan should Birdwhistle be willing to give her if the prevailing benchmark rate of return for home improvements is 4%?

Question 3. Alice Ainsworth opens a comedy school where students pay USD200 a month for 20 months. What is the present value of the tuition for each student if the relevant risk-adjusted annual required return on school tuition is 6%?

Question 4. Louis Perrier has a great year with his spa de valeur actuelle—or present-value spa (a spa where people get therapeutic benefits from working present-value math problems). He anticipates that the spa will generate FRF2 million in profits next year and that the profits should grow by 3% per year. What is the value of the spa if the relevant risk-adjusted hurdle rate on health profits is 10%?

Question 5. Margaret Berrycloth owns an oil well that produces profits of GBP2 million per year. The output is depleting such that profits are expected to decline by 2% per year. What is the value of the oil well if the relevant risk-adjusted benchmark return on oil well profits is 8%?

[28] GBP = United Kingdom pound.

SECTION V
BUSINESS FINANCING

Y ou may recall that balance sheets have two sides: the asset side and the liabilities and equity side. The asset side is commonly the "stuff" side—it's the side that has all the stuff (computers, trucks, office supplies, and the like) that businesses use to do what they do.

This section is about the other side of a balance sheet. The liabilities and equity side indicates how the business raises the money for (or finances) all those assets. As you might imagine, financing stuff is another thing that finance people are into.

At first pass, this business financing section might seem less interesting—like the kind of material that should be relegated to the back of the book. But with further study, you will find that this section is filled with all sorts of concepts that are just as interesting. Here are some of the questions you will grapple with in this section:

Why are the owners of some businesses cash poor while the owners of other businesses are well off, and what does the life cycle of a tomato plant have to do with it?

How many slices should you cut a pizza into, and what does that have to do with the effect of debt on the risk and value of a business?

How do the operating decisions that businesses make (like how much inventory to hold) affect the financing needs of the business?

Three chapters make up this final section. Chapter 14 showcases the concept of the *cash cycle*, a measure of how long it takes the operations of your business to convert "cash out" into "cash in." Bad cash cycles have been at the heart of all sorts of business failures throughout history. Your task will be to recognize the financing effects of cash cycles and to know what to do about them. Chapter 15 explores the fundamentals of capital structure policy. Capital structure policy deals with the value gains and losses associated with how a business is financed. For example, should a company be financed with lots of debt or little debt? This chapter examines how changes in the amount of debt financing affect (or don't affect) a business's value or risk profile. Chapter 16 finishes up with an extension of financial modeling that includes both the left and right sides of the balance sheet. By modeling both sides of the balance sheet, we will be confronted with the fact that the sources and uses of cash must be equal. This reality helps us gain an appreciation of all the levers that affect how cash runs through a business. Moreover, we'll find out what happened to Dillon Adams and Bart Zamboni, the teenagers who ran the food truck for their entrepreneurial grandmothers at Goodtimes Senior Center.

14

The Cash Cycle and the Calaboose Challenge

PROFESSOR RAINWEATHER AND HORTICULTURE 1

It was class time at Calaboose U. A group of 20 students gathered around a tomato plant while Bud Rainweather, their horticulture professor, explained the details of a tomato plant's life cycle.

"This tomato follows the classic life cycle pattern of angiosperms," Rainweather began. "With careful attention, the entire life cycle can be expedited to under 60 days. Can anyone run through the life cycle stages?"

The eager students leaned in closer. Digger Melon, whose primary motivation for taking the class was getting more high-volume eating opportunities, raised his hand. Once called on, he volunteered, "Tomato fruit contains seeds. When placed in most soil that is about 75 degrees Fahrenheit for an extended period, the seeds begin to germinate."

"Don't forget about the radicles, cotyledons, and plumules!" interrupted Rake Root, who tended to be both particularly exacting with his horticulture studies and jealous of the success of others.

"He's got it, Rake," asserted Rainweather.

Melon continued, "Upon germination, the radicle—the part of the embryo that becomes the root—grows downward, and the plumule—the part of the embryo that becomes the stem—grows upward, along with the cotyledons—the part of the embryo that becomes the leaves. Over a few days, the seed transforms from seed to seedling. With the appropriate conditions, the seedling continues to mature, and after a few weeks, buds form, and then flowers bloom."

"When you think about the transformation, it is such a wonder!" blurted Wilder Legume, a tear running down his cheek. Leaf Hoe, a former soybean farmer, put an arm around Legume and acknowledged the miracle of it all.

"Please continue," urged Rainweather.

"What makes the flower of an angiosperm unique is the male chromosomes contained in the gametes inside the tiny pollen grain and the female chromosomes contained in the gametes of the flower's ovule," Melon said. "Pollination occurs as the pollen grains are moved by wind or insects from the stamen to the stigma. Once the pollen makes its way down the style to the flower ovary, fertilization occurs as the male gametes and the female gametes combine to form an embryo. Upon fertilization, the ovary grows into the tomato fruit and the fertilized ovules grow into seeds within the fruit."

Suddenly, over half of the students erupted into enthusiastic cheers.

Rainweather brought the crowd back to attention with a click of his fingers. "Yeah, yeah, yeah, but don't let yourself get carried away in the botany. Remember that horticulture is not about simply watching plants grow. What does this tomato plant really need?"

"Nitrogen, phosphorus, and potassium," Root replied quickly. "Nitrogen stimulates vine growth, phosphorus stimulates root growth, and potassium stimulates strong stems and disease resistance. It is the fertilizer that accelerates the life cycle and helps grow a robust product. Have a look at this chart. It shows what I see as the minimum life cycle for a tomato cultivar." Root displayed for all to see the drawing he had made of the accelerated life cycle of a tomato plant (**Figure 14.1**). He explained that it took 7 days for seed to transform into seedling, 25 days for seedling to transform into flower, and 28 days for flower to become fruit. Summing the total days in the life cycle gave him 60 days.

"Nice work, Root," Rainweather said. Addressing the entire group of 20 students, he raised his shovel and proclaimed, "I think we're ready for the Calaboose Challenge!"

Suddenly the group got quiet and uncomfortable.

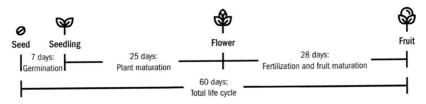

FIGURE 14.1. Accelerated life cycle of a tomato plant.

CONCEPT

Just like a plant's life cycle of renewal, businesses maintain a cycle of cash renewal across a business's production and sales cycle. Finance people call this cycle the *cash cycle* or *cash conversion cycle* and recognize its importance in understanding a business's cash needs.

As plants maintain a life cycle from seed to plant to flower to fruit, so do businesses experience a cycle of cash from purchasing to producing to selling to collecting. Conceptually, the cash cycle measures how long it takes from the time money flows out of the business (with the purchasing and production of inventory) to the time money flows into the business (with collections on the sales). Technically, the cash cycle measures the number of days the business holds its inventory plus the number of days it takes to collect on the sales minus the days it takes to pay its suppliers. The cash cycle captures the amount of time it takes for cash outflows to turn into cash inflows. The cash cycle matters to finance people—they appreciate that investors finance the business operations over the cash cycle. The longer the cash cycle, the larger the financing needs of the business.

TERMINOLOGY

Cash cycle. The cash cycle or *cash conversion cycle* of a business represents the amount of time between the cash outflow a business makes to buy or make a good or service and the cash inflow a business receives when collecting on the sale. The typical cash cycle is equal to the average number of inventory days (days inventory outstanding, DIO) plus the average number of accounts receivable days (days sales outstanding, DSO) minus the average number of payable days (days payable outstanding, DPO), or DIO + DSO − DPO. Because the costs of production must be financed by the business, longer cash cycles are associated with greater business financing needs.

Days inventory outstanding (DIO). The number of DIO represents the average number of days a business holds its inventory from delivery to sale. It captures the number of days that a business is holding the inventory that it sells. DIO is also known as *inventory days*. A common way DIO is calculated is

$$DIO = \frac{\text{inventory}}{\text{cost of goods sold}} \times 365 \text{ days},$$

where inventory is the average amount of inventory that the business keeps on hand, and cost of goods sold (COGS) is the cost of the inventory that the business sells in a year. It is customary to use COGS rather than revenue to measure the amount of sales, since inventory is valued at its production cost rather than its sales value. The ratio tells how many days the business holds inventory on average. For example, suppose that inventory was equal to the annual COGS. If we calculate the ratio, we find that the DIO is 365 days. This makes sense because the business is holding a full year's worth of inventory.

Days payable outstanding (DPO). The number of DPO represents the average number of days a business holds its payables from delivery of the inputs to payment for the inputs. It captures the number of days a business is holding the accounts payable before paying the supplier. DPO is also known as *payable days*. A common way to calculate DPO is

$$DPO = \frac{\text{accounts payable}}{\text{cost of goods sold}} \times 365 \text{ days},$$

where accounts payable is the average amount of payables owed to the suppliers of the business, and COGS is the amount of inventory that the business sells in a year. Finance people often use annual purchases as an alternative to COGS: since purchases correspond more closely to accounts payable, annual purchases can be a more accurate number.

Days sales outstanding (DSO). The number of DSO represents the average number of days a business holds its accounts receivable, meaning the average number of days between a sale and collection of payment for that sale. DSO captures the number of days a business is holding the receivables associated with its sales. DSO is also known as *accounts receivable days* or simply *receivable days*. A common way to calculate DSO is

$$DSO = \frac{\text{accounts receivable}}{\text{revenue}} \times 365 \text{ days,}$$

where accounts receivable is the average amount of receivables owed by the customers of the business, and revenue is the amount of sales that the business has made for the year. The ratio tells how many days the business holds accounts receivable on average. For example, suppose that accounts receivable was equal to the annual revenue. If we calculate the ratio (it would equal 1), we find that the DSO is 365 days. This makes sense because the business is holding a full year's worth of receivables.

THE CALABOOSE CHALLENGE

The Calaboose Challenge was a commercial agricultural challenge and a requirement for all horticulture students. In the challenge, each student received a common set of unknown resources and had to live off their own horticulture business for six months.

The morning before the challenge, the group gathered in anticipation. Each student received a bag of edible dried red beans and USD 10,000 in cash. Each student took a vow to live off only the gains they could get from these two resources for the next six months. With the bags of beans over their shoulders and the cash in their pockets, the group of Calaboose horticulture students then scattered to the wind.

Legume, Melon, and Root traveled south together. After two days of arduous foot travel, they found themselves in a prosperous farming community. Legume and Melon agreed to partner on the purchase of a tract of farmland with a beautiful southwestern exposure. They called their land Solanum Tomato Farm. Root used his funds to purchase a large roadside fruit stand. Calling his business Root's Reds, he focused on retailing produce with a heavy emphasis on tomatoes.

Within one week, Legume and Melon had prepared the ground at their farm. Remembering Rainweather's counsel, they spent the rest of their remaining cash on fertilizer, which they secured at a local farm supply store. Although they couldn't afford enough fertilizer to meet Rainweather's standards, they added all the nitrogen, phosphorus, and potassium they could to the soil. They planted their tomato seeds and anticipated a great harvest.

Over the next two months, while they waited for the plants to fruit, Legume and Melon lived on the dried red beans. The first month went fine, but by the second month the physical and psychological effects of a one-food diet were beginning to reveal themselves. They began to long for their days back in the Calaboose U cafeteria, eating canned peas and dry Salisbury steak.

Finally, their first tomatoes turned red. After eating the first fruits of their labor and finding them to be of exceptional quality, the pair contacted several tomato wholesalers. Legume and Melon negotiated hard to get high prices for their product. One buyer agreed to the price but demanded 40 days credit on the purchase, meaning that the buyer wouldn't pay for the tomatoes until 40 days after the purchase. This 40-day period allowed the buyer sufficient time to sell the fruit and collect the money.

Seeing no other alternative, Legume and Melon agreed to the terms and harvested their first tomato crop. The next day, 75 days after planting, a truck collected the fruit and the driver gave them an invoice for a tidy sum with the promise of payment to Solanum Tomato Farm in 40 days.

After 10 weeks of nothing but beans (and a few tomatoes) on the menu, Legume and Melon had had enough. In search of another meal, they walked into town to pay a visit to their friend Root. Business looked brisk at Root's Reds, and Root greeted them warmly as he welcomed them to his office. On the credenza was a large spread of Buffalo chicken wraps, along with a selection of cheese and celery. Legume and Melon's mouths began to water and they immediately questioned Root's fidelity to his vow of honesty to the challenge.

"Gentlemen," Root began, "rest assured that this meal is completely on the up and up. I'm still an honest Calaboose man. Fill yourself a plate first and then let me enlighten you on what Professor Rainweather really taught us back in class."

Legume and Melon needed no further encouragement. Scarfing sounds ensued and soon their plates were clean. Holding a piece of celery, Root began in a manner reminiscent of their beloved professor, "Remember that horticulture is not botany. Botany studies the wonder of plants. Horticulture, on the other hand, is practical. Horticulture is about maximizing the beneficial effects of plants. Remember the plant cycle?" Both Legume and Melon nodded. "The plant cycle takes time. In the case of tomato plants, that cycle of seed to fruit takes at least 60 days. You may recall that for Rainweather, that cycle time was the enemy. His quest was to push the tomato cycle time to its minimum."

"Okay," Legume said. "So what?"

"*So what* is that businesses also have cycle times—the cash cycle is the time it takes for cash outflows incurred in the costs of producing or purchasing inventory or services to turn into cash inflows incurred from collecting cash on the sales of inventory or services. Let's look at the cash cycle time for Solanum Tomato Farm." Following several pointed questions to Legume and Melon to ascertain some details, Root picked up his notepad (see **Figure 14.2**).

"What do you notice from the timeline?" asked Root.

"Well, I see that cash goes out at the beginning when we buy fertilizer, and cash comes in at the end, when we collect on our sales—not when we actually sell the tomatoes," offered Melon. "Our inventory sits for 75 days, then our receivables sit for 40 days, so in total it takes us 115 days for our cash outflows to be offset by our cash inflows."

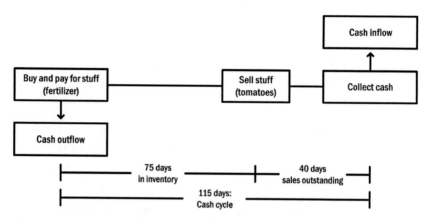

FIGURE 14.2. Cash cycle timeline for Solanum Tomato Farm.

"Professor Rainweather would be proud. Does that 115-day cash cycle matter?"

"I don't know. It all seems kind of academic to me," confessed Legume.

"Academic?? #$*&!!," Root retorted. "Don't you appreciate that the reason I've been eating Buffalo chicken and you've been eating dried beans is entirely because of your 115-day cash cycle? The two of you are starving for cash inflow while I'm awash in it. Let me show you." He returned to his notepad to sketch a cash cycle for another business (see **Figure 14.3**). "What do you notice from the timeline for my business?"

"Your cash inflows occur before your cash outflows," acknowledged Legume. "How do you manage that? You've got a negative cash cycle?"

"Yep, that is the magic," boasted Root.

"But how do you do that?" continued Legume.

"Well, one feature is that I have an advantage," Root said. "I'm leaning on farms like yours to fund the time it takes to grow the tomatoes. A retailer like me could prepay to help you out, but I haven't. That inventory time matters because your costs are simply sitting out in the field. Once the tomatoes are ready for market, I don't load up on inventory—I'd rather leave that with my suppliers. Instead, I take just the inventory that I can sell that week. This keeps my days inventory outstanding, or DIO, to 5. Next, let's look at my sales. I sell all my produce for cash only.

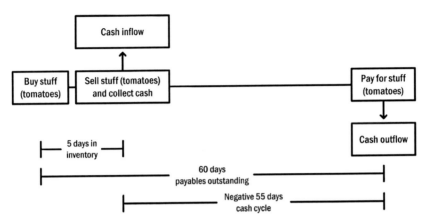

FIGURE 14.3. Cash cycle timeline for Root's Reds.

I might be able to get a higher price if I sold on credit, but it isn't worth it to me. I want cash now. You, on the other hand, have sold on credit, giving your customers 40 days to pay."

"But they demanded the 40 days! There was nothing we could do," insisted Melon.

"Maybe," responded Root, "but I expect that it was because you demanded a premium price. When paying those kind of prices, I also require generous credit."

"So that's why you aren't paying your suppliers for 60 days?"

"Yes, that's right. Paying a higher price is worth it to me to reduce my cash cycle time. Overall, I'm sitting on a business that generates cash inflows first and cash outflows 55 days later. I can use that cash surplus to fund growth in my business."

Legume and Melon pondered Root's insights for a few minutes. Finally, Legume argued, "I still think you are overdoing this cash cycle thing. I mean, doesn't the cash cycle time only matter for business start-ups? Once Digger and I start collecting on our sales, I'm anticipating that all our cash problems will go away. It's all profit!"

"That's what it seems," Root said, with a note of caution in his voice, "but unless your cash cycle changes, you will always continue to have to fund 115 days of your business. Remember what's going to happen to that cash inflow once you get it? You'll plow it back into buying seed and fertilizer, and the process will repeat itself. You'll be able to keep the profit, but you're going to have to continue to fund a hundred days of operating costs, including your wages. Businesses that have long cash cycles, like yours, require additional money to fund their large inventory and receivable balances. Eventually and with enough time, you will build up that money. But you won't be able to spend it—that money will be locked in your business. Meanwhile, my business requires very little investment because of its negative cash cycle."

"I think I mostly get it," Legume acknowledged.

"Let me try one more time with the specifics of your balance sheet," suggested Root. He tabulated the assets, liabilities, and equity of Solanum Tomato Farm (see **Table 14.1**).

"So here we go," he continued. "You spent USD12,000 on your farm, and now you have USD4,000 locked up in inventory in the field and USD4,000 locked up in receivables that your customers owe you. Since you have nothing in cash, your total assets are USD20,000. Since your suppliers haven't provided any credit, you have financed the entire business out of the USD20,000 you started with. The cash challenge you are facing is that you have a lot of receivables and inventory and you are financing all of it yourselves."

"Except for our zero cash balance, I'm not sure I understand what is wrong with that," admitted Legume.

"Well, let's compare your situation to mine," continued Root as he noted down the balance sheet for Root's Reds (see **Table 14.2**). "There

TABLE 14.1. Balance sheet for Solanum Tomato Farm (in thousands of US dollars).

Cash	0.0	Payables	0.0
Receivables	4.0	Equity	20.0
Inventory	4.0		
Land and equipment	12.0		
Total	20.0	Total	20.0

TABLE 14.2. Balance sheet for Root's Reds (in thousands of US dollars).

Cash	10.0	Payables	12.0
Inventory	1.0	Equity	5.0
Store and equipment	6.0		
Total	17.0	Total	17.0

are a couple of things to see. First, you spent USD6,000 each on your land and equipment and I spent USD6,000 total on my store and equipment. Next, the only other operating asset I have is USD1,000 in inventory; that's 5 days of sales for me. Because my suppliers are willing to fund 60 days of my sales, my accounts payable balance is a whopping USD12,000. Thanks to all of that funding I'm getting from my suppliers, I have been able to accumulate a sizable amount of cash this season: USD10,000."

"Are you kidding me?" retorted Melon. "You've already accumulated USD10,000 in cash?!"

"Well, yes," admitted Root. "And that's not all. Notice how my equity balance has dropped to USD5,000. That's because I already paid out USD5,000 to myself as a cash dividend. Not only am I eating Buffalo chicken every day, I've managed to buy myself a little motorcycle to get around town."

"Flaming tomatoes!" shrieked Legume. "What are we doing, Digger? It's the cash cycle that has us yearning to be back in the Calaboose cafeteria. We've got to fix our cash cycle!"

Root excused himself to help some customers who had just pulled up at his stand. Legume and Melon were grateful for some time to themselves to think through how to salvage the cash cycle of Solanum Tomato. Melon was ready to get on the phone to negotiate better credit terms with their customers and suppliers.

Root returned in a few minutes. "Those customers are looking for more tomatoes than I can provide. Would Solanum Tomato be interested in becoming one of my suppliers?" he asked with his characteristic charm.

Legume and Melon looked at each other and then slowly back to Root. "Of course we are," replied Legume with a smile. "How about you give us the cash now at a discount and we'll deliver the fruit in 40 days? We've got a cash cycle to fix."

"Dratted radicles, cotyledons, and plumules!" groused Root, offering his hand to shake on the deal. "You have figured this out."

CONCEPT WRAP-UP

The cash cycle captures the amount of time it takes for business cash outflows to turn into cash inflows. Three components—DIO (the average time the business holds its inventory), DSO (the average time the business takes to collect the money on its sales), and DPO (the average time the business takes to pay its suppliers)—play important roles in the length of the cash cycle and function as operating levers for adjusting it. The typical cash cycle is equal to DIO, meaning the average number of inventory days, plus DSO, meaning the average number of accounts receivable days, minus DPO, meaning the average number of payable days:

$$\text{Cash cycle} = \text{DIO} + \text{DSO} - \text{DPO}.$$

The cash cycle is very important to finance people because investors must finance business operations over the cash cycle. The longer the cash cycle, the larger the financing needs are likely to be. Financing needs become particularly acute when businesses with long cash cycles are growing. Finance people are aware of the relations among the cash cycle, growth, and financing need.

Table 14.3 provides the cash cycle values for a select number of large US companies. The table indicates that the cash cycle varies tremendously—the cash cycle for Apple Inc., a technology company, is −40 days; and for the Boeing Company, an aircraft manufacturer, it is 455 days. The other cash cycle values are 5 days for the Coca-Cola

TABLE 14.3. Estimates of cash cycle values for select US companies in 2022.

	DIO	DSO	DPO	Cash cycle (DIO + DSO – DPO)
Apple	8	56	105	–41
Boeing	452	62	59	455
Coca-Cola	81	33	109	5
Johnson & Johnson	122	59	130	51
Merck	125	57	97	85
Walmart	48	5	47	6

Source: Calculated based on financial statements for each company.

Company, a beverage maker; 6 days for retailer Walmart Inc.; 51 days for health care company Johnson & Johnson; and 85 days for health care company Merck & Co., Inc.

Using the formula DIO + DSO – DPO, it is easy to ascertain the cause of the variation in cash cycle. On the two extremes, we see that Boeing's large cash cycle is caused by a tremendously large DIO of 452 days. While Boeing's receivable days and payable days are not necessarily that large, its tendency to maintain a large amount of inventory days creates a massive financing need for the company and a cash drain for investors. In contrast, Apple's negative cash cycle is due to a large number of payable days (105 days) relative to its small number of inventory days (8 days) and receivable days (56). Because of how Apple has structured its terms with its customers and suppliers, Apple is receiving the cash for its sales *before* it is paying for those sales. Such an arrangement shrinks its financing need and is beneficial to investors. In reference to the chapter example, Boeing is like Solanum Tomato Farm and Apple is like Root's Reds.

It is interesting to see how other companies structure their cash cycle. Johnson & Johnson has the longest term of payable days, at 130 days. This allows it to finance a relatively large number of DIO, 122 days. Merck has a similar level of inventory days and receivable days, but Merck's lower number of payable days results in a longer cash cycle.

Coca-Cola also uses long payable days (109 days) to reduce its cash cycle to just 5 days. Walmart excels at a low level of inventory days (48 days). Because Walmart sells little on credit, it also has a very low term of receivable days. These two arrangements result in a low cash cycle for Walmart, at 6 days.

REVIEW QUESTIONS

Calaboose student Leaf Hoe has acquired a tomato-canning operation just outside of a major urban center. He has negotiated the following terms with his suppliers and customers:

- Suppliers to be paid within 20 days of delivery.
- Customers to pay within 40 days of purchase.

Hoe runs an efficient operation in which he produces to order with frequent deliveries. As such, his days of inventory outstanding is just three days.

Question 1. What is the length of the cash cycle for Hoe's operation?

Question 2. Hoe doesn't understand the importance of the cash cycle to his business. How would you explain to him the relevance of the definition of the cash cycle?

Question 3. Hoe has struggled to fill big orders for his canned tomatoes— every time a large order comes in, he doesn't have enough inventory, and those customers go elsewhere. How can Hoe work with his customers so that he can increase the amount of inventory he is able to stock (an increase in his inventory days) while keeping his cash cycle constant?

15

Financial Leverage and Thru-Hiking the Appalachian Trail

BAREFOOT HILLS HOSTEL

A late morning in February found two friends, now known by their trail names, Ozone and Sunshine, sitting in a room at the Barefoot Hills Hostel near Amicalola Falls at the southern terminus of the Appalachian Trail (AT), a 2,200-mile trail that wound its way through the Appalachian Mountains along the eastern part of the United States from Georgia to Maine. Thru-hiking the AT (doing the entire trail without going home) was a notable American challenge: several thousand people attempted it each year, and about a quarter completed it. Ozone and Sunshine anticipated hiking about 15 miles per day and hoped to reach Mount Katahdin—the northern terminus of the trail—by August. The pair had been planning the adventure for years and were excited and anxious about the journey ahead.

Ozone had left a job as an equity analyst for a large security brokerage house. She was known for her ability to identify both the rewards and the risks associated with stock investing. After her time on the trail, she planned to return to equity investing on her own through a hedge fund she was organizing. Sunshine also worked in the financial sector, but her role was with debt markets—she worked for the syndicated loan arm of a major commercial bank. Sunshine had a low tolerance for risk and was willing to pay a premium (meaning she would accept a low interest rate) to keep risk at a minimum. She had taken a six-month leave and hoped to return to the bank at the end of the summer.

At the hostel, the two were packing their gear into their backpacks. All their personal gear was packed, but allocating the shared gear involved an important joint decision. "In the name of all that is freeze-dried!" Sunshine erupted as she looked at the large pile in the center of the room: tent, stove, water filter, bear bag rope, toilet paper (TP), cooking gear, solar shower, and a week's worth of food. "Our highest summit may be this mountain of shared stuff!"

While the obvious solution was to simply split the weight in half, Ozone was considering an alternative proposal. "It is a lot, but maybe there is a trade to be had." She offered, "What if I carry the entire mountain of shared gear and food, except the TP?" Then she paused briefly and added, "But as compensation, you do all the cooking and water filtering?"

A liberating smile stole over Sunshine's face as she considered the proposal carefully. Without all that extra weight to carry, the entire hike suddenly seemed much more doable. But Sunshine knew her friend well enough to appreciate that Ozone had fully considered both the upside and downside to the trade. For Ozone's willingness to take on the weight, she would get a substantial increase in rest time. The tradeoff between pack weight and rest time was meaningful. Still, they both knew that Ozone was physically more capable of carrying weight and that Sunshine was easily the better cook.

"This sounds eerily like a leveraged finance deal," Sunshine joked. "It's like you are taking the equity position by bearing more risk in return for an upside gain, while I take the debt position by offloading my risk exposure for lower free-time returns."

"Ha! I guess that's right," Ozone confirmed. "It is true that I have always been willing to bear risk for the right price!"

Sunshine said, "Since I've always been willing to trade away the risk, and you are always willing to accept it, why not do that now?"

The two shook hands to complete the deal. Sunshine closed and tightened up her backpack with a smile, while Ozone was relieved that she had brought her massive 70-liter pack. An hour later, having left the hostel and put boots to trail, they began to climb Frosty Mountain, their first peak. With the joint gear very unequally distributed, they looked at each other and cheered, "Hike on!"

CONCEPT

Businesses tend to have two types of investors: debt holders and equity holders. The debt holders accept a relatively low-risk first claim on the profits of the business, while the equity investors get the remaining, or "what is left over," share of the profits. Financing decisions, such as choosing the mix of debt and equity financing, are fundamental decisions for any business. If a business tilts toward more debt, finance people say that the business is financially *leveraged*. Financial leverage is associated with substituting debt financing for equity financing. As the mix of debt to equity increases, financial leverage increases. The term *leverage* is used because, as with mechanical leverage, which enhances one's ability to move something, debt allows the business owner to enhance her buying power: by taking on debt, she can leverage her equity to finance additional assets. For example, a USD500,000 house purchased by someone with their own cash involves no leverage, since no debt financing is involved. Alternatively, someone who acquires a USD500,000 house with just USD50,000 of their own cash and USD450,000 of debt financing is using substantial financial leverage. This second homeowner is considered to be levered 10 to 1 since they have put in only 10% of the financing for the house.

As we explore financial leverage, there are five core principles with which to get comfortable.

1. **Cash flow outcome is uncertain.** Business performance is rarely certain. Things may turn out well, with high cash flow, or things may turn out poorly, with low cash flow. The actual outcome is unknown beforehand. This uncertainty in business cash flow is called *business risk*.

2. **Investors require a fair return for bearing risk.** Investors care about risk and work hard to receive fair compensation for it. Because

of finance people's resolve to be compensated for bearing risk, markets maintain a positive relation between the risk investors bear and the return they can anticipate. As we saw back in chapter 6, when investors perceive an investment as low risk, they don't require much expected return for it. When investors perceive an investment as risky, they price it in a way that enables them to anticipate a higher compensatory return premium for the risk they bear. The security price is the mechanism for adjusting the expected return. As an investment increases in risk, the value (or price) of the investment must decline to allow the expected returns to increase and compensate investors for the expected increase in risk. Prices are determined based on investors' risk tolerance. For our thru-hikers, it was important for both Ozone and Sunshine to determine whether the pack-weight-for-rest-time bargain they struck was fair.

3. **Risk doesn't have to be allocated to investors evenly.** Just as Ozone took on more of the weight than Sunshine did, so equity holders take on more of the cash flow uncertainty than debt holders do. One important way to think about debt is simply to consider it as a financing contract that has disproportionately lower risk. Likewise, then, we can think of equity as simply a financing contract that has disproportionately higher risk. The total firm risk gets spread across the investors in the business, with equity investors bearing all the risk the debt holders don't bear.

4. **As financial leverage increases, the concentration of risk among equity investors increases proportionally.** Although a business's mix of debt and equity financing changes, it is important to recognize that the mix of debt and equity doesn't change the business's total business risk. The total amount of risk is conserved—it must stay the same regardless of how much leverage there is, even though it is allocated differently. If we think back to Ozone and Sunshine preparing for their trip, although Ozone took a larger proportion of gear and food, the amount of gear and food didn't change—it was simply allocated differently. This principle can be called the *law of conservation of risk*; it states that even though risk is allocated

disproportionately among debt and equity holders, total business risk is the same regardless of the level of financial leverage (in a frictionless world, meaning an idealized market without transaction costs).

5. **In a frictionless world, as leverage increases, value should be unchanged, since the total cash flow and total risk haven't changed.** This is commonly called the *pizza principle*, in that just as the total value of a pizza shouldn't change based on how it is sliced, so the total value of the cash flow and the total amount of risk of a business shouldn't change based on how it is divided among debt holders and equity holders. The total value of the business should remain the same regardless of the mix of debt and equity financing. This principle can also be called the *law of conservation of value*. The law of conservation of value states that total business value is the same regardless of the level of financial leverage in a frictionless market.

To illustrate these important principles, we will return to the story of Ozone and Sunshine, after a quick detour to define some terms.

TERMINOLOGY

Debt holders. Debt holders (also called *debt investors*) are one type of investor. In exchange for lending money to the business, debt holders have the following two claims: (1) a promise of a set of fixed future payments and (2) the right to exert control over the assets of the business in the event that the promised fixed payments are not paid. Suppose Boris gives USD1 million to Jumbo Airlines in exchange for a promise of annual interest payments of 10% of the USD1 million loan for 10 years, plus a return of the USD1 million at the end of the 10-year loan. As a debt holder, Boris can expect to receive annual payments of USD100,000 every year for the next 10 years. As long as those payments are made, Boris has no right to exert influence on the company's business decisions. But if Jumbo Airlines fails to make its promised payment, Boris is assured that he will have influence. The structure of the debt contract gives the debt holder assurance that others in the company won't take advantage of them.

Equity holders. Equity holders are another type of investor. The term *equity holder* is synonymous with the terms *equity investor, stockholder,* and *shareholder.* In exchange for their investment in the business, equity holders have the following two claims: (1) the right to exert control over the assets of the business as long as the promises to other claim holders (i.e., debt holders) are made and (2) the right to the residual profits of the business. Equity holders are residual claim holders, meaning they get what is left over after everyone else has been paid. Sometimes it is good to be a residual claim holder and sometimes it is not. Suppose Ivana gives USD1 million to Jumbo Airlines for a promise of shared equity in the company—meaning she shares the equity with people who have similar claims—and a promise of the residual profits. As an equity holder, Ivana can expect to have voting rights on company policies and the leadership of Jumbo Airlines. If she doesn't like the decisions that the board of directors is making, she can vote the board members out. The company provides cash payments to Ivana through board-approved cash dividends and through equity buybacks (when the company buys back shares). If the company is acquired or liquidated, Ivana gets her share of what is left over after all other claim holders are paid. The structure of the equity contract gives the equity holder assurance that others in the company won't take advantage of them.

Financial leverage. Financial leverage is a concept that captures the mix of debt and equity used to finance a business. By leverage, finance people mean the ability of debt financing to give more power to the amount of equity financing being used. Using debt allows someone to buy more assets with the same amount of equity; in other words, they leverage their equity by using debt. That power to enhance their equity to buy more assets is what finance people refer to as *leverage.* Suppose Isabel has USD50,000 in cash to invest in a house. Without debt financing, she is only able to afford a house priced at under USD50,000. However, suppose she can find a bank to lend her USD50,000. With the USD50,000 of bank financing, she is able to afford a house priced at USD100,000. With the bank as the debt holder, Isabel, the equity holder, has leveraged her equity at a proportion of two times, in that she has acquired an asset worth two times her equity investment. Now suppose she is able to find another a bank that will lend her

USD450,000. With the USD450,000 of bank financing, she is able to afford a house priced at USD500,000. Isabel has leveraged her equity at a proportion of 10 times, in that she has acquired assets worth 10 times her equity investment. Note that she also increased her risk level by 10 times.

Business risk and **financial risk.** Business risk is the potential variation in financial outcome to investors due to uncertainty in business performance. Business risk is different from financial risk. *Financial risk* is the variation in business risk caused by financial leverage. If a firm's equity is levered two times, then debt holders have financed half the assets, but they have not taken their proportional share of the business risk. If, for example, the debt holders have contracted to bear no risk, then the leverage has doubled the risk the equity holders are bearing. Changes in the value of the business assets are associated with twice the change in the value held by the equity holders, since they bear all the asset risk despite providing half the investment.

Law of conservation of risk. The law of conservation of risk states that the overall risk associated with a business remains the same regardless of how the business is financed. This is a powerful principle for thinking clearly about assessing a business's risk. Two firms can have the same overall business risk, even if the first is financed mostly with equity and the second is financed mostly with debt. The law of conservation of risk implies that businesses with lots of debt aren't necessarily any riskier than those with none. This law is foundational to understanding how the risks for debt holders and for equity holders change as the mix of debt and equity changes.

Law of conservation of value. The law of conservation of value states that the value of a business remains the same regardless of how the business is financed. Two firms can have the same business value, even if the first is financed mostly with equity while the second is financed mostly with debt. The law of conservation of value implies that debt financing doesn't necessarily change firm value. It is based on the notion that firm value is determined by the size of firm's cash flow, not by how that cash flow is divvied out. The law of conservation of value is foundational to understanding how the values of the debt holder and equity holder positions change as the mix of debt and equity changes.

DAMASCUS FOOD SUPPLY

Two months and 500 miles later, Sunshine and Ozone celebrated as they crossed the Tennessee–Virginia border and descended into the famed trail town of Damascus, Virginia. The hike to Damascus had been harder than they had originally envisioned. Ozone and Sunshine had reveled in every aspect of their thru-hike except for one important element—the quality of the trail food. Their experience, they believed, couldn't be unique to them. One evening at the Roan High Knob Shelter, the two concocted a business idea to meet the nutrition needs of AT thru-hikers. The idea was to provide a quality food-delivery service up and down the AT. They believed that with the help of an unemployed friend of theirs, the business concept would be pretty simple to implement. They thought they could get it off the ground by stopping in Damascus and pausing their hike for just a month of concerted effort.

Based on interviews with fellow thru-hikers and estimates of production and shipping costs, Ozone and Sunshine agreed that the business would result in one of two outcomes. If demand for their food was strong, annual cash flow was expected to be USD60,000. If demand was weak, annual cash flow was expected to be USD20,000. They thought the probability of either outcome was 50%. Based on the two possible outcomes and the associated probabilities, the expected cash flow for the enterprise was USD40,000. The USD40,000 expected cash flow came from multiplying the possible USD60,000 outcome by its probability of 50% and the possible USD20,000 outcome by its probability of 50%, to give an expected value of USD40,000 [50% × USD60,000 + 50% × USD20,000]. Based on their understanding of the risk of the cash flows, they determined (using the concepts discussed in earlier chapters) that a discount rate of 8% was appropriate for valuing the business.

The two considered how much money they were willing to put into a business like that. "We can use the perpetuity formula to value the business," Sunshine offered. "Since we expect the business to generate cash flow of USD40,000 per year in perpetuity, the business's present value could be estimated by simply dividing the expected annual cash flow of

TABLE 15.1. Total cash flow and values for Damascus Food Supply (figures in thousands of US dollars).

	Cash flow	Probability	
Strong demand	60	50%	
Weak demand	20	50%	
Expected cash flow (weighted average of possible outcomes)			40
Risk-adjusted discount rate			8.0%
Perpetuity value of business ($V = C/R$)			500

USD40,000 by the discount rate of 8%.[29] That value is USD500,000 (see **Table 15.1**). One way to structure our ownership is for us to both be equity partners—splitting the USD500,000 equity value in two, at USD250,000 each."

"But of course, you know," Ozone countered, "there is another way."

The friends grinned at each other, knowing full well where this conversation was leading.

"Let's suppose that instead, you take a risk-free debt position worth USD250,000," Ozone continued. "Since your debt claim carries lower risk, I expect the fair return on your risk-free debt claim to be the risk-free rate of 6%, rather than 8%. A 6% return on a USD250,000 investment would necessitate that the business pay you an interest payment of USD15,000 per year. You can expect to get that amount under both outcome scenarios for the business. As your debt contract doesn't bear risk, you get the USD15,000 payment each year regardless of the strength of demand in the business. I expect that since the investment is risk free, you are happy with the 6% return." (See **Table 15.2**.)

Sunshine nodded. "Yes, I'd be happy with that. And now let's consider your expectations as the equity holder. Since my interest payment of USD15,000 gets paid no matter what, the equity cash flows need to be

---

[29] According to the perpetuity formula featured in chapter 13, one could calculate the present value (V) of an expected perpetual stream of cash flow (CF) by dividing CF by the relevant discount rate, $V = CF/R$. So if the expected annual cash flow is USD100 for forever and the risk-adjusted discount rate is 10%, an investor should be indifferent between receiving USD1,000 in cash today or an expected payment of USD100 a year for forever. This makes sense, since if one has cash of USD1,000, one may home cook the USD100 annual payment by investing the USD1,000 at the 10% rate and peel off the expected USD100 payments every year for forever.

TABLE 15.2. Debt contract cash flow and values for Damascus Food Supply (figures in thousands of US dollars).

	Cash flow	Probability	
Strong demand	15	50%	
Weak demand	15	50%	
Expected cash flow (weighted average of possible outcomes)			15
Risk-adjusted discount rate			6.0%
Perpetuity value of business ($V = C/R$)			250

adjusted to accommodate the interest payments. You could do this by subtracting the cash flows in the second table (**Table 15.2**) from those in the first table (**Table 15.1**). Now, instead of getting USD60,000 in the strong-demand scenario, you, as the equity holder, get USD45,000 because of the interest payment of USD15,000 that goes to me. In the weak-demand scenario, you get just USD5,000 instead of USD20,000, again because of the USD15,000 interest payment to me." Sunshine wrote out the revised expected equity cash flow profile, which looked like **Table 15.3**. "How much would you be willing to pay for the revised equity profile?"

Ozone responded, "Well, one thing to note is that the business's risk is now more concentrated with me because you, the debt holder, didn't take any risk—your USD250,000 is risk free since you get your USD15,000 no matter what. All the variability in the cash flow outcome is now concentrated with me, the equity holder. Because of this additional risk, I need a higher return. Rather than requiring just 8%, as was the case in the first table (**Table 15.1**), I will now require 10% because of the extra risk I'm bearing. The 4% risk premium associated with anticipating a 10% return rather than the 4% you are getting compensates me for holding all the business risk on half of the investment capital."

"Excellent," piped back Sunshine. "Since your expected equity cash flow is USD25,000 [50% × USD45,000 + 50% × USD5,000], we can now use the perpetuity formula to value your equity position as USD250,000. That's USD25,000 divided by 10%." (See **Table 15.3**.)

"So, the math works," Ozone concluded. "Rather than being 50% equity partners, we can divide the risk, with you taking none of the risk

TABLE 15.3. Equity contract cash flow and values for Damascus Food Supply (figures in thousands of US dollars).

	Cash flow	Probability	
Strong demand	45	50%	
Weak demand	5	50%	
Expected cash flow (weighted average of possible outcomes)			25
Risk-adjusted discount rate			10.0%
Perpetuity value of business ($V = C/R$)			250

and earning 6% and me taking all of the risk and earning an expected but uncertain return of 10%. Overall, the total risk hasn't changed with leverage. Instead, the risk has been reallocated."

"And of course the value hasn't changed," added Sunshine. "The business is still worth USD500,000. But the value has been reallocated. The laws of conservation of risk and conservation of value hold. The firm is still worth USD500,000, no matter how the cash flow and risk are divided among investors."

"Now that we've got a financing plan," Ozone said, "let's get this business together so we can get back to hiking . . ."

". . . and eating better!" Sunshine added, grinning.

CONCEPT WRAP-UP

Ozone and Sunshine's example illustrates a number of important concepts.

1. **Funding with equity isn't cheaper than funding with debt.** There is a common misconception that equity funding is cheap since equity holders don't require interest payments. As seen from the above example, Ozone is careful to build in an expected return that will compensate her for the additional risk she now bears as the equity holder. Her return comes through the residual profits of the business. In good times, those profits would be large, and in bad times, they would be small. Still, the expected return is sufficient to compensate for the risk and certainly larger than the return experienced by the debt holders.

2. **Debt funding isn't a bargain.** Another common misconception is that debt funding is cheap, since the interest rates lenders require are always lower than the rates equity holders require. While it is true that the returns required by debt investors are lower than those required by equity investors, the two are highly interrelated. As a business increases its financial leverage by borrowing more, an increasing amount of risk is concentrated among a smaller pool of equity. Suppose that Sunshine provided two-thirds of the capital for the Damascus Food Supply business with a no-risk debt contract. In that case, Ozone would bear even greater risk on a similar investment since Sunshine would still have a claim on a larger interest payment regardless of the state of demand. Because of the greater risk, Ozone would require an even greater return to compensate for the additional risk that is now concentrated in her smaller holdings. The overall borrowing cost wouldn't necessarily decline, because the increase in lower debt financing would be offset by a higher cost of equity financing. The law of conservation of risk implies that the cost of borrowing must remain the same since the overall risk hasn't changed: it has simply been reallocated.

3. **Financial leverage doesn't create easy investment opportunities with dazzling returns.** Financial leverage has the effect of magnifying the operating returns for any investment. This magnification makes good operating returns better and poor operating returns worse.

   To illustrate this principle, consider the example of Lola and Nina, two sisters who bought identical neighboring houses on Market Street, each for USD300,000. Lola paid for her house with USD300,000 in cash, while Nina paid for hers with USD30,000 in cash and a USD270,000 loan from a local bank. The next week, while both sisters were doing yard work, they discussed their different approaches to the capital structure of their housing investments. Nina bragged about how bank debt was going to goose up the returns she got from her housing investment. She explained that since housing prices on Market Street would be up 10% in the coming year, her house would be worth USD330,000. Since the bank took none of the upside, Nina's USD30,000 investment in the house would be worth USD60,000—generating a quick 100% return on her one-year investment. She also explained that since Lola had put all her money into the house, the USD30,000 gain she would also realize on the house would represent only a 10% return on Lola's USD300,000 investment, much smaller than Nina's 100% return.

Lola humored her younger sister for a while, but then encouraged her to consider that leverage had two sides. Lola acknowledged that Nina's leverage created an important amplification of investment returns, but warned Nina that there was nothing certain about her 10% expected increase in house prices. She explained that there was a real possibility that house prices on Market Street might fall 10% in the coming year. If that happened, their houses would be worth USD270,000. Since Nina's bank was not interested in absorbing the downside risk, Nina's stake in the house would now be worth nothing—representing a −100% return on her USD30,000 investment. In contrast, since Lola had put all her money into the house, the house decline of USD30,000 would represent only a −10% decline on her USD300,000 investment. Lola warned that leverage was always the friend of equity holders when asset prices were appreciating, but never friendly when asset prices were in decline. Lola sketched out the math (see **Table 15.4**).

Lola reminded her sister that leverage amplifies both risk and return, and when one accepts the possibility of tempting upside gains, one also has to accept the possibility of equally impressive downside losses.

TABLE 15.4. Housing prices for Lola and Nina (in US dollars).

Scenario 1. 10% house price appreciation
Value of house = value of debt + value of equity
Nina: 330,000 = 270,000 + 60,000
Lola: 330,000 = 330,000

Scenario 2. 10% house price depreciation
Value of house = value of debt + value of equity
Nina: 270,000 = 270,000 + 0
Lola: 270,000 = 270,000

REVIEW QUESTIONS

The World Pizza Association Conference was an annual three-day meeting that gathered the greatest pizza experts from around the globe to discuss the leading ideas and most pressing challenges in the world of pizza. This year, the meeting was taking place at a hotel on the east coast of Sicily, nestled between the slope of Mount Etna and a beautiful Mediterranean bay just north of Catania.

In a particularly anticipated session, a group of high-profile academics and practitioners had gathered to discuss one of the most important matters to New York–style pizza cooking: "What is the optimal number of slices in a single pizza pie?"

Lorenzo Gallo, known as the Dazzling Pizzaman, was presenting some of his research. "As you can see from this slide, if I cut a 16-inch pizza into 8 slices, I can sell the pie for USD12. But if I cut the same pizza into 12 slices, I can sell the same pie for USD18. I believe that customers are willing to pay 50% more for the pie because they get 50% more slices."

"What kind of nonsense pizza pizzazz are you serving, Lorenzo?!" asked Maria Romano, a pizza critic for a large news agency. "Why should slicing matter at all? I can understand that people care about ingredients, size, and taste, but why should they care about slicing? Paying 50% more for a pizza that isn't any bigger or better but just has more slices—that seems like nonsense pizza pizzazz!"

Question 1. Romano's critique of pizza slicing applies to how claims on the cash flows of businesses are sliced, since debt and equity partitioning is similar to the slicing of a pizza. Please explain this connection and include a reference to the implications of financial leverage on the value of businesses.

Question 2. How does Romano's critique of pizza slicing apply to the allocation of risk across claim holders in a business? Please include a reference to the implications of financial leverage for the value of businesses.

16

Sources and Uses of Cash and a Yellow '69 Stingray

A RETURN TO GRANNY'S GREEK

Dillon Adams and Bart Zamboni prepared for another onslaught. It was 11:00 a.m. on a Tuesday, and the two teenage boys were preparing their food truck in anticipation of the 11:30 a.m. rush from the residents of Goodtimes Senior Center. With materials for a thousand Greek sandwiches, they expected to sell out within three hours. Sponsored by their grandmothers, who both resided at Goodtimes and were motivated to improve the quality of food at the senior center, the boys had made their food truck venture, Granny's Greek, an iconic phenomenon in their small town over the past few years. In fact, the signage that welcomed travelers to town now read, "Welcome to Rockville, Home of Granny's Greek."

Today, the food truck shared the parking lot with a van and crew from a major national news network. Inspired by the scene of travelers, community members, and nursing home residents mingling each day over tasty Greek gyros, the network planned to tell the story of Granny's Greek to a national audience. Before the rush began, the reporter approached Dillon and Bart and asked them about the source of their success.

Dillon was quick to explain that Granny's Greek was launched for the primary purpose of providing quality food to nursing home residents. "What's been a surprise is the broad support we've seen for that vision.

There seem to be a lot of people who can get behind the concept of No More Corn," he said.

Bart nodded, then added, "But you should know that the success of this business is not just due to quality food. No, our grandmothers' core skill is well outside the realm of food innovation."

"Really? What is their core skill that's led to such success?" asked the reporter with great curiosity.

The boys paused to heighten the anticipation, then Bart slowly responded with a smile, "Financial modeling. Not a day goes by that we don't get a steady flow of financial modeling analysis from our grandmothers. They're relentless in their discipline."

"That's right," continued Dillon. "My Grandma Agnes doesn't allow herself to waste time with aimless innovation—no, she's focused on viable innovation. She's never naive because she always knows what matters to the business. Why? Because she's modeled it. What's more, she and Bart's Grandma Zina don't just look at the profit and loss—they model the entire organization to understand the implications of business decisions, including balance sheet effects and the sources and uses of cash. To understand the secret of Granny's Greek, you gotta know that these women model with an absolute vengeance!"

CONCEPT

As discussed in chapter 10, finance people like to model. This chapter extends that introduction to financial modeling by looking at how to model not just the income statement but also the balance sheet. This is an important skill for understanding the overall implications of business decisions, and it is also a great way to integrate the principles and skills we've explored throughout this book.

One important insight that comes from modeling both sides of the balance sheet is an appreciation for the sources and uses of cash. Businesses are constrained such that the uses of cash (such as investment in the business or disbursements to investors) must be equal to the sources of cash (such as business profits or new cash infusions from investors). A model of the full financial statements ensures that the forecast is feasible, meaning the uses of cash are matched to the sources of cash.

It is common for finance people to rely on financial ratios to forecast various line items, for two main reasons: ratios preserve important relationships that exist across financial statements, and ratios facilitate interpretation. For example, rather that forecasting the specific amount of accounts receivable, finance people forecast a financial ratio associated with accounts receivable, such as days sales outstanding (DSO) or receivable days, and then use that ratio to back into the amount of receivables implied by the ratio. By using a ratio that has interpretable meaning to forecast the figures, they ensure that their forecast is grounded in economic reality.

B&D MUSCLE CARS

Along with their food truck venture, Dillon and Bart shared a long-standing affinity for classic automobiles. Their deepest love by a long shot was the unique shape, smooth handling, and raw power of a 1970s-era Chevrolet Corvette. To Bart and Dillon, there was something truly otherworldly about flying down the open road in an old Corvette with the top down and the engine opened up. After they cashed in on their success by selling Granny's Greek to their grandmothers' neighbors in Room 37, the pair decided to build a business retailing vintage Corvettes to the elderly. They named the business B&D Muscle Cars.

Using the entire USD400,000 payout from the business sale, Bart and Dillon bought 20 cars of inventory and a suitable warehouse garage. The USD400,000 they spent on the business assets included USD150,000 for a warehouse, USD200,000 in inventory, and USD50,000 in a checking account. They easily chose individual roles in the business: Bart oversaw the sourcing of quality vehicles at reasonable prices, and Dillon managed the sales end. To honor the deep friendships the pair had developed with the Goodtimes residents over the years, they offered residents Corvette test-drives; this became an important and enjoyable feature of the new venture. In his sales role, Dillon joined the Goodtimes residents each morning for breakfast and then returned to the parking lot by 10 a.m. to give test-drives to residents in the cars they had selected at breakfast.

Many residents had ample discretionary income, and having a good-looking Corvette to park in the Goodtimes lot provided significant value to many an elderly owner, even if they no longer had a valid driver's license. In the first year, the business had a strong start—Dillon and Bart sold 20 cars, at an average sales price of USD12,500 apiece. Since the average purchase price was USD10,000, the two achieved an average gross profit of USD2,500 per car. **Table 16.1** provides the financial statements for the business over its first year. Total revenue was USD250,000, and total gross profit was USD50,000. The USD10,000 selling and administrative (S&A) expenses reflected the costs of maintaining the warehouse, website, and other business expenses. The USD40,000 operating profit resulted in USD32,000 of net income after taxes.

On a recent evening visit to the senior center, both boys were particularly ecstatic about their business, and they gushed about their success to their grandmothers, Agnes Adams and Zina Zamboni. "I'm telling you,"

TABLE 16.1. Financial statements for B&D Muscle Cars (in thousands of US dollars).

	Year 1
Income Statement	
Revenue	250
Cost of sales	200
Gross profit	50
S&A expenses	10
Operating profit	40
Taxes	8
Net income	32
Balance Sheet	
Cash	50
Inventory	200
Property and equipment	150
Total assets	400
Equity	400

Bart enthused, "we have strong demand and we are getting good at meeting it. Look at these financials—in our first year, we've cleared an impressive USD32,000 in profit!"

"This business could be another Granny's Greek, don't you think?" Dillon victoriously thrust the set of first-year financial statements at the two grandmothers while they sat together peacefully in the TV room, sipping large smoothies. Neither Agnes nor Zina said a thing, and their grandsons started to think they might be reluctant to celebrate.

"Aren't you impressed?" Bart asked. "You must admit that we've done well for a first year. We know that we're not yet making enough to live on, but we have a plan to expand inventory by 50% next year to grow profits."

Finally, the two women looked at each other and smiled. Zina graciously took the proffered financial statements and motioned for the two young men to pull up a rocking love seat while Agnes reached into her walker basket for her laptop. "We're so happy and proud of you two boys," Zina began. "We are glad to hear how well your car business is doing. We often remark on the stir you always create at the senior center. You know, around here, most of the ladies' daily schedules turn on when they expect Dillon to pull up to offer test-drives in some good-looking 'vette."

"But while we are proud of you," Agnes continued, her smile fading, "We are also well aware that you are running this business by the seat of your threadbare pants. You know what Granny's Greek was built on: financial modeling analysis. I'd recommend that you refrain from any delusion that your venture compares to Granny's Greek until you have grounded your business in the modeling analysis it needs."

"Agreed," said Zina. "But all is not lost. We've got a proposal for you. Agnes and I have both had our eyes on that salacious yellow '69 Stingray you've got. How about we spend some time with you working on some modeling of next year's financials, if you agree to take us both for a long test-drive tomorrow? Deal?"

"Deal," said both boys willingly.

"Let's get modeling!"

With some effort, the group transitioned to the cafeteria and settled around a four-person table so they could all see Agnes's laptop screen.

"You said your plan is to grow profits by expanding your inventory 50%," she said. "Let's see how that models."

Agnes opened a blank spreadsheet. "Let's start with the balance sheet. You've got three items: cash, inventory, and property and equipment—or P&E for short. I take it the only thing you plan to change is increasing inventory from USD200,000 to USD300,000?" The boys nodded. After some quick typing and work with her computer mouse, Agnes highlighted a portion of her screen: "So your Year 2 business assets will look like this, right?" (See **Table 16.2.**)

"Yes, that is exactly right," replied Bart. "We'll still need the USD50,000 in our bank account to run the business, and we plan to maintain USD150,000 invested in the warehouse. And just so you know, there is plenty of room in our warehouse to store another 10 vehicles."

"Okay, so let's look at some financial ratios from last year," continued Agnes. "Let's start with gross margin. This measure indicates what percentage of your sales price goes to profit after the direct cost of your product is covered. Dividing gross profit by revenue for last year gives a gross margin of 20%—that's USD50,000/USD250,000. Next, let's look at your inventory turnover ratio. That represents the times per year that your inventory is turning over in a sale. Since your cost of sales is exactly equal to your inventory level, your inventory turnover ratio is equal to 1.0—we get that from USD200,000/USD200,000. A related measure is days in inventory, or DIO, which is defined as inventory divided by cost of sales multiplied by 365 days in a year. DIO tells you, on average, how many days inventory sits until it's sold. In this case, your DIO is 365."

TABLE 16.2. Business assets for B&D Muscle Cars (in thousands of US dollars).

	Year 1	Year 2
Cash	50	50
Inventory	200	300
Property and equipment	150	150
Total assets	400	500

"Calculating financial ratios again makes my ticker dance, Agnes!" Zina laughed. "Now that we have some historical ratios, it is time to forecast them. How do you believe those ratios will change in the coming year with your larger operation?"

"Actually, I don't think they will change," Dillon replied. "We plan to continue to price our cars with the same gross margin; we need a similar level of selling and administrative, or S&A, expenses; and I expect that our inventory turnover will remain at just one turn per year, or 365 inventory days."

"That makes our model easy, then," returned Zina. "As a base case, let's make the assumption that revenue will grow 50% to USD375,000 and that gross margin will remain at 20%. These two assumptions result in a gross profit of USD75,000—because USD75,000 is equal to 20% margin multiplied by revenue of USD375,000. The inventory turnover is still 1.0, since the cost of sales is equal to the inventory level: both are at USD300,000."

Turning from her spreadsheet to the two boys, Zina asked, "What is the nature of your S&A expenses—are they variable or fixed costs?"

"I think they are mostly fixed," answered Bart. "I don't see them changing much next year despite the increase in volume. I expect that we will continue to spend about USD10,000 in S&A expenses."

"Good, then our pro forma income statement is pretty much done," Zina said. "Your assumptions suggest that the anticipated operating profit is USD65,000. And with a 20% tax rate, you can anticipate USD52,000 in net profit. So here is what we have." She turned her laptop so everyone could see the spreadsheet she'd made (see **Table 16.3**).

"Well, look at that . . . USD52,000 in profit!" exclaimed Dillon. "This is looking like a viable business now!"

"Don't get too excited, Dillon," cautioned his grandmother Agnes. "Our work is not done. The problem is that profit is not all that matters. It is important to understand that changes in balance sheet investment don't come out of thin air—someone has to finance the USD100,000 increase in inventory that is on the left-hand side of the balance sheet. We have yet to model the right-hand side of the balance sheet. Now, we know that

TABLE 16.3. Base-case pro forma financial statements for B&D Muscle Cars (in thousands of US dollars).

	Year 1	Year 2	Forecast Calculation
Income Statement			
Revenue	250	375	Maintain margin: USD12,500 × 30 cars
Cost of sales (COS)	200	300	Maintain inventory turnover of 1
Gross profit	50	75	Revenue less COS
S&A expenses	10	10	Keep fixed at 10
Operating profit	40	65	Gross profit less S&A expenses
Taxes	8	13	Operating profit × 20%
Net income	32	52	Operating profit less taxes
Balance Sheet			
Cash	50	50	Keep fixed at 50
Inventory	200	300	200 × (1 + 50%)
Property and equipment	150	150	Keep fixed at 150
Total assets	400	500	Sum of assets
Equity	400	500	Previous equity + net income + equity investment − dividends and must balance with total assets
Dividend	32	(48)	Net income + equity investment − change in equity
Financial Ratios			
Gross margin	20%	20%	Gross profit / revenue
Taxes	20%	20%	Taxes / operating profit
Inventory turnover	1.0	1.0	Cost of goods sold / inventory
Revenue growth rate		50%	Percentage change in revenue

both sides of the balance sheet have to balance. We also know that the equity account increases with equity funds that come in, less equity funds that are paid out. More precisely, the Year 2 balance of equity is equal to the old equity balance of USD400,000, plus net income generated for the year of USD52,000, plus new equity investment, minus dividends. I'll write that out." On a pad of Goodtimes stationery, Adams wrote:

New equity balance = previous equity balance + net income
+ new equity investment − dividends.

"To make the balance sheet balance," Agnes continued, "we can adjust the equity account up by USD100,000, from USD400,000 to USD500,000. That difference has to be funded with either net income or new equity. Since the net income is estimated at USD52,000, this model implies that you two boys need to inject another USD48,000 into the business to finance the USD100,000 growth in your balance sheet. Again, your USD100,000 increase in inventory doesn't come out of thin air."

"Woah!" Bart's eyes widened. "Is that right? In order to scale up the business, you're saying we should expect that not only are we going to make less than we made last year, when we dividend all the profits out to ourselves, but we are also going to have to come up with an additional USD48,000 to put into the business?"

"Yes, my boy," counseled his grandmother Zina. "Now you appreciate the important implications of financial modeling. But don't worry, Agnes and I have been down this road before. We have a lot of tricks up our sleeves. What shall we lay on them, Agnes?"

"Hmm," Agnes thought for a moment. "The most obvious solution is to borrow USD100,000 from a bank to finance the inventory increase. That would leave equity unchanged and add a bank debt line to the right-hand side of the balance sheet. Then you two can keep the full amount of the USD52,000 net income for yourselves as a dividend. But we have other ways, and I don't think you want to take on debt at this point. An alternative approach is to crank up the inventory turnover—which is the same thing as reducing DIO. This means that you increase the revenue without increasing the inventory investment. One way to do that is to reduce your profit margin to drive more sales. Let's say you reduced the gross margin by half, from 20% to 10%. This would mean that the average car would sell for USD11,111 rather than USD12,500 you priced them at last year. I believe this change would increase the volume you are selling from 20 cars per year to 36 cars. This seems reasonable from what I know of Goodtimes residents' sensitivity to price reductions on your inventory. It may surprise you to know that some of them are making money by buying Corvettes from you then reselling them on online markets."

"With your margin-turnover relation estimate," continued Zina, "I think you can run a much more efficient operation with your inventory. I believe you can get more out of your inventory by increasing inventory turnover to 2.0 from 1.0. That way you get more sales, but with less inventory investment. If we put these numbers into the model, we get the following pro forma financial statements." (See **Table 16.4.**) "Let's see if you can recreate how the model builds."

"Sure," agreed Dillon. "The forecasted revenue of USD400,000 comes from 36 cars times the new average sales price of USD11,111. The gross

TABLE 16.4. Low-margin and high-inventory-turnover scenario pro forma financial statements for B&D Muscle Cars (in thousands of US dollars).

	Year 1	Year 2	Forecast calculation
Income Statement			
Revenue	250	400	USD11,111 × 36 cars
COS	200	360	USD10,000 × 36 cars
Gross profit	50	40	Revenue less COS
S&A expenses	10	10	Keep fixed at 10
Operating profit	40	30	Gross profit less S&A expenses
Taxes	8	6	Operating profit × 20%
Net income	32	24	Operating profit less taxes
Balance Sheet			
Cash	50	50	Keep fixed at 50
Inventory	200	180	Increase inventory turnover to 2.0 times [360/2]
Property and equipment	150	150	Keep fixed at 150
Total assets	400	380	Sum of assets
Equity	400	380	Previous equity + net income + equity investment − dividends and must balance with total assets
Dividend	32	44	Net income + equity investment − change in equity
Financial Ratios			
Gross margin	20%	10%	Gross profit / revenue
Taxes	20%	20%	Taxes / operating profit
Inventory turnover	1.0	2.0	Cost of goods sold / inventory
Revenue growth rate		60%	Percentage change in revenue

profit of USD40,000 is based on the implied gross margin of 10% on the USD400,000 revenue."

"Spot on," encouraged Agnes.

"The only other tricky figure is inventory," Bart said. "The USD180,000 comes from the inventory turnover value. Since we're assuming an inventory turnover of 2.0, and inventory turnover is defined as cost of sales divided by inventory, the inventory value must be USD180,000, since the cost of sales is USD360,000—or USD360/USD180 = 2.0 times inventory sold."

"Bravo!" shouted Zina, raising her arms in victory and showering the remains of her smoothie around her chair. "So how does this scenario differ in terms of the business cash flow that goes to the two of you?"

"I think the answer is USD44,000 of cash flow," offered Dillon timidly.

"That's my boy!" shrieked Agnes, sending melted smoothie remains flying a second time. "Show me how you got that!"

"Well," began Dillon, "the net income is USD24,000. We'll keep all of that, because rather than having our assets increase with the 60% revenue growth, we are shrinking our assets from USD400,000 to USD380,000 due to increased inventory efficiency. That shrinkage of USD20,000 in assets generates USD20,000 of investor cash flow. So our total cash flow is the sum of USD44,000."

"Let's test-drive one of those muscle cars!" exulted Zina.

"Hold on, Grandma. Can we try one more model?" asked Bart.

"Of course, sweetheart."

"How about this scenario?" Bart ventured. "We increase the price to USD14,000 to drive out our customers who are upselling. To justify the higher price, we'll need to spend USD5,000 more on S&A expenses to keep our inventory washed and cleaned. We'll tighten up our inventory by purchasing only the cars we know we can sell, which can increase inventory turnover to 2.0. I think this is a scenario that Dillon and I can pull off. Can we see what the numbers look like for that one?" Dillon took his grandmother's laptop and began modeling like the Granny's Greek veteran he was.

TABLE 16.5. Dillon's scenario pro forma financial statements for B&D Muscle Cars (in thousands of US dollars).

	Year 1	Year 2	Forecast calculation
Income Statement			
Revenue	250	350	USD14,000×25 cars
COS	200	250	USD10,000×25 cars
Gross profit	50	100	Revenue less COS
S&A expenses	10	15	Increase by 50%
Operating profit	40	85	Gross profit less S&A expenses
Taxes	8	17	Operating profit×20%
Net income	32	68	Operating profit less taxes
Balance Sheet			
Cash	50	50	Keep fixed at 50
Inventory	200	125	Increase inventory turnover to 2.0 times [250/2]
Property and equipment	150	150	Keep fixed at 150
Total assets	400	325	Sum of assets
Equity	400	325	Previous equity+net income+ equity investment−dividends and must balance with total assets
Dividend	32	143	Net income+equity investment− change in equity
Financial Ratios			
Gross margin	20%	29%	Gross profit/revenue
Taxes	20%	20%	Taxes/operating profit
Inventory turnover	1.0	2.0	Cost of goods sold/inventory
Revenue growth rate		40%	Percentage change in revenue

"As expected," Dillon shouted, showing off the figures on the screen (see **Table 16.5**). "Bart's scenario turns out USD143,000! That'll give us enough money to take you both on a weeklong Corvette cruise up and down the coast!"

"Flaming tailpipes, I believe you are right," admitted Agnes with admiration. "That scenario generates USD68,000 in net income and USD75,000 less asset investment, for a combined investor cash flow of USD143,000. Maybe this business *is* the next Granny's Greek."

"Why don't you ladies get your driving jackets?" suggested Bart. "I think it is time to take a night ride in a yellow Stingray."

CONCEPT WRAP-UP

In this chapter, we've learned how to model both the income statement and the balance sheet of a business. Finance people do this because they care about cash flow—and modeling both sides of the balance sheet explicitly shows the sources and uses of cash, yielding important insights into cash flow. Cash in businesses doesn't just come out of thin air or get consumed into thin air. Rather, a business (or any organization, for that matter) is a constrained system: the uses of cash (such as investment in the business or disbursements to investors) are constrained to be equal to the sources of cash (such as business profits or new cash infusions from investors). A model of the full financial statements ensures that the forecast is fully modeled, in that the uses of cash are matched to feasible sources of cash. If, in the model, the sources do not equal the uses of cash, then the analyst can use the model to identify ways to increase the sources of cash or decrease the uses of cash. To avoid cash going into or coming out of thin air, the sources of cash must always equal the uses of cash.

Modeling is an important skill that will help you understand the overall implications of business decisions. For example, models help us appreciate how cash is flowing through or being consumed by a business. Financial models depend on the prudent use of financial analysis, cash flow estimation, and an appreciation of the cash cycle; they help us come up with forecasts that are grounded in the prevailing macroeconomic reality, the ongoing industry dynamics, and the strategy of the business being analyzed. Thoughtfully reflecting the macroeconomic reality, ongoing industry dynamics, and the strategy of the business is what discriminates good forecasts from garbage forecasts.

REVIEW QUESTIONS

This is the last question in the book, and it's a challenge—one that is analytically pretty difficult. But you are ready for this! Just do your best!

The American sports equipment company Under Armour experienced strong growth through the year 2021, and debt levels for the company declined from USD2.0 billion in 2020 to USD1.5 billion in 2021 (see **Table 16.6**).

Question 1.   Please build a financial model of the expected 2022 financial statements for Under Armour using the following assumptions. Do you expect the anticipated debt levels to decline? Please note that you may experience a circularity in the logic of your spreadsheet. In order to avoid this circularity error, you may need to activate iterative calculations in your spreadsheet options.

Modeling assumptions for the year 2022:

a) Revenue grows by 20%.
b) Gross margin remains at 50%.
c) Selling, general, and administrative (SG&A) expenses are at 45% of revenue.
d) Interest expense is USD0.17 billion.
e) Income taxes are 10% of operating profit.
f) Cash needs are 20% of revenue.
g) Receivable days (days sales outstanding, DSO) is 40 days.
h) Inventory days (days in inventory, DIO) is 110 days.
i) Property, plant, and equipment (PP&E) turnover is 5.0 times.
j) Payable days (days payable outstanding, DPO) is 120 days.
k) Under Armour elects to not pay a cash dividend in 2022.

Question 2.   How does your answer change if the company wants to pay out a USD0.25 billion dividend? Assume that interest expense is USD0.20 billion.

Question 3.   What is your best recommendation for a change in operating policy to reduce the debt by USD0.5 billion? Assume that interest expense is USD0.14 billion.

TABLE 16.6. Financial statements for Under Armour (figures in billions of US dollars).

	2020	2021
Revenue	4.48	5.68
Cost of sales	2.32	2.82
Gross profit	2.16	2.86
SG&A expense	2.17	2.34
Operating income	(0.01)	0.52
Interest expense	0.48	0.13
Pre-tax profit (PTP)	(0.49)	0.39
Taxes	0.06	0.03
Net profit	(0.55)	0.36
Cash	1.52	1.70
Receivables	0.53	0.57
Inventory	0.90	0.81
Other current assets	0.28	0.29
Net PP&E	1.20	1.06
Other long-term assets	0.60	0.56
Total assets	5.03	4.99
Payables	1.25	1.31
Debt	2.01	1.50
Equity	1.77	2.18
Total liabilities and equity	5.03	4.99
Revenue growth		27%
Gross margin	48%	50%
SG&A expense percentage	48%	41%
Operating margin	0%	9%
Interest expense / debt	24%	8.7%
Tax percentage PTP	−12%	8%
Cash percentage revenue	34%	30%
Receivable days (DSO)	43.2	36.6
Inventory days (DIO)	141.6	104.8
PP&E turnover	3.7	5.4
Payable days (DPO)	196.7	169.6

Source: Financial statements for Under Armour, Inc.

17

Bringing It Together and the Legendary J-Song

ROOM 120

It was the last day of finance class in Room 120. Jenn Song timidly entered the room, slid her backpack off her shoulder, and sat down in her customary seat in the second-to-last row. She was relieved to have made it to the last day of class but anxious about the upcoming exam. Over the term, Song had worked hard to learn the ins and outs of finance, studying both individually and with a team. Despite having been terrified of the subject at the beginning of the course, she had been surprised at how much of the material she had actually enjoyed, and especially at how it had opened up an important part of society that had previously been opaque to her. She also recognized that none of her understanding had come easy.

For the last day of class, the study material was a review of the previous year's exam. Each student received a 10-page description of the high-profile acquisition of European media company EuroArt by Asian tech giant NCOM. This case study provided the context for a litany of exam questions. Song had thrown herself into preparing the case by answering the questions and thinking about the implications. Now, as she fired up her laptop and prepared her notes, the other students in the section filed in and took the seats around her. An enjoyable banter filled the air as other students shared their happiness at having made it to this point, as well as their apprehension about the next phase of the process.

As the clock struck the hour, Professor Joseph strode into the room. Dressed in a tie, a well-pressed dark shirt, and highly polished shoes, Joseph was a no-nonsense, "old-school" instructor who saw everything through the lens of his discipline. He demanded excellence and didn't hold back from vigorously recognizing performance that failed to meet his high expectations. Planting himself firmly in the center of the room, Joseph scanned the space, reminding the students of a hungry tiger at dusk surveilling a flock of grazing sheep. "Song," he announced, then turned slowly in her direction. "What do you want to talk about today?"

With her biological vital signs running wild, Song looked at Joseph and mustered her inner strength, then began.

"Thank you," she acknowledged. "Let's talk through the economics of the acquisition of EuroArt by NCOM." Joseph nodded and began writing on the board as Song continued. "To date, NCOM has been quite active but extremely careful in its acquisition strategy. Led by CEO Sanjay Baseer, NCOM has been highly disciplined in paying only for tangible merger gains. In response to the takeover interest, EuroArt management claimed that EuroArt will not approve any takeover offer less than EUR25 billion. NCOM management needs to determine whether EuroArt is worth that. I ran the numbers to see if NCOM can justify an offer of EUR25 billion for EuroArt. I built a model of the annual incremental cash flows associated with the acquisition. My model identified the anticipated individual merger gains, including specific increases in revenue growth and operating margin for EuroArt. I also identified specific opportunities for increases in asset turnover, including a reduction in the cash cycle from 78 days to 32 days due to improvements in receivable collections, inventory management, and better bargaining with suppliers. All my cash flow forecasts included the effects of expected inflation."

Joseph was writing furiously on the board, attempting to keep up with Song's analysis. He looked harried, but she kept going.

"I spent a considerable amount of time analyzing the appropriate discount rate for my valuation model. I evaluated EuroArt's mix of debt and equity and that of some of its peer firms and concluded that the current mix seemed appropriate. I used prevailing credit rating and equity beta estimates to estimate the opportunity cost of capital that reflected the business risk associated with a media company such as EuroArt. I felt that 9.4% was the appropriate discount rate to use; this rate reflects a 5% risk premium over the risk-free rate in euros."

Joseph finished filling a second board. Chalk dust filled the room, and all the other students seemed entirely focused on assimilating every word. Song kept going.

"Using the cash flow forecast and the discount rate, I estimated a value for EuroArt in the terminal year using the perpetuity formula with a steady-state growth rate of 4.5%. I felt that a 10-year planning period was appropriate because the return on capital in the terminal year was close to the cost of capital, suggesting that the firm was no longer generating abnormal returns. I verified the value using peer companies' existing market-valuation multiples. This model gave a base-case valuation including the merger gains of EUR21 billion. I adjusted various assumptions to identify the nature of gains needed to justify a valuation of EUR25 billion. I needed to double the margin gains in order to justify the higher price, and I believe NCOM is unlikely to achieve this. Given the analysis, I can strongly recommend that NCOM not make a full-price offer. It may be justified by some other media firm with more strategic complementarity than that of NCOM, but I don't see those kinds of gains coming from an NCOM–EuroArt deal."

With that, Song paused to invite further scrutiny of her recommendation. Instead, there was complete silence for a few seconds, followed by a rush of applause. Students threw papers in the air, then pens, empty coffee cups, and even laptops as they stormed forward in Song's direction. Lifting her to their shoulders, the other students paraded Song around the classroom, shouting out inspiring quotations from her analysis: "A reduction in the cash cycle!"; "Reflected the business risk associated with a media company!"; and "I needed to double the margin gains in order to justify the higher price!" Meanwhile, Joseph had secured a piece of blank cloth and markers and was finishing a banner that read *J-SONG*, followed by the year and a single word: *LEGENDARY*. Climbing on the backs of four eager students, Joseph secured the banner to the classroom rafters.

CONCEPT WRAP-UP

While this example, like much of what you have read in this book, is fictitious hyperbole, the transformation Song experienced—from highly hesitant finance student to competent finance analyst—occurs with great regularity. While a banner proclaiming you *legendary* may not be hung anywhere, you, like so many who are also intimidated by finance concepts, have the capacity to understand the basics and think like finance people.

This book has introduced you to the foundations of financial thinking. With an understanding of this fundamental material, you are now ready to go, equipped to discuss these ideas and explore them further, to master all the ways finance people think. We have not covered all the concepts Song talked about in her analysis of the EuroArt acquisition, but you are ready to learn them by building on the foundation you now have. While you've acquired a significant amount of finance understanding, you have only begun the journey. There is much to be done to deepen your understanding of the principles discussed and to refine your application of these principles to real-world decision-making.

As you begin this process, it is good to appreciate that finance is commonly broken into three major areas of study and practice: corporate finance, investments, and financial institutions.

The study of *corporate finance* examines how businesses interact with investors and other participants in financial markets. Corporate finance concerns include especially how businesses raise new money (e.g., by issuing debt or equity) and how they allocate their money (e.g., NCOM either buying EuroArt or building a new plant in Paraguay). Corporate finance decisions involve evaluating the merits of potential investment projects, deciding how much debt financing to use, and determining a dividend that is appropriate to issue to shareholders. Corporate finance decisions are immensely important in society.

Analysis of *investments* examines how investors interact with businesses and other participants in financial markets. Investment concerns include especially how investors allocate their money (e.g., buying debt or equity securities) and how they measure risk exposure and required returns. Investment decisions involve evaluating the merits of potential investment opportunities and deciding how much debt financing to use. Investment decisions are immensely important in society.

And a focus on *financial institutions* includes especially how these institutions interact with businesses and other participants in financial markets. Primary concerns include how banks allocate their money (e.g., issuing debt or accepting deposits) and how they measure risk exposure and required returns. Financial institutions' decisions involve evaluating the merits of potential investment opportunities (such as extending a loan to a particular customer) and deciding how to finance the investments. Financial institutions' decisions are immensely important in society.

As you move forward in your study of finance and learn how its people think, remember that the terminology, the institutions, and the lore of finance will all continue to be formidable barriers to the inexperienced. The process you followed throughout this book should serve you well as you continue to build comfort with this new territory, its language, and its people.

Some Good Answers to the Review Questions

This section provides some potential good answers to the review questions asked at the end of each chapter. The responses provided here are not meant to be the only possible correct responses—they are illustrations of what good responses might contain. The responses are organized by book chapter.

CHAPTER 3. ECONOMIC VALUE CREATION AND SUSTAINABILITY AT CAMP BIG FISH

Question 1. **A well-respected report defines sustainability as "meeting the needs of the present without compromising the ability of future generations to meet their own needs." How does this definition of sustainability help define the focus in finance on economic value creation?**

Economic value creation demands that decisions seek to create, not destroy, economic resources. This discipline anticipates that the resources of the future will be greater than the resources today. An economic value-creation orientation encourages all organizations to add to—and not take away from—the ability of future generations to have access to greater resources.

Question 2. **Why is economic value creation such a good decision metric for finance people?**

A commitment to seek economic value creation gives decision-makers a framework for evaluating the outcomes of any decision. An orientation toward value creation contrasts with other decision orientations, such as doing what is in one's sole best interest or what hurts rivals. Economic value creation is about increasing the size of the pie for everyone. Since finance decisions can be framed in way that estimates the specific economic value implications, value creation provides an extraordinarily helpful decision metric for finance decisions.

CHAPTER 4. OPPORTUNITY COST OF CAPITAL AND WAIT TIMES AT THE DMV

Question 1.   **What is the opportunity cost of the following activities in your life?**

a) Going on a trip by car this weekend.

The opportunity cost is the cost above what you would spend if you didn't go on the trip. If the weekend trip will create an additional USD100 out-of-pocket expenses like gas and wear on the car (above what you would normally spend anyway) and use up the time you could spend doing something else with your weekend (like working or doing your laundry), the opportunity cost is the value of what you would do with the time plus the USD100 in incremental expenses. It makes sense to go on the trip if the benefits of the trip exceed the opportunity cost.

b) Going on the same trip in a plane this weekend.

If flying to the location costs an additional USD200 but saves two hours of drive time, the opportunity cost is the value of the USD200 cash less the value of what you would do with the additional two hours of leisure time on the trip. The opportunity cost of flying is less than driving if the additional two hours of nontravel time is worth more than USD200.

c) Spending the evening watching a movie instead of studying for a test.

The opportunity cost of watching the movie is the value of what you would do with the additional time not watching the movie. If you would use that time to study, and that study time would help you do significantly better on the test, the opportunity cost represents the net value you would obtain by doing better on the test. If that value or opportunity cost is high, it's better to study.

d) Adopting a pet.

The opportunity cost of adopting a pet is the value of the money, time, and effort that you would give up by having the pet. If this value is substantial, it would be important to consider this opportunity cost before agreeing to adopt the pet.

e) Spending a year as a full-time student.

The opportunity cost of spending a year as a full-time student is the value of your best alternative to that year as a student. If the best alternative activity is working at a restaurant, then the value of the year spent at the restaurant is the measure of the opportunity cost. If the best alternative activity is launching a business endeavor, then the expected value of the year spent launching the business is the measure of the opportunity cost of attending school.

Question 2. **Investors have invested INR30 million in Saba Motors. If the opportunity cost of capital is 8% per year, what amount of profit do investors need in order to exceed their opportunity cost?**

If the opportunity cost of capital is 8%, then investors expect that they could take their INR30 million and invest it in something else with similar risk and earn 8%. This 8% on INR80 million amounts to profits of INR2.4 million per year [8% × INR30 million]. Because of this opportunity cost for their investment money, investors will not be pleased if the expected annual profits at Saba Motors are below INR2.4 million. In such a case, the opportunity cost is higher than the expected profits and they will seek to invest their money elsewhere. Investors need the expected annual profits to exceed INR2.4 million.

CHAPTER 5. INFLATION AND RETURNS AT CACKLING HEN COLLECTIBLES

Question 1. **The inflation rate over the past year was 5%.**

a) **If a pizza was priced at USD10 a year ago, what do you expect it to be priced at this year?**

Since the inflation rate was 5%, one can expect pizza prices to have gone up by 5% this year. The 5% inflation means the new expected price is USD10.50, which is calculated as the old price multiplied by 1 plus the inflation rate [USD10.00 × (1 + 5%)].

b) **What are the nominal prices and real prices for the pizza? Has the real price of pizza changed?**

The nominal prices are the prices you expect to observe in the pizza store: USD10.00 last year and USD10.50 this year. The real prices are the prices that strip out the effects of inflation. Since the price of pizza has changed only because of inflation, the real price of pizza hasn't changed. The real price is USD10.00 in both years if we define it based on last year's prices, or USD10.50 in both years if we define it based on this year's prices. The observation that the real prices don't change indicates that inflation is the only reason for the price change. Finance people might share the following insight: "In real terms, pizza prices haven't changed from last year to this year."

c) **What is the value of one dollar today in terms of the value of one dollar a year ago?**

Since the inflation rate is 5%, the value of one dollar has declined by 5%. This means that a dollar this year is worth only USD0.952 of last year's dollars.

A dollar today buys the amount of goods and services that USD0.952 purchased a year ago. Because of inflation, the value of the dollar has declined. The value today of USD0.952 is calculated as USD1.00/(1+5%).

Question 2.　**The price for similar new cars has increased from USD20,000 five years ago to USD28,000 this year.**

a) What appears to be the compound annual inflation rate for new cars?

The compound inflation rate over the five-year period is calculated by finding or solving for R in the following equation. This equation indicates that there is some rate (R) that gets USD20,000 to grow to USD28,000 over five years:

$$USD20,000(1+R)^5 = USD28,000.$$

Rearranging the equation to solve for R, we get the compound annual growth rate (CAGR) formula:

$$R = \left(\frac{28,000}{20,000}\right)^{1/5} - 1.$$

Solving this equation, we find that the implied inflation rate for new cars is 7.0%. That means that if one were to grow USD20,000 at 7.0% compounded for five years, one would have USD28,000. If we expected that same inflation rate to continue, we would anticipate that these cars would be selling for over USD39,000 in five more years.

b) If the annual inflation rate had been half of that, what would be the implied price of new cars this year?

To find the current car price with half the inflation, we can substitute 3.5% (half of 7%) into the compounding formula USD20,000 $(1+3.5\%)^5$ to get USD23,754. Because of compounding, the amount of the increase over the USD20,000 initial value with 3.5% inflation is less than half of what the price was with an inflation rate of 7.0%.

Question 3.　**Your business pays USD30 per meter for an important raw material. You read that the raw material is supposed to increase in price by 4% per year over the next three years. What do you anticipate the price per meter to be in three years?**

To find out what the price of the raw material should be in three years, one can put 4% into the compounding formula, USD30$(1+4\%)^3$, to get USD33.75. The anticipated price in three years is USD33.75. Please note that USD30.00 and USD33.75 are both nominal prices.

Question 4.　**A stock investment increased from USD30 per share to USD50 per share over the past 10 years. The annual general inflation rate was 6% over the** same 10 years. What was the nominal return on the stock investment (the return implied by the two nominal prices)? What was the real return on the investment (the return above the inflation rate of 6%)?

This is the kind of question finance people are really into. In the chapter, it is how Jane Yellen thought about investment returns. The answer compares the stock returns to simply keeping up with inflation. The nominal return is the CAGR over the 10 years of prices rising from USD30 to USD50. This amount is 5.24%, which is equal to the R in the compounding formula that makes USD30 increase to USD50:

$$USD30(1+R)^3 = USD50.$$

The 5.24% nominal return comes from the CAGR formula:

$$R = \left(\frac{50}{30}\right)^{1/10} - 1.$$

Since the general inflation rate is 6%, the stock return is lagging general inflation by 0.76% [5.24% − 6.0%]. Thus the nominal return is 5.24%, and the real rate of return is −0.76%. The appreciation of the stock has not been enough to offset prevailing inflation. One might say that investors would have been better off investing in goods or collectible toys than putting their money in the stock, since the goods or toys might have kept up with inflation.

CHAPTER 6. RETURN BENCHMARKS AND THE BUS DRIVER LEADERBOARD

What is problematic about the following statements regarding hurdle rates? Recall that hurdle rate is just another term for benchmark rate or cost of capital.

Question 1.   Mick: "We use 10% as our company hurdle rate. It is simple and clear. It has always worked."

It appears that Mick's hurdle rate is arbitrary: it just is what it is. Mick's hurdle rate may lead to poor investment decisions. Good benchmarks are not arbitrary—they are grounded in market-oriented measures of the opportunity cost of capital, which undoubtedly changes over time. As the forgone cost of investing in similar investments (the opportunity cost of capital) changes, the hurdle rate should adjust to reflect that prevailing economic reality. If the 10% rate is too high, the company will tend to underinvest by passing on projects that are above the true cost of capital (see the smiley-face projects in **Figure 6.1**), and if the 10% rate is too low, the company will tend to overinvest by accepting projects that are below the true cost of capital (see the frowny-face projects in **Figure 6.1**).

Question 2.   **Yua: "We did a ton of analysis five years ago to establish an appropriate cost of capital of 8.4% for our business. At some point we will review it, but for now we are just focusing on building the business."**

Yua's hurdle rate may lead to poor investment decisions because it is stale. Good benchmarks are updated to reflect the current opportunity cost of capital. As the forgone cost of investing in similar investments changes, the hurdle rate is updated to reflect that economic reality. Realistically, companies don't adjust their hurdle rates minute by minute with ever-changing market prices. But they do update their rates regularly (at least annually) or when there are important changes in market prices.

Question 3.   **Miguel: "Business forecasts always have optimistic bias built into them. You'd be a fool to take a forecast at face value. In order to combat that bias, I add 2% to the cost of capital to neutralize the optimism before evaluating any project."**

Miguel's hurdle rate may lead to poor investment decisions because it is arbitrary. While it may be common to boost hurdle rates in an arbitrary way to beat down optimistic forecasts, the better approach is to scrutinize the forecasts and get them right. It is impossible to know if Miguel's 2% adjustment is the right amount. Maybe 1% or 3% is the better correction? There is no way to know without analyzing the forecast head-on.

CHAPTER 7. DIVERSIFICATION GAINS AND PROFIT RISK IN KATANGA

Question 1.   **In Table 7.2, the standard deviation of Year 1 profits is USD1,734 for Boule de Neige and USD1,691 for Ours Polaire. Why is the standard deviation of the profits in the 50-50 partnership not the average of the two, or USD1,713, rather than the standard deviation of USD1,271 reported for the portfolio? How can the standard deviation of the portfolio be less than that of the standard deviation of both Boule de Neige and Ours Polaire?**

This is a classic example of the diversification effect. Since the profits at the two mines are uncorrelated (they don't tend to move together), there tends to be a large amount of idiosyncratic risk in the two profit series. This means that there is a lot of random variation in profit that tends to get washed out. When Boule de Neige profits are down, it is often true that Ours Polaire profits are up. This tendency for the portfolio of the two mines to cover up the extreme movements in either individual mine generates profits in the 50-50 partnership that are substantially less volatile. The reduction in volatility is what drives the reduction in standard deviation. This is an example of diversification magic and creates the strong incentive for investors to diversify their investments.

Question 2.   **Suppose that the operating returns on investment for the first three months of Year 3 are as shown in Table 7.3.**

TABLE 7.3. Operating return on investment (monthly profit / amount of investment).

	Boule de Neige	Ours Polaire
January	1%	3%
February	−1%	1%
March	3%	−1%

a) **If the two brothers form a 50-50 partnership on the two mines, what is the monthly return on the partnership for each of the three months (note that the partnership return is the average return for the two mines)?**

The monthly return on the partnership is 2.0% in January, 0.0% in February, and 1.0% in March. This is the simple average of the two mines' returns for each month.

b) **Over the first three months, what is the average monthly return for Boule de Neige, Ours Polaire, and the 50-50 partnership?**

Boule de Neige's average monthly return is 1.0%, Ours Polaire's is 1.0%, and the 50-50 partnership's is 1.0%. The average return is 1.0% for all three. This is calculated by taking the average across the three months for each mine, and then the three-month average of the 50-50 partnership, which is the average of both mines each month. For example, the 1.0% for Boule de Neige is the three-month average of the 1.0% return in January, the −1.0% return in February, and the 3.0% return in March.

c) **Over the first three months, what is the standard deviation of monthly returns for Boule de Neige, Ours Polaire, and the 50-50 partnership?**

Boule de Neige's standard deviation is 2.0%, Ours Polaire's is 2.0%, and the 50-50 partnership's is 1.0%. This is calculated by taking the standard deviation across the three months by mine. For example, the 2.0% for Boule de Neige is the standard deviation of the 1.0% return in January, the −1.0% return in February, and the 3.0% return in March. Most people use an electronic function (e.g., in Excel) to calculate standard deviation,

TABLE A7.1. Returns by mine and in combination.

	Boule de Neige	Ours Polaire	50-50
January	1.0%	3.0%	2.0%
February	−1.0%	1.0%	0.0%
March	3.0%	−1.0%	1.0%
Average	1.0%	1.0%	1.0%
Std. Deviation	2.0%	2.0%	1.0%

but for the hard-core people who want to do it by hand, the calculation of the 2.0% standard deviation for Boule de Neige is as follows:

1. Sum the squared deviations from the average together to get 0.08%:

$$(1\% - 1\%)^2 + (-1\% - 1\%)^2 + (3\% - 1\%)^2 = 0.08\%.$$

2. Divide 0.08% by the number of observations less 1 $(3 - 1 = 2)$ to get the variance of 0.04%:

$$\frac{0.08\%}{3-1} = 0.04\%.$$

3. Take the square root of the variance to get the standard deviation of 2.0%:

$$\sqrt{0.04\%} = 2.0\%.$$

d) **Explain the result. How can the 50-50 partnership maintain the same return as either mine, but have a standard deviation that is so much lower than that of either mine?**

The statistics asked for in question 2a, 2b, and 2c are summarized in Table A7.1. To answer question 2d, one wonders, "How can the 50-50 partnership maintain the same return as either mine (1.0% in all three), but a standard deviation that is half of either one (1.0%, not 2.0%)?" This example shows particularly strong diversification gains because the returns of the two mines tends to strongly offset each other (their correlation is not only low, like that of the example in the chapter, but actually negative, because they offset each other). When the returns are low for one mine, they tend to be high for the other mine. The result of this strong offsetting effect is that the returns of the 50-50 portfolio are much less volatile (the range between the highest and lowest monthly return is 2.0% for the 50-50 portfolio, while the high-to-low range for each individual mine is 4.0%). This example demonstrates the risk-reducing effect of diversification in a powerful way. If you can earn 1.0% (average return) with risk of 1.0% (standard deviation) for the 50-50 portfolio, why would you ever want to just hold one mine and face twice the risk with the same average return?

Question 3. **Ski Afrique**

. . . **"We like cheap money," was Lilian's response.**

Using the concept of diversification, explain the intuition behind Lilian's response. Why is a ski sweater business in the DRC arguably less risky, with all sorts of mining investments to consider? Why should investors want to invest in such a business?

Jacques Kasongo raised his eyebrows. "But why should ski sweaters in Kinshasa merit cheap money?"

"We're on to you, Papa," said Madeleine with a smile. "Everyone knows that the Congolese economy is concentrated in mining. This concentration results in common booms and busts for the country's businesses. Investors in the DRC recognize the risk of putting all their eggs in one basket and are willing to pay extra for something with a very different risk profile. A ski sweater business in the DRC is just the thing!"

"Avoid putting all your eggs in one basket, huh? I hadn't realized it, but it does seem that you are on to me," Jacques admitted. "You are correct that the ski sweater business is uncorrelated with our mining-concentrated economy. Since the systematic risk of ski sweaters is much lower, investors are willing to pay more for exposure to ski sweater risk, since it reduces their overall portfolio risk."

CHAPTER 8. FINANCIAL STATEMENTS AND THE MUSIC OF CHABYON KWA DAEBYON

Question 1. **Go through each of the eight transactions in Table 8.12 and record the accounting transactions by identifying the pairs of accounts affected and the precise financial effect.**

Transaction 1. Deposited KRW15 million in a bank account under the name BAK EUMAG.

For Transaction 1, the two accounts being impacted are the cash account and the equity account.

Cash: +15
Equity: +15

Transaction 2. Paid KRW1 million in cash to rent woodshop space for year.

For Transaction 2, the two accounts being impacted are the cash account and the general expense account.

Cash: −1
General expense: +1

Transaction 3. Paid KRW5 million in cash to purchase KRW5 million in woodshop equipment.

For Transaction 3, the two accounts being impacted are the cash account and the general expense account.

Cash: −5
Equipment: +5

Transaction 4. Paid KRW2 million in cash to purchase high-quality wood and hardware for woodshop inventory.

For Transaction 4, the two accounts being impacted are the cash account and the inventory account.

Cash: −2
Inventory: +2

Transaction 5. Paid KRW1 million in wages for neighbor to help in shop.

For Transaction 5, the two accounts being impacted are the cash account and the general expense account.

Cash: −1
General expense: +1

Transaction 6. Received KRW4 million in cash to be recorded as revenue for selling 10 instruments. The inventory sold was on the books at KRW2 million.

For Transaction 6, two pairs of accounts are affected. The first two accounts being impacted are the cash account and the revenue account, to record the cash coming in. The second two accounts being impacted are the inventory account and the cost of goods sold (COGS) account, to record the inventory going out.

Cash: +4
Revenue: +4

Inventory: −2
COGS: +2

Transaction 7. Bought KRW2 million of high-quality wood and hardware for woodshop inventory. Agreed to pay suppliers in January.

For Transaction 7, the two accounts being impacted are the accounts payable account and the inventory account. The accounts payable account is affected since we haven't yet paid the invoice on the goods received.

Accounts payable: −2
Inventory: +2

Transaction 8. Spent KRW1 million in cash on tax expense.

For Transaction 8, the two accounts being impacted are the cash account and the tax expense account.

Cash: −1
Tax expense: +1

Question 2. **Using your responses to question 1, build out the financial statements for BAK EUMAG, including both a balance sheet and an income statement.**

Accumulating the transactions above gives the financial statements below (see **Table A8.1**).

TABLE A8.1. BAK EUMAG balance sheet and income statement (in millions of Korean won).

Balance Sheet				
Assets			Liabilities and equity	
Cash	9		Accounts payable	2
Inventory	2		Equity	14
Equipment	5			
Total assets	16		Total liabilities and equity	16

Income Statement	
Revenue	4
COGS	2
General expense	2
Operating profit	0
Tax expense	1
Net profit	−1

Note that because of the KRW1 million loss recorded in the income statement, the equity account on the balance sheet is reduced by KRW1 million to recognize the loss in equity incurred by losing money during the year.

Question 3.   **What can you tell about Bak's business based on the financial statements you prepared?**

Bak's business lost KRW1 million last year—the net profit is −1 million. Her operating profit is zero because her total operating expenses are the same as her revenue. Bak may consider raising her prices or reducing her costs. This KRW1 million net profit loss resulted in the equity account dropping by KRW1 million to KRW14 million. The business is mostly financed with Bak's own money—she didn't use debt to acquire her equipment. Accounts payable of KRW2 million is financing the KRW2 million in inventory. The rest of her assets are funded with equity. Once that account payable comes due next month, the cash account will decline by KRW2 million and the accounts payable will decline by KRW2 million, to zero. At that point she will have assets of KRW14 million, which can all be applied to generating future profit.

CHAPTER 9. FINANCIAL ANALYSIS AND THE DIAGNOSIS OF AZUL

Question 1.   **Use the given information to build an income statement for Mafalda's repair business. This should include the number of bikes and scooters repaired for each of the two years and the resulting revenue for the two years. Subtracting the COGS from revenue gives the gross profit for the two years. Subtracting the G&A expenses from gross profit gives the operating profit. See the template in Table 9.6. What does the income statement tell Mafalda about her business?**

The information provided should allow you to build an income statement for Mafalda's repair business that looks a lot like what is provided in **Table A9.1**. The approach is different from what we did in the previous chapter since we are building it directly rather than through the specific

TABLE A9.1. Financial statements for Mafalda's bike and scooter repair business.

	Year 1	Year 2
Income Statement		
Bikes and scooters repaired (number)	20	23
Revenue	120	138
COGS	70	103
Gross profit	50	35
G&A expenses	5	5
Operating profit	45	30

double-entry accounting entries. Each figure follows from the description in the question. The income statement tells Mafalda how her costs compare to her revenue by year. In both years, her costs are smaller than her revenue.

Question 2. **Use the given information to build a balance sheet for Mafalda's repair business. This should include the cash balance, the receivables (invoices that haven't yet been paid), and the inventory for each of the two years. Adding these three items up gives the current assets for both years. The tools Mafalda owns are the business's equipment. Summing the current assets and the equipment gives the total assets she owns. Since she doesn't owe anything to anyone, the right-hand side of her balance sheet contains only one account—equity. The amount of equity must equal the total assets amount so that the balance sheet balances. See the template in Table 9.7. What does the balance sheet tell Mafalda about her business?**

The information provided should allow you to build a balance sheet for Mafalda's repair business that looks a lot like what is provided in **Table A9.2.** The balance sheet is harder than the income statement. To complete it, you'll need to notice that the EUR10 Ana owes is a receivable to Mafalda; the inventory and equipment have stayed constant at EUR20 and EUR30, respectively; and all the assets are financed by Mafalda's equity (no one else has claims on the business). The balance sheet tells Mafalda about the operating assets she is using to generate the revenue and profits and how those assets are financed.

TABLE A9.2. Financial statements for Mafalda's bike and scooter repair business (in euros).

	Year 1	Year 2
Balance Sheet		
Cash	50	70
Receivables	0	10
Inventory	20	20
Current assets	70	100
Equipment	30	30
Total assets	100	130
Equity	100	130

Question 3. **Based on the financial statements you created in questions 1 and 2, perform a financial analysis of the business. In your analysis, calculate the following financial ratios: the unit and revenue growth rate, return on equity (ROE), gross and operating margin, asset turnover, and financial leverage.**

TABLE A9.3. Financial ratios for Mafalda's bike and scooter repair business.

	Year 1	Year 2	Calculation
Unit growth (change in units repaired/Year 1 units repaired)		15%	[3/20]
Revenue growth (change in revenue/Year 1 revenue)		15%	[18/120]
ROE (operating profit/equity)	45%	23%	[30/130]
Gross margin (gross profit/revenue)	42%	25%	[35/138]
Operating margin (operating profit/revenue)	38%	22%	[30/138]
Asset turnover (revenue/total assets)	1.20	1.06	[138/130]
Leverage ratio (total assets/equity)	1.00	1.00	[130/130]

Based on the financial statements, the requested financial ratios are calculated as in **Table A9.3.** The table shows the figures used to calculate each ratio.

Question 4. **What do you observe about Mafalda's business? Is the unit growth and revenue growth the same? What does that suggest? Is the ROE increasing or decreasing? What is the cause? How do the other ratios help you identify the cause of changes in ROE?**

Based on the financial ratios in **Table A9.3,** one can observe the following:

1. The unit growth and revenue growth are exactly the same. This means that Mafalda hasn't changed her pricing policy—she's charging the same amount for each bike repair in both years because the units and revenue are growing together.

2. The ROE is declining sharply, from 45% to 23%. This should be a cause for concern. While Mafalda is getting good returns (23% is probably a pretty good return), it would be good to know the cause of the decline. The leverage ratio is constant because there is no leverage (no debt) being used. Some of the decline in ROE is due to a decline in asset productivity (the asset turnover is down from 1.20 to 1.06). This appears to be primarily due to the increase in cash balance. Mafalda has chosen to keep her profits in the business rather than remove that cash from the business. Some is also due to her financing Ana's receivable. The largest driver of the decline in ROE is Mafalda's large decline in gross margin. Since growth is constant, the margin decline is due to rising COGS.

Question 5. **What would you say to Mafalda about the financial health of her business?**

Mafalda would benefit from reviewing her cost structure and investigating the source of her rising direct cost of repairs. She could consider implementing cost efficiencies or price increases to maintain gross margin. If she has additional questions, her friend Pedro is likely to be interested in helping her out.

CHAPTER 10. FINANCIAL MODELING AND OPERATION NO MORE CORN

Question 1.   **Using the template in Table 10.6, replicate Agnes Adams and Zina Zamboni's financial model for the high-price scenario detailed in Table 10.4. Your replicated model should use assumption input values for all of the cells colored gray, including plate 1 gross profit, unit 1 demand, plate 2 gross profit, unit 2 demand, wages, rent, and other fixed costs as specified in the table. All other values in the template (those not colored gray) should be calculated based on these assumption input values. The end result should be a model that matches Table 10.4. Consider doing this using electronic spreadsheet software.**

The replicated model for the high-price scenario should look identical to that of Table 10.4. Please see the following help notes:

The total revenue is equal to the plate 1 price times the units of plate 1 plus the plate 2 price times the units of plate 2.

The gross profit is equal to the plate 1 per-unit gross profit times the units of plate 1 plus the plate 2 per-unit gross profit times the units of plate 2.

Wages are equal to the USD16-per-hour wage rate times the expected hours worked each week under the two scenarios (25 or 29 hours) times the number of grandsons (2).

Operating profits are equal to the gross profit less wages, less rent, and less other fixed costs.

Question 2.   **Imagine an even-higher-price scenario. Suppose Tom O'Brien tested a demand scenario for even higher prices and found the estimated demand values outlined in Table 10.7. Adjust the financial model you created in response to question 1 to include these new assumptions. Would you recommend that Adams and Zamboni consider pricing their sandwiches even higher?**

The even-higher-price scenario generates per-unit gross profit for the submarine offering that offsets the loss in demand such that modeled profits for subs are now slightly positive (USD8 per week). The expected profits for the Greek offering are also positive, but less so than in the high-price scenario. The USD7 and USD9 price points seem to generate the best outcome. The financial model should look similar to **Table A10.1.**

TABLE A10.1. Financial model of even-higher-price scenario (monetary values in US dollars).

	Granny's Greek	Granny's Subs
Plate 1 price	9.00	9.00
Units 1	155	140
Gross profit 1	5.00	5.50
Plate 2 price	11.00	11.00
Units 2	110	75
Gross profit 2	6.00	6.50
Total revenue	2,605	2,085
Total gross profit	1,435	1,258
Wages	928	800
Rent (equipment and parking)	400	350
Other fixed costs	100	100
Operating profit	7	8

Question 3. For the last several years, O'Brien and Mary Marino have lived off WOW Sauce, a hot sauce that their granddaughters concocted to help their grandparents mask the bland taste of the Goodtimes food. O'Brien and Marino chatted about starting a business to market bottles of WOW Sauce to the other Goodtimes residents. Their granddaughters' production costs were USD5 per bottle of WOW Sauce. The weekly hours were low, such that the wage costs were expected to be just USD160 per week for both granddaughters. The other fixed costs were USD100 per week. Weekly demand was estimated at 100 bottles per week, if priced at USD8 per bottle, and 75 bottles per week, if priced at USD10 per bottle.

Build a financial model that indicates the business profits under the following two scenarios: a price of USD8 per bottle and a price of USD10 per bottle.

The assumptions can be organized into a model that looks somewhat like **Table A10.2.** Total revenue is equal to the price times the respective units. Total gross profit is equal to the per-unit gross profit times the units. Wages are equal to the USD16-per-hour wage rate times the expected hours worked each week (5) times the number of granddaughters (2). Operating profits are equal to the gross profit less wages less other fixed costs.

The model suggests that the USD10 price maintains sufficient gross profit to offset the loss in demand. As such, it maintains the higher profits and seems superior to the USD8 price scenario for Goodtimes.

TABLE A10.2. Financial model of WOW Sauce business with USD8 and USD10 prices (monetary values in US dollars).

	8.00 price	10.00 price
Price	8.00	10.00
Units	100	75
Total revenue	800	750
Total gross profit	300	375
Wages	160	160
Other fixed costs	100	100
Operating profit	40	115

CHAPTER 11. CASH FLOW AND EL RANCHO DE LAS VACAS BAILANDO

Use the financial statements in Table 11.2 to calculate the following figures for 2022:

Question 1.   **Working capital**

Working capital is calculated as total current assets less total current operating liabilities. The total current assets include cash of UYU5.0 million plus receivables of UYU3.0 million plus inventory of UYU20.0 million. Those three items sum to UYU28.0 million. The total current operating liabilities match the amount of payables, which is UYU3.0 million. Subtracting UYU3.0 million from UYU28.0 million gives a working-capital amount of UYU25.0 million. This working-capital balance of UYU25.0 million is the net amount of current business assets investors have financed. In other words, investors have put up UYU25 million to support the working capital the business is using.

Question 2.   **Total capital**

Total capital is calculated in one of two ways.

One way to find total capital is to find the sum of working capital and fixed assets. Since working capital in 2022 is UYU25.0 million (from question 1), and fixed assets is simply equal to the property and equipment balance of UYU17.0 million, the total capital balance is the sum of those two items: UYU42.0 million.

The second way is to find the sum of total debt and total equity. Since total debt is the 2022 debt balance of UYU5.5 million, and total equity is the 2022 equity balance of UYU36.5 million, the total capital balance is the sum of those two items: UYU42.0 million.

Regardless of how you calculate it, the total capital of UYU42.0 million is the amount of asset investment in el Rancho de las Vacas Cantoras that is financed by the business investors.

Question 3.   **The year's investment (change) in working capital**

The year's investment in working capital is equal to the change in the working-capital balance over the year. Since the 2022 working-capital balance is UYU25.0 million, and the 2021 working-capital balance is UYU35.0 million [cash of UYU5.0 million + receivables of UYU5.0 million + inventory of UYU30.0 million − payables of UYU5.0 million], the investment in working capital is the difference of those two amounts, or UYU10.0 million. Since the working-capital balance has declined, the investment amount is negative by the amount of UYU10 million. This amount is a disinvestment rather than an investment—the investors have effectively drawn UYU10 million from the business due to the reduction in working-capital investment.

Question 4.   **The year's investment (change) in fixed assets**

The year's investment in fixed assets is equal to the change in the fixed-asset balance over the year. Since the 2022 fixed-asset balance is simply the property and equipment balance of UYU17.0 million, and the 2021 fixed-asset balance is unchanged at UYU17.0 million, the investment in fixed assets is the difference of those two amounts, or 0.0. Since the fixed-asset balance has remained the same, the investment amount for the year is zero, meaning that investors are unaffected in the year by investment needs in fixed assets.

Question 5.   **Total cash flow**

Total cash flow is measured by the inflows from the operations less the outflow due to investment. We can measure this as the business profits of UYU9.0 million minus the total investment of −UYU10.0 million [working-capital investment of −UYU10.0 million plus fixed-asset investment of 0]. Putting these two effects together gives a total cash flow of UYU19.0 million.

Question 6.   **How do you interpret the total cash flow figure that you calculated? How are investors affected financially by their investment in el Rancho de las Vacas Cantoras?**

Since the total cash flow amount is negative (UYU19.0 million), it is really a disinvestment rather than an investment. Investors have actually gotten UYU19 million out of the business rather than put money into it. The most important reason for this cash outflow is the reduction of inventory investment for UYU10 million. Investors have benefited from the sales without having to replenish the cost of the inventory. Note that since interest expense is a cash flow to debt investors, it is common to not deduct interest when calculating total cash flow to investors. If we do that and don't deduct interest expense, cash flow increases by UYU1 million.

CHAPTER 12. VALUATION AND RUPERT'S HOME COOKING

Question 1.   Take on Rupert Rudolfinquist's investment challenge yourself by solving the same five problems, Alpha through Epsilon. For some of the questions (particularly Delta and Epsilon), it will be easier to use an electronic spreadsheet to automate the calculation of all the terms.

Your responses should follow the responses provided in the chapter.

Question 2.   Having gone through investment challenges Alpha through Epsilon, you should be able to value many financial contracts. Here's another one: Suppose that Rupert is considering buying a fishing boat and has the budget to afford a monthly payment of CAN100 over the next three years. How large a loan should he be willing to take, with no down payment, if prevailing interest rates are 6% per year for a similar loan?

This question is identical to the Epsilon challenge. Rupert should be able to borrow CAN3,287 if he is willing to pay CAN100 per month for three years and the prevailing interest rate is 6%. This is the approach lenders use all over the world to establish the value of any loan, from home mortgages to insurance contracts.

Question 3.   If the amount in question 2 is not enough to get Rupert the boat of his dreams, how large a loan should Rupert be willing to take if he were able to double the payment and the interest rate declined to just 3%?

By substituting in the different CAN200 payment for the previous CAN100 payment and the 0.25% monthly rate [0.25% = 3.0%/12 months] for the previous 0.5% monthly rate [0.50% = 6.0%/12 months] into the pricing equation

$$\text{Value} = \frac{\text{CAN200}}{(1+0.25\%)} + \frac{\text{CAN200}}{(1+0.25\%)^2} + \cdots + \frac{\text{CAN200}}{(1+0.25\%)^{35}} + \frac{\text{CAN200}}{(1+0.25\%)^{36}},$$

we get the loan value to increase to CAN6,877. Hopefully, Farout has some good fishing boats selling for under CAN6,877. This increase from CAN3,287 is mostly due to the increase in the monthly payment and only somewhat due to the improvement in interest rates. Interest rates don't matter as much since the loan is only for three years.

CHAPTER 13. PERPETUITIES AND THE CHAMPAGNE OF TABLE WATER

Question 1.   James Thornberry opens a barber shop in the Midlands that generates profits of GBP40,000 per year. Thornberry expects that the shop can operate forever. What is the value of the barber shop if the relevant risk-adjusted benchmark return on hair cutting profits is 5%?

Using the present value of a perpetuity formula, Thornberry's barber shop has a value of GBP800,000. The present value of a perpetuity is equal to C divided by R. In this case, the annual perpetual cash flow is GBP40,000, and the risk-adjusted discount rate is 5%. Dividing GBP40,000 by 5% gives the value of GBP800,000.

Question 2. **Jane Carmichael offers to pay Arthur Birdwhistle GBP200 a year for 10 years on a loan to finance the construction of a mineral water cellar at her house. How much of a loan should Birdwhistle be willing to give her if the prevailing benchmark rate of return for home improvements is 4%?**

Using the present value of an annuity formula, Carmichael's loan has a value of GBP1,622.

Putting the appropriate values into the present value of a 10-year annuity formula—cash flow of 200, discount rate of 4%, and maturity of 10 years—gives

$$V = \frac{200}{4\%} - \frac{200}{4\%(1+4\%)^{10}} = 1,622.$$

Birdwhistle should be willing to loan Carmichael GBP1,622 to build her cellar.

Question 3. **Alice Ainsworth opens a comedy school where students pay USD200 a month for 20 months. What is the present value of the tuition for each student if the relevant risk-adjusted annual required return on school tuition is 6%?**

Using the present value of an annuity formula, the tuition has a value of USD3,797.

Putting the appropriate values into the present value of a 20-month annuity with cash flow of 200, discount rate of 0.5% per month (0.5% = 6%/12 months), and maturity of 20 months gives

$$V = \frac{200}{0.5\%} - \frac{200}{0.5\%(1+0.5\%)^{20}} = 3,797.$$

The present value of the tuition for each student is USD3,797.

Question 4. **Louis Perrier has a great year with his spa de valeur actuelle—or present-value spa (a spa where people get therapeutic benefits from working present-value math problems). He anticipates that the spa will generate FRF2 million in profits next year and that the profits should grow by 3% per year. What is the value of the spa if the relevant risk-adjusted hurdle rate on health profits is 10%?**

Using the present value of a growing perpetuity formula, the value is FRF28.6 million.

Putting the appropriate values into the present-value formula—first cash flow of FRF2 million, discount rate of 10%, and a growth rate of 3%—we get

$$\text{Present value of a perpetuity with growth } g = \frac{2\,\text{M}}{10\% - 3\%} = 28.6\text{M}.$$

Question 5. **Margaret Berrycloth owns an oil well that produces profits of GBP2 million per year. The output is depleting such that profits are expected to decline by 2% per year. What is the value of the oil well if the relevant risk-adjusted benchmark return on oil well profits is 8%?**

Using the present value of a growing perpetuity formula, the value is GBP20 million.

Putting the appropriate values into the present-value formula—the first cash flow of GBP2 million, discount rate of 8%, and a growth rate of −2%—we get

$$\text{Present value of a perpetuity with growth } g = \frac{2\,\text{M}}{8\% + 2\%} = 20\text{M}.$$

CHAPTER 14. THE CASH CYCLE AND THE CALABOOSE CHALLENGE

Question 1. **What is the length of the cash cycle for Hoe's operation?**

Days in inventory (DIO) is 3. Days sales outstanding (DSO) is 40. Days payable outstanding (DPO) is 20. Using the cash cycle formula (cash cycle = DIO + DSO − DPO), we find that the cash cycle is equal to 3 + 40 − 20, or 23 days.

Question 2. **Hoe doesn't understand the importance of the cash cycle to his business. How would you explain to him the relevance of the definition of the cash cycle?**

The cash cycle measures the number of days it takes for cash outflows used for purchasing tomato and can inventory to turn into cash inflows through collected sales. Due to Hoe's 23-day cash cycle, he needs to finance 23 days of his business operation. If he is doing USD10,000 of business on an average day, Hoe will need to put up or get another investor to put up USD230,000 [USD10,000 times 23 days] to finance the amount of money he has tied up in his business on an average day.

Question 3. **Hoe has struggled to fill big orders for his canned tomatoes—every time a large order comes in, he doesn't have enough inventory, and those**

customers go elsewhere. How can Hoe work with his customers so that he can increase the amount of inventory he is able to stock (an increase in his inventory days) while keeping his cash cycle constant?

Hoe can observe that a day saved on his DSO can be substituted for a day on his DIO. If he negotiates to have his customers pay him 5 days earlier (35 days), he would be able to increase his inventory levels to 8 days in inventory (8 days = 3 days + 5 days) without changing the cash cycle (3 + 40 − 20 = 8 + 35 − 20 = 23). With the larger DIO, Hoe would be able to fill bigger orders.

CHAPTER 15. FINANCIAL LEVERAGE AND THRU-HIKING THE APPALACHIAN TRAIL

Question 1. **Romano's critique of pizza slicing applies to how claims on the cash flows of businesses are sliced, since debt and equity partitioning is similar to the slicing of a pizza. Please explain this connection and include a reference to the implications of financial leverage on the value of businesses.**

The value of a business is determined by the size and riskiness of the expected cash flows. Businesses with large expected cash flows are worth a lot, while the risk of the cash flows dampens that value. Just as it shouldn't matter how a pizza is sliced, so too it shouldn't matter how a firm's cash flows are sliced. The law of conservation of value tells us that the total value of the firm should not change simply because its cash flows are divided differently between debt holders and equity holders. Business value should be neutral to changes in financial leverage in a frictionless market.

Question 2. **How does Romano's critique of pizza slicing apply to the allocation of risk across claim holders in a business? Please include a reference to the implications of financial leverage for the value of businesses.**

The total risk of a business's expected cash flows should not change simply because it is sliced and diced in a different way. The risk doesn't disappear into thin air; it is conserved across different levels of financial leverage, just as the amount of a pizza doesn't change if it is sliced differently. The law of conservation of risk reminds us that total firm risk is neutral to changes in financial leverage in a frictionless market.

Since the return required by debt holders is lower than that required by equity holders, it is easy to assume that relying more on debt financing lowers the overall total cost of financing. But that ignores the fact that as the firm borrows more, the risk of the firm becomes more concentrated on the remaining equity holders. With the additional concentrated risk, the equity holders will require a higher return for their riskier position. The increase in return must be just enough to offset any gains from increased reliance on debt financing, since the overall risk remains unchanged.

CHAPTER 16. SOURCES AND USES OF CASH AND A YELLOW '69 STINGRAY

Question 1. **Please build a financial model of the expected 2022 financial statements for Under Armour using the following assumptions. Do you expect the anticipated debt levels to decline? Please note that you may experience a circularity in the logic of your spreadsheet. In order to avoid this circularity error, you may need to activate iterative calculations in your spreadsheet options.**

Modeling assumptions for the year 2022:

a) **Revenue grows by 20%.**
b) **Gross margin remains at 50%.**
c) **Selling, general, and administrative (SG&A) expenses are at 45% of revenue.**
d) **Interest expense is USD0.17 billion.**
e) **Income taxes are 10% of operating profit.**
f) **Cash needs are 20% of revenue.**
g) **Receivable days (days sales outstanding, DSO) is 40 days.**
h) **Inventory days (days in inventory, DIO) is 110 days.**
i) **Property, plant, and equipment (PP&E) turnover is 5.0 times.**
j) **Payable days (days payable outstanding, DPO) is 120 days.**
k) **Under Armour elects to not pay a cash dividend in 2022.**

No, the anticipated debt is not expected to decline. Instead, it is expected to rise from USD1.5 million to USD1.9 billion. This is because assets increase by USD0.4 billion, from USD4.99 billion to USD5.39 billion; payables decline almost USD0.2 billion, while net profit is less than USD0.2 billion. See **Table A16.1** for calculations.

Question 2. **How does your answer change if the company wants to pay out a USD0.25 billion dividend? Assume that interest expense is USD0.20 billion.**

Issuing the dividend reduces the equity account by the amount of the dividend, or USD0.25 billion. This decline in equity gives rise to an increase in debt financing of USD0.28 billion, relative to question 1. The USD0.28 billion increase in debt is due to the loss of equity financing of USD0.25 billion plus the increasing interest expense from the increased debt. See **Table A16.2**.

TABLE A16.1. Under Armour financial forecast, assuming no dividend.

	2020	2021	2022	Assumption
Revenue	4.48	5.68	6.82	20% growth rate
Cost of sales	2.32	2.82	3.41	Plug
Gross profit	2.16	2.86	3.41	Gross margin of 50%
SG&A expense	2.17	2.34	3.07	SG&A expense/revenue of 45%
Operating income	−0.01	0.53	0.34	
Interest expense	0.48	0.14	0.17	Interest expense of 9% of debt
Pre-tax profit (PTP)	−0.49	0.39	0.17	
Taxes	0.06	0.03	0.02	Tax rate of 10%
Net profit	−0.55	0.36	0.15	
Cash	1.52	1.67	1.36	Cash % of 20% of revenue
Receivables	0.53	0.57	0.75	DSO of 40 days
Inventory	0.90	0.81	1.03	DIO of 110 days
Other current assets	0.28	0.29	0.29	Keep constant because there is no other guidance
Net PP&E	1.20	1.06	1.36	PP&E turnover at 5.0 times
Other long-term assets	0.61	0.60	0.60	Keep constant because there is no other guidance
Total assets	5.03	4.99	5.39	
Payables	1.25	1.31	1.12	DPO of 120 days
Debt	2.01	1.50	1.93	Plug (total assets − payables − equity)
Equity	1.77	2.18	2.33	Previous equity + net profit (no dividend)
Total liabilities and equity	5.03	4.99	5.39	
Revenue growth		27%	20%	
Gross margin	48%	50%	50%	
SG&A expense percentage	48%	41%	45%	
Operating margin	0%	9%	5%	
Interest expense/debt	24%	8.7%	9.0%	
Tax percentage of PTP	−12%	8%	10%	
Cash percentage of revenue	34%	30%	20%	
DSO	43.2	36.6	40.0	
DIO	141.6	104.8	110.0	
PP&E turnover	3.7	5.4	5.0	
DPO	196.7	169.6	120.0	
Debt/assets	0.4	0.3	0.4	

TABLE A16.2. Under Armour 2022 financial forecast, assuming USD0.25 billion dividend.

	2020	2021	2022	Assumption
Revenue	4.48	5.68	6.82	20% growth rate
Cost of sales	2.32	2.82	3.41	Plug
Gross profit	2.16	2.86	3.41	Gross margin of 50%
SG&A expense	2.17	2.34	3.07	SG&A expense/revenue of 45%
Operating income	−0.01	0.53	0.34	
Interest expense	0.48	0.14	0.20	Interest expense of 9% of debt
PTP	−0.49	0.39	0.14	
Taxes	0.06	0.03	0.01	Tax rate of 10%
Net profit	−0.55	0.36	0.13	
Cash	1.52	1.67	1.36	Cash % of 20% of revenue
Receivables	0.53	0.57	0.75	DSO of 40 days
Inventory	0.90	0.81	1.03	DIO of 110 days
Other current assets	0.28	0.29	0.29	Keep constant because there is no other guidance
Net PP&E	1.20	1.06	1.36	PP&E turnover at 5.0 times
Other long-term assets	0.61	0.60	0.60	Keep constant because there is no other guidance
Total assets	5.03	4.99	5.39	
Payables	1.25	1.31	1.12	DPO of 120 days
Debt	2.01	1.50	2.21	Plug
Equity	1.77	2.18	2.06	Previous equity + net profit less USD0.25 billion dividend
Total liabilities and equity	5.03	4.99	5.39	

Question 3. **What is your best recommendation for a change in operating policy to reduce the debt by USD0.5 billion? Assume that interest expense is USD0.14 billion.**

Return Under Armour's DPO to a previous level in 2020 or 2021, such as 190 days. This change in trade credit has a dramatic effect: debt drops from USD2.22 billion to USD1.50 billion. This USD1.5 billion figure implies that debt remains the same as the level of debt in 2021. Since suppliers allowed for 190-day credit in 2020, Under Armour may be able to achieve that this year. See **Table A16.3.**

TABLE A16.3. Under Armour 2022 financial forecast, assuming USD0.25 billion dividend and increase of DPO to 190 days.

	2020	2021	2022	Assumption
Revenue	4.48	5.68	6.82	20% growth rate
Cost of sales	2.32	2.82	3.41	Plug
Gross profit	2.16	2.86	3.41	Gross margin of 50%
SG&A expense	2.17	2.34	3.07	SG&A expense/revenue of 45%
Operating income	−0.01	0.53	0.34	
Interest expense	0.48	0.14	0.14	Interest expense of 9% of debt
PTP	−0.49	0.39	0.21	
Taxes	0.06	0.03	0.02	Tax rate of 10%
Net profit	−0.55	0.36	0.19	
Cash	1.52	1.67	1.36	Cash % of 20% of revenue
Receivables	0.53	0.57	0.75	DSO of 40 days
Inventory	0.90	0.81	1.03	DIO of 110 days
Other current assets	0.28	0.29	0.29	Keep constant because there is no other guidance
Net PP&E	1.20	1.06	1.36	PP&E turnover at 5.0 times
Other long-term assets	0.61	0.60	0.60	Keep constant because there is no other guidance
Total assets	5.03	4.99	5.39	
Payables	1.25	1.31	1.77	DPO of 120 days
Debt	2.01	1.50	1.50	Plug
Equity	1.77	2.18	2.11	Previous equity + net profit less USD0.25 billion dividend
Total liabilities and equity	5.03	4.99	5.39	
Revenue growth		27%	20%	
Gross margin	48%	50%	50%	
SG&A expense percentage	48%	41%	45%	
Operating margin	0%	9%	5%	
Interest expense/debt	24%	8.7%	9.0%	
Tax percentage of PTP	−12%	8%	10%	
Cash percentage of revenue	34%	30%	20%	
DSO	43.2	36.6	40.0	
DIO	141.6	104.8	110.0	
PP&E turnover	3.7	5.4	5.0	
DPO	196.7	169.6	190.0	

The Vocabulary of Finance

This appendix provides explanations of some of the common terms used by finance people. Please know that this is not a comprehensive list, but it does include many of the most common and foundational terms.

Accounts payable. *See* payables.
Accounts payable days. *See* days payable outstanding (DPO).
Accounts receivable. *See* receivables.
Accounts receivable days. *See* days sales outstanding (DSO).
Amortization. *See* depreciation and amortization.
Annuity. An annuity is a promised payment of expected cash flow that repeats at a regular interval and then ends at some defined point. A common example of an annuity is a loan where the borrower agrees to make a specific payment every month for a specified number of months. The formula for calculating the present value of an annuity is

$$V = \frac{C}{R} - \frac{C}{R(1+R)^T},$$

where V is the present value of the annuity, C is the regular promised payment, R is the risk-adjusted periodic discount rate, and T is the expected number of periods until maturity. As an example, suppose that Ingrid has agreed to make payments of USD290 per month to her bank for five years to finance USD15,000 of the classic antique car she is buying. If the prevailing annual interest rate for car loans of this type is 6%, is the loan fair for both Ingrid and the bank? To figure this out, we first note that Ingrid has agreed to pay a monthly annuity to the bank. If the annual relevant risk-adjusted rate is 6%, then the monthly periodic rate is 0.5% (which comes from 0.5% = 6.0%/12 months in a year). The number of periods to maturity is 60 months (which comes from 60 months = 5 years × 12 months per year). Inputting the appropriate values into the annuity present-value formula, we get a present value of USD15,000:

$$V = \frac{USD290}{0.5\%} - \frac{USD290}{0.5\%(1+0.5\%)^{60}} = USD15,000.$$

Since the present value of the annuity is equal to USD15,000, the bank's willingness to offer Ingrid USD15,000 seems appropriate. The terms of the loan seem fair for both parties.

Asset turnover. Asset turnover measures the productivity or efficiency of the business assets. It is defined as a measure of flow (i.e., sales) divided by investment (i.e., total assets). Productive or efficient assets are able to generate a lot of sales proportionally. A business that can generate two dollars of revenue for every one dollar of assets is more productive or efficient than a business that can only generate one dollar of revenue for every one dollar of assets. Turnover measures the times the assets are turning over with revenue.

Balance sheet. Businesses need physical things such as cash, inventory, and equipment to carry out their operations. The balance sheet is a financial statement that indicates all the assets and liabilities of the business at a point in time (e.g., at the end of the year). The assets and liabilities are commonly listed on the balance sheet at their cost (i.e., what it cost to acquire the asset). The balance sheet provides a tabulation of all the business's assets (e.g., cash, inventory, and equipment) on the left-hand side, and a tabulation of how those assets were financed (e.g., trade credit, debt claims, or equity claims) on the right-hand side. By the rules of accounting, the balance sheet balances, meaning the tabulation on the left-hand side always equals the tabulation on the right-hand side. This balancing of the balance sheet isn't magic—it's the result of standard double-entry accounting that matches the cost of the assets acquired to how the business paid for them.

Bankruptcy. When a company is not able to make the payments it has promised to debt holders (an impending default), the board may file for *bankruptcy protection*. Bankruptcy protection means that a legal court organized by the local government becomes the arbiter with the power to renegotiate the claims by the claim holders. In the extreme example (chapter 7 bankruptcy in the United States), a trust appointed by the bankruptcy court liquidates the assets of the company and distributes them, as negotiated by the court, to all the claim holders in the company, including employees, suppliers, customers, debt holders, and possibly equity holders. In the more common example (chapter 11 bankruptcy in the United States), the company continues to operate, and the bankruptcy court renegotiates the claims of the claim holders. For example, it may be determined that debt holders will do better if they simply miss a couple of interest payments to allow the business to get back on its feet and begin repaying its debt. In this case, the board and management team may continue to run the company, or the court could decide that it is best for the management team to be replaced.

Beta. *See* capital asset pricing model (CAPM).

Beta risk. *See* systematic risk.

Board (board of directors). Some businesses have very few equity holders, while other businesses have millions. When there are lots of equity holders, it is common for the equity holders to elect a body of people responsible for overseeing the management team and big company policy decisions. These board members represent all the equity holders and often come from a wide range of backgrounds.

Bonds. *See* financial securities.

Business risk. Business risk is the potential variation in financial outcome to investors due to uncertainty in business performance. Business risk is different from financial risk. *Financial risk* is the variation in business risk caused by financial leverage. If a firm's equity is levered two times, then debt holders have financed half the assets, but they have not taken their proportional share of the business risk. If, for example, the debt holders have contracted to bear no risk, then the leverage has doubled the risk the equity holders are bearing. Changes in the value of the business assets are associated with twice the change in the value held by the equity holders, since they bear all the asset risk despite providing half the investment.

CAGR. *See* compound annual growth rate (CAGR).

Capital asset pricing model (CAPM). The CAPM (often pronounced *cap-em*) is a specific equation for the risk premium required by investors. It is a theory for the risk-return relation. This theory says that investors insulate themselves from idiosyncratic risk through their tendency to diversify their investment portfolios. Because of the diversification effect, investors only care about systematic or nondiversifiable risk. The theory uses the term *beta* as a measure of systematic risk: beta measures how the prices of any investment comove with the prices of other investments. According to the CAPM, the fair risk-adjusted return investors should expect of any investment opportunity should be reflected in the following formula:

Expected return = risk-free rate + beta risk of investment × market risk premium.

Capital gains. *See* return on investment (ROI).

Capitalize versus expense. *See* property, plant, and equipment (PP&E).

Cash. *Cash* is a term used to indicate the amount of currency that the business has, including the cash currency and the liquid currency in bank accounts and other financial securities. The term *liquidity* refers to the ease with which the asset can be turned into currency. For example, money held in bank accounts is considered liquid because businesses can typically turn bank account holdings into cash currency very quickly and at low cost.

Cash conversion cycle. *See* cash cycle.

Cash cycle. The cash cycle or *cash conversion cycle* of a business represents the amount of time between the cash outflow a business makes to buy or make a good or service and the cash inflow a business receives when collecting on the sale. The typical cash cycle is equal to the average number of inventory days (days inventory outstanding, DIO) plus the average number of accounts receivable days (days sales outstanding, DSO) minus the average number of payable days (days payable outstanding, DPO), or DIO + DSO − DPO. Because the costs of production must be financed by the business, longer cash cycles are associated with greater business financing needs.

Cash flow. Cash flow is the net amount of money a business generates for its investors. Cash flow represents the financial effect on investors of the business or a business project. Positive cash flow means a current positive payout to investors. Negative cash flow means a current negative cash effect to investors (i.e., investors pay money into the business). Investors care about how businesses consume or produce cash, because the only way they get compensated for investing in the business is through business cash flow or selling their investment to someone else. Investors recognize that measures of profit have a number of distortions that can make business profit differ substantially from business cash flow. One of these distortions is noncash expenses like depreciation and amortization. Another distortion occurs when management doesn't distribute profits but instead plows them back into the business by buying additional assets. Technically, a standard definition of cash flow is equal to net operating profit after tax (NOPAT), adding back depreciation and amortization, subtracting capital expenditures in fixed assets, and subtracting net investment in working capital. The intuition behind this formula is that cash flow starts with the operating profits of the business and adds back any depreciation or amortization expenses since those expenses don't really require cash payment—they are only allocations included to reduce taxes. Finally, the business investment, which is equal to changes in net working capital and capital expenditures, is subtracted.

Compound annual growth rate (CAGR). There are two standard ways to average growth rates over multiple periods: the *average annual growth rate* and the *compound annual growth rate* (CAGR—often pronounced *cay-grr*). The CAGR is the annual rate that, when compounded over the relevant number of years, changes the beginning amount to the ending amount. For example, suppose the price of chocolate is USD10 in Year 1, then grows by 50% to USD15 in Year 2, and then declines by 20% to USD12 in Year 3. The average annual growth rate is calculated by simply taking the average of the two annual growth rates (+50% and −20%), which gives an average annual growth rate of 15%. The *compound* annual growth rate, which we can call R for *return*, is calculated by finding what growth rate would grow USD10 (the start point) to USD12 (the end point) over two years, if compounded for those two years. That amount is found by finding the R that makes the following equality true: $USD10 (1+R)^{2 \text{ years}} = USD12$. Note that the "two years" value is an exponent, as $(1+R)$ is raised to the power of 2. When solving this equation for R, we get $(USD12/USD10)^{1/2} - 1$, which is equal to 9.5%. This means that if we start with USD10 and grow it for two years at a compound rate of 9.5%, we can expect to have USD12 in two years. To calculate the CAGR for any series, one divides the ending value by the starting value and then takes that value to the power of 1 over T, which is the same as taking that value to its Tth root, where T is the number of years. In the above example, we found the 9.5% CAGR by finding the square root of 12/10 and then subtracting 1.

Corporate governance. Lots of people have an interest in the affairs of a business: one term for all these people is *stakeholders*. Stakeholders are all those who care about the business outcomes. These stakeholders include managers and employees, customers, suppliers, investors, the government, and community members. As you might imagine, the varying stakeholders have varying ideas about what should be done with the business. Corporate governance deals with the rules, laws, and norms about who gets to decide what the business (or firm or company—all synonyms) does.

Cost of capital. *See* required return.

Cost of goods sold (COGS). *See* income statement.

Coupon rate. *See* yield.

Covariance risk. *See* systematic risk.

Days inventory outstanding (DIO). The number of DIO represents the average number of days a business holds its inventory from delivery to sale. It captures the number of days that a business is holding the inventory that it sells. DIO is also known as *inventory days*. A common way DIO is calculated is

$$DIO = \frac{\text{inventory}}{\text{cost of goods sold}} \times 365 \text{ days},$$

where inventory is the average amount of inventory that the business keeps on hand and cost of goods sold (COGS) is the cost of the inventory that the business sells in a year. It is customary to use COGS rather than revenue to measure the amount of sales, since inventory is valued at its production cost rather than its sales value. The ratio tells how many days the business holds inventory on average. For example, suppose that inventory was equal to the annual COGS. If we calculate the ratio, we find that the DIO is 365 days. This makes sense because the business is holding a full year's worth of inventory.

Days payable outstanding (DPO). The number of DPO represents the average number of days a business holds its payables from delivery of the inputs to payment for the inputs. It captures the number of days a business is holding the accounts payable before paying the supplier. DPO is also known as *payable days*. A common way to calculate DPO is

$$\text{DPO} = \frac{\text{accounts payable}}{\text{cost of goods sold}} \times 365 \text{ days},$$

where accounts payable is the average amount of payables owed to the suppliers of the business, and cost of goods sold (COGS) is the amount of inventory that the business sells in a year. Finance people often use annual purchases as an alternative to COGS: since purchases correspond more closely to accounts payable, annual purchases can be a more accurate number.

Days sales outstanding (DSO). The number of DSO represents the average number of days a business holds its accounts receivable from sale to collection of payment for that sale. It captures the number of days a business is holding the receivables associated with its sales. DSO is also known as *accounts receivable days* or simply *receivable days*. A common way to calculate DSO is

$$\text{DSO} = \frac{\text{accounts receivable}}{\text{revenue}} \times 365 \text{ days},$$

where accounts receivable is the average amount of receivables owed by the customers of the business, and revenue is the amount of sales that the business has made for the year. The ratio tells how many days the business holds accounts receivable on average. For example, suppose that accounts receivable is equal to the annual revenue. If we calculate the ratio (it would equal 1), we find that the DSO is 365 days. This makes sense because the business is holding a full year's worth of receivables.

DCF. *See* discounted cash flow (DCF) analysis.

Debt holders. Debt holders (also called *debt investors*) are one type of investor. In exchange for lending money to the business, debt holders have the following two claims: (1) a promise of a set of fixed future payments and (2) the right to exert control on the assets of the business in the event that the promised fixed payments are not paid. Suppose Boris gives USD1 million to Jumbo Airlines in exchange for a promise of annual interest payments of 10% of the USD1 million loan for 10 years, plus a return of the USD1 million at the end of the 10-year loan. As a debt holder, Boris can expect to receive annual payments of USD100,000 every year for the next 10 years. As long as those payments are made, Boris has no right to exert influence on the company's business decisions. But if Jumbo Airlines fails to make its promised payment, Boris is assured that he will have influence. The structure of the debt contract gives the debt holder assurance that others in the company won't take advantage of them.

Default. When a company does not pay its promised payments to debt holders, the company is in default. Default typically triggers specific conditions that are written into the debt contract. Default can be messy, as debt holders and other claim holders battle to maximize their payout. To protect the firm from a disorderly unraveling as claim holders look out for their own best interests, the board of directors may seek the more orderly process of bankruptcy protection.

Depreciation and amortization. Businesses often make investments in long-term assets, such as buying a building or investing in a patent. Since the productive life of these assets may be many years, finance people spread the cost of those long-term investments over the investment's life. This cost-spreading technique is called depreciation and amortization. The annual charge for depreciation and amortization is put on the income statement and reduces profit by capturing the costs associated with use of the fixed assets. *Depreciation* refers to the annual charge of tangible assets like property, plant, or equipment. *Amortization* refers to the annual charge of intangible assets like patents. It is important to note that depreciation and amortization expenses aren't ever really paid, since they are just accounting allocations of investment expenditures made previously. As an example, suppose Jumbo Airlines spent USD1 million on a new building it expected to use for 10 years: How should it charge that USD1 million against profits? One way to account for that expenditure would be to incur the expense in the year it occurs. In that case, Jumbo would have a big USD1 million building expense on the income statement in the year of the expenditure, which would make business profits in that year low and profits in future years high (since there would be no charge in subsequent years). An alternative way to account for the expenditure would be to spread the USD1 million charge over all 10 years by allocating a USD100,000 building depreciation charge each year over the 10 years of the building's life. This allocation of the investment expenditure smooths out profits by matching the expenditure not to when it is made but instead to when it benefits the business. This approach to smoothing profits is at the heart of depreciation and amortization charges.

DIO. *See* days inventory outstanding (DIO).

Discounted cash flow (DCF) analysis. Investments commonly have multiyear implications. A common cash flow profile for an investment is negative cash flow in the early years and positive cash flow in the later years. DCF analysis is a way of distilling the multiyear financial effects of an investment to a single value. Suppose that Burt is considering a USD2 million investment in a piece of equipment. The equipment is expected to save his business USD1 million in the subsequent three years. Should Burt make the investment? The naive response is "Duh, yes. The USD2 million investment is less than the USD3 million savings." But a finance person might instead say, "Dude, let's run a DCF." By *run a DCF*, they mean, "Let's discount the future cash flows to the present at the appropriate discount rate and then add them up to see if the value is greater than the required investment." To do this, they estimate an appropriate risk-adjusted discount rate (let's say 10%), then they calculate the present value of each future payment at a discount rate of 10%. It turns out that the discounted value of the three USD1 million savings at a 10% discount rate is USD2.5 million. Since the cost of the investment is USD2 million, the investor gains USD0.5 million by making the investment. Thus, the post-analysis finance person's response is, "Duh, yes. The DCF gains are positive!"

Discount rate. *See* required return.

Dividends. Equity holders receive payments on their stock investments through dividend payments that companies make. These dividend payments are made at the discretion of the company's board of directors. Suppose that Jumbo Airlines makes a profit of USD10 million. If the board decides to pay out all company profits to shareholders, then the total cash dividend is USD10 million. Since there are 1 million shareholders, each shareholder will receive USD10 in cash per share. Alternatively, suppose that the board decides that it is best for shareholders to invest USD5 million of the profits into replacing some of the aging equipment on its airplanes and to pay out the other half of profits to shareholders. In this case, the total cash dividend is USD5 million. Since there are 1 million shareholders, each shareholder will receive USD5 in cash per share. Shareholders can be compensated in other ways besides cash dividends. One way is *stock buybacks*. Suppose that the board decides to use the USD10 million profit to do a USD10 million stock buyback instead of a cash dividend. In this case the board will offer to buy back USD10 million of stock at the prevailing price of USD100. Since USD10 million divided by USD100 per share equals 100,000 shares, the buyback will be for 100,000 shares. In this case, the USD10 million will still flow back to the shareholders of the company, and those who want the cash can sell their shares and those who don't want the cash will not take the buy back. The share price will adjust so that 10% of the shares will be repurchased by Jumbo.

DPO. *See* days payable outstanding (DPO).

DSO. *See* days sales outstanding (DSO).

Earnings. *See* profit.

Earnings before interest and tax, and **earnings before interest, tax, depreciation, and amortization.** *See* EBIT and EBITDA.

EBIT and EBITDA. The acronyms EBIT and EBITDA are common finance terms that stand, respectively, for *earnings before interest and tax* and *earnings before interest, tax, depreciation, and amortization* (with such a mouthful, it is easy to appreciate why finance people like the acronym EBITDA). EBIT is generally the same as *operating profit*, since it includes all operating expenses but does not include interest and taxes. EBIT and operating profit are useful concepts because they capture the profitability associated with the true operations of the company without any distortion for how the company is financed (e.g., how much debt financing is used) or its particular tax policy. EBIT measures pure operating profitability—well, maybe. A lot of finance people don't like EBIT because it contains the ad hoc noncash investment expense of depreciation and amortization. Finance people recognize that businesses never really pay depreciation and amortization expenses. As such, the true cash operating profit that a business generates excludes the noncash depreciation and amortization allocation. This is what EBITDA captures: the cash operating profit of the business before any depreciation or amortization allocation is made. If a business has USD100,000 in EBIT for the year, but depreciation and amortization expenses are USD200,000 for the year, the actual cash profits are best represented as EBITDA, or USD300,000, rather than the EBIT of USD100,000. This is because the depreciation and amortization expense of USD200,000 was never really paid out. This USD200,000 is simply an allocation of some of an investment expenditure that occurred in a previous period. Both EBIT and EBITDA are measures of operating profits that go to all investors—both debt and equity holders.

Economic value. When making a business decision, economic value is the difference between the value of the long-term gains created and the value of the long-term resources consumed. Economic value is created when the expected long-term economic gains created by a decision exceed the expected long-term economic costs of the resources consumed by that decision. Economic value captures the economic gains accrued to owners by any decision.

Equity holders. Equity holders are a type of investor. The term *equity holder* is synonymous with the terms *equity investor, stockholder,* and *shareholder.* In exchange for their investment in the business, equity holders have the following two claims: (1) the right to exert control over the assets of the business as long as the promises to other claim holders (i.e., debt holders) are made and (2) the right to the residual profits of the business. Equity holders are residual claim holders, meaning they get what is left over after everyone else has been paid. Sometimes it is good to be a residual claim holder and sometimes it is not. Suppose Ivana gives USD1 million to Jumbo Airlines for a promise of shared equity in the company—meaning she shares the equity with people who have similar claims—and a promise of the residual profits. As an equity holder, Ivana can expect to have voting rights on company policies and the leadership of Jumbo Airlines. If she doesn't like the decisions that the board of directors is making, she can vote the board members out. The company provides cash payments to Ivana through board-approved cash dividends (cash payments made to equity holders where each share of stock entitles the shareholder to a certain cash payment) and through equity buybacks (when the company buys back shares). If the company is acquired or liquidated, Ivana gets her share of what is left over after all other claim holders are paid. The structure of the equity contract gives the equity holder assurance that others in the company won't take advantage of them.

Financial leverage. Financial leverage is a concept that captures the mix of debt and equity used to finance a business. By leverage, finance people mean the ability of debt financing to give more power to the amount of equity financing being used. Using debt allows someone to buy more assets with the same amount of equity; in other words, they leverage their equity using debt. That power to enhance their equity to buy more assets is what finance people refer to as *leverage.* Suppose Isabel has USD50,000 in cash to invest in a house. Without debt financing, she is only able to afford a house priced at under USD50,000. However, suppose she can find a bank to lend her USD50,000. With the USD50,000 of bank financing, she is able to afford a house priced at USD100,000. With the bank as the debt holder, Isabel, the equity holder, has leveraged her equity at a proportion of two times, in that she has acquired an asset worth two times her equity investment. Now suppose she is able to find another bank that will lend her USD450,000. With the USD450,000 of bank financing, she is able to afford a house priced at USD500,000. Isabel has leveraged her equity at a proportion of 10 times, in that she has acquired assets worth 10 times her equity investment. Note that she also increased her risk level by 10 times.

Financial model. A financial model is a financial forecast of a business outcome based on various assumptions. Financial models are commonly built using electronic spreadsheet software. A financial model is like a prototype of a product, as it allows the analyst to examine and test a "mocked-up" business scenario without actually pursuing the project in real life. Good models allow the analyst to adjust assumptions and easily see how the outcomes vary. Financial models are powerful tools for financial decision-making.

Financial risk. *See* business risk.

Financial securities. Debt and equity holders have claims on the profits and governance of the business. Sometimes investors will find it advantageous to be able to trade these claims.

The ability to trade gives owners flexibility to buy into or sell out of claims in the business at a lower cost. To facilitate trading, financial securities are created; these formalize the claim into a uniform contract. For equity holders, the uniform contracts are called *shares* or *stocks*. Suppose the total equity holdings in Jumbo Airlines are divided into 1 million shares. The shares or stocks delineate the portion of equity that is traded, such that one share of stock in Jumbo is a claim on one-millionth of the voting privilege and the profit payouts of the equity. A similar thing can be done for debt, where claims on a debt contract are divided into financial securities called *bonds*. If Jumbo issues 1,000 bonds in a USD1 million bond offering, then each bond has a claim on USD1,000 of the debt raised. To facilitate the trading of financial securities, financial markets are created for investors to buy and sell financial securities. Shares of stock are commonly bought and sold on *stock exchanges* such as the London Stock Exchange, Euronext, or NASDAQ. These exchanges provide gathering places for buyers and sellers of stock to trade with each other. Stock exchanges maintain listing requirements—companies or investors must comply with these listing requirements in order for shares of their stock to be traded on the exchange. Bonds are commonly bought and sold on *over-the-counter exchanges*—informal networks of traders who buy and sell bonds. *Security brokers* are organizations (e.g., Interactive Brokers, TD Ameritrade) that help investors with securities trading by providing access to *securities markets* (formal exchanges or informal networks) and managing all the logistic details that the investor doesn't want to deal with. When investors buy or sell their stocks or bonds, they typically do so with the help of a security broker.

Firm-specific risk. *See* idiosyncratic risk.

Fixed assets (net fixed assets). The total investment in both long-term assets, such as property, plant, and equipment (PP&E), and intangible assets is called fixed assets. Fixed assets are different from working capital because fixed assets are long-term assets while working capital exists in the short term.

General and administrative (G&A) costs. *See* income statement.

Gross margin. *See* profit margin.

Gross profit. *See* profit.

Hurdle rate. *See* required return.

Idiosyncratic risk. Idiosyncratic risk measures the risk that is not associated with common risk factors. Suppose the value of a pharmaceutical firm depends mostly on the outcome of a drug trial. If the trial shows the drug to be effective at treating a certain illness, the firm is worth tons. If the trial shows the drug to not be effective at treating a certain illness, the firm is worth nothing. In that case, the firm has lots of idiosyncratic risk, since the outcome of the firm's drug trial is not likely to be a risk factor for other firms in the economy. Common alternative terms for idiosyncratic risk include *nonmarket risk* and *firm-specific risk*. These terms are used interchangeably in finance. *See also* systematic risk.

Income. *See* profit.

Income statement. When businesses sell stuff, they create sales or revenue, but creating that revenue entails business costs. The income statement is a financial statement that indicates, over a period of time, the magnitude of the business sales relative to the magnitude of the business costs. The net difference in sales and costs over a period of time is the profit of the business. The costs listed on the income statement are commonly divided in several categories. *Cost of goods sold (COGS)* are the direct costs associated with making or buying the products or services that the business sells. *Selling, general, and administrative (SG&A)*

costs are the indirect costs associated with operating the business such as water and energy costs, management salary, and advertising expenses; alternative names for SG&A costs include general and administrative (G&A) costs, and selling and administrative (S&A) costs. COGS and SG&A costs are considered operating costs in that they are directly associated with the operations of the business. Other costs, such as interest expense or income taxes, are not operating costs and tend to be listed lower in the income statement. A typical period for an income statement is a year, but a month or a quarter are also common. Finance people have other terms for the income statement, including *profit and loss statement (P&L)*.

Inflation rate. Inflation is a general rise of prices for goods and services in the economy. Inflation results from the same amount of money buying less over time—it is a decline in the purchasing power of money. Inflation occurs in an economy when the supply of money grows faster than the demand for goods and services. For example, inflation may result from government efforts to stimulate the economy or stimulate employment by giving money to businesses through stimulus checks, tax breaks, or low interest rates. The inflation rate measures the percentage increase in prices, which is the same as the percentage of a currency's reduction in purchasing power. If the inflation rate is 10% over the course of the year, that means that it takes 10% more money this year to buy the same basket of goods as it did last year. In other words, the value of the currency has declined by 10%. A common measures of inflation in many countries is the Consumer Price Index (CPI). The inflation rate matters to investors as they seek returns that compensate them for declines in purchasing power. By choosing to invest their money, investors are, by definition, deferring, planning to spend that money later rather than now. In order to convince investors to spend their money later rather than now, investors naturally need to be compensated for expected inflation in prices.

Intangible assets. Businesses also make investments in assets that are not tangible—meaning that there isn't much one can handle or take a picture of. Such intangible assets include the benefits of productive research and development. If a company has been able to generate an asset with commercial value (e.g., a new drug, a promising patent, or a valuable copyright or trademark), the cost of developing that asset is considered an intangible asset.

Internal rate of return (IRR). The IRR is a way of distilling the multiyear financial effects of an investment to a single value. This is done by identifying the rate of return that would be needed to generate the financial benefits of the investment. This amount represents the rate of return that investors are expected to achieve by making the investment. In Burt's example (*see* discounted cash flow [DCF] analysis), the IRR is 23%. This means that Burt can expect to make 23% on his money by buying the equipment for USD2 million. Another implication of Burt's expected IRR is that he should expect net present value (NPV) to be positive so long as the discount rate is less than 23%. As another example, suppose that an investment of USD1,000 is expected to generate a payoff of USD2,000 in five years. The increase from USD1,000 to USD2,000 is a 100% increase, but the increase occurs over five years. The IRR is calculated by solving for R in the equation,

$$\text{USD1,000 investment} \times (1 + R)^5 = \text{USD2,000 expected payoff}.$$

The exponent 5 refers to the five years of delay in realizing the USD2,000 payment. Solving for R gives an IRR of 15%. This means that 15% is the annual percentage return that transforms USD1,000 into USD2,000 in five years.

Inventory. Businesses commonly produce goods for sale. In order to have material to sell, businesses typically hold a stock or supply of these goods. This stock of goods is referred to as inventory. Since the business typically pays for the inventory prior to selling it, inventory can be a sizable investment asset for a business. Inventory does not refer to the assets used to make those goods, like equipment; it refers only to items that are made for sale.

Inventory days. *See* days inventory outstanding (DIO).

Investors. Finance has lots of terms for investors. Investors provide the money that firms need to operate. If a firm needs a warehouse or a truck, investors put up the money. If a firm needs a pile of inventory to sell, investors put up the money. If a firm needs to fund the development of a drug or a computer system, investors put up the money. To compensate investors for all that money, firms issue *claims* on the business to investors. These claims promise two things: (1) various monetary payouts and (2) influence on firm decisions. The investor arrangement works well for both parties—the business gets the money it needs to operate, and the investors exert power over the business decisions and get a share of the profits.

IRR. *See* internal rate of return (IRR).

Law of conservation of risk. The law of conservation of risk states that the overall risk associated with a business remains the same regardless of how the business is financed. This principle is a powerful principle for thinking clearly about assessing a business's risk. Two firms can have the same overall business risk, even if the first is financed mostly with equity and the second is financed mostly with debt. The law of conservation of risk implies that businesses with lots of debt aren't necessarily any riskier than those with none. This is foundational to understanding how the risks for debt holders and equity holders change as the mix of debt and equity changes.

Law of conservation of value. The law of conservation of value states that the value of a business remains the same regardless of how the business is financed. Two firms can have the same business value, even if the first is financed mostly with equity while the second is financed mostly with debt. The law of conservation of value implies that debt financing doesn't necessarily change firm value. It is based on the notion that firm value is determined by the size of firm's cash flow, not by how that cash flow is divvied out. The law of conservation of value is foundational to understanding how the values of the debt holder and equity holder positions change as the mix of debt and equity changes.

Liquidity. *See* cash.

Management. In some small businesses, there is a single owner and employee, and all the decisions are made by one person. But as businesses get larger, it is common for there to be a separation of ownership (the investors) and management (the people who make the day-to-day decisions). This makes sense because (1) growing businesses are better served by pooling the resources of lots of investors, and (2) the skills required to invest in a business may be very different from the skills needed to run a business. It is typical for the management team to serve at the discretion of the equity holders. If the management team works hard and impresses the equity holders, the equity holders keep them on. If the management team loafs around or makes lots of bad decisions that frustrate the equity holders, the equity holders step in and find a new management team.

Market risk. *See* systematic risk.

Net assets. *See* total capital.

Net fixed assets. *See* fixed assets.

Net margin. *See* profit margin.

Net operating profit after tax (NOPAT). Taxes have real cash effects on businesses and how much they can return to investors. As such, it makes sense to consider tax effects on investor returns. NOPAT, the abbreviation for *net operating profit after tax*, is a measure of the after-tax profits available to all investors in the business, both debt holders and equity holders. To calculate this value, start with the EBIT for the business and then subtract the taxes that would be paid on those operating profits. The exact calculation is

$$\text{NOPAT} = \text{EBIT} \times (1 - \text{tax rate}).$$

NOPAT provides a measure of the after-tax profit of the business that is neutral to how it is financed (i.e., NOPAT is the same whether the company has no debt or lots of debt). In that way, NOPAT is different from net profit, because interest payments to debt holders have not been deducted. This difference is useful because it measures the business's after-tax profits that are available to both debt holders and equity holders. As an example, if a business's EBIT is USD100,000 and the tax rate is 30%, then the business's NOPAT is USD70,000. This USD70,000 NOPAT is calculated by removing the USD30,000 taxes implied by the 30% tax rate from the operating profit of USD100,000, using the above equation.

Net present value (NPV). NPV is a way of distilling multiyear financial effects of an investment to a single value. This is done by identifying the financial amount that would be needed to generate the financial benefits of the investment less the amount required to make the investment. The net difference measures how the investors' wealth is affected by the investment. In Burt's example (*see* discounted cash flow [DCF] analysis), the present value of the benefits is USD2.5 million and the present value of the investment is USD2 million. That means that the NPV is USD0.5 million. This NPV equals the expected wealth impact of making the investment. Burt is financially better off by USD0.5 million for having made the USD2 million investment.

Net profit. *See* profit.

Net working capital. *See* working capital.

Nominal rates. Nominal rates include inflation; they tend to be how people think about rates of price or value changes in everyday living. *Real rates* are adjusted nominal rates that exclude inflation. Inflation is baked into nominal rates but removed from real rates. For example, suppose that over the year, the price of lumber has increased 10%. This rate of 10% is considered a nominal rate because it is the rate of increase that people see in lumber prices. If the general currency inflation rate was 4%, then finance people would say that the real rate of increase for the lumber price was 6% [the 10% nominal rate less the 4% inflation rate]. This real rate of 6% excludes inflation, as it means that the rate of price increase is 6% above the general inflation rate of money. Finance people would say that nominal lumber prices are up 10% and real lumber prices are up 6%. Thus, nominal figures have inflation baked in, while real figures have inflation removed.

Nonmarket risk. *See* idiosyncratic risk.

NOPAT. *See* net operating profit after tax (NOPAT).

NPV. *See* net present value (NPV).

Operating margin. *See* profit margin.

Operating profit. *See* EBIT *or* profit.

Opportunity cost of capital. *See* required return.

P&L. *See* income statement.

Payable days. *See* days payable outstanding (DPO).

Payables. The opposite of receivables, payables is used to refer to bills that the company owes. When an invoice creates a receivable for the seller, it also creates a payable for the buyer. In the hospital example (*see* receivables), the hospital's receivable is a payable for the insurance company. The term *accounts payable* refers to bills the business has received for goods it has purchased but not paid for. Payables also includes other operating liabilities that the business may have incurred but not paid for. For example, suppose a business pays its employees once per month. In this case, the business accrues *wages payable* throughout the month for all the work its employees have completed and that it will pay them for at the end of the month. Payables can be an important form of financing for businesses.

Payback. Payback is usually defined as the number of years it is expected to take for the cash inflows of an investment to make up for the initial cash outflows required. It is the number of years it takes to "break even" on the investment. In Burt's example (*see* discounted cash flow [DCF] analysis), it takes Burt two years to break even on his USD2 million investment, since it is expected to take two years before the expected annual USD1 million savings sum up and make up for the initial USD2 million investment.

Perpetuity. A perpetuity is a promised payment of expected cash flow that repeats at a regular interval forever. An example of a perpetuity is a promise of a USD100 payment every year forever. The formula for calculating the present value of a perpetuity is

$$V = \frac{C}{R},$$

where V is the present value, C is the promised payment or expected cash flow, and R is the risk-adjusted discount rate. As an example, suppose that Jumbo Airlines is considering offering new flight service between San Jose and Santo Domingo. Jumbo expects that the service will generate USD1 million of cash flow per year. Since Jumbo has no expectation for ending the service, investors might expect that the USD1 million cash flow to go on forever and value this business opportunity as a perpetuity. If the relevant discount rate is 10%, the formula for calculating the present value of the San Jose–Santo Domingo business is

$$V = \frac{\text{USD1 million}}{10\%} = \text{USD10 million.}$$

If you think about it, a value of USD10 million seems reasonable, since if an investor had USD10 million and invested it at an expected rate of return of 10%, the investor would earn USD1 million each year forever. In effect, a sum of USD10 million allows one to home cook an annual USD1 million payment for forever. Finance people also commonly use an *alternative present-value formula* that accommodates cash flow that is expected to grow at a constant rate (instead of remaining constant without growing). The present-value formula for this growing perpetuity is

$$V = \frac{C_1}{R-g},$$

where V is the present value of the growing perpetuity, C_1 is the first promised payment, R is the risk-adjusted discount rate, and g is the expected growth rate for the cash flow.

PP&E. *See* property, plant, and equipment (PP&E).

Present value. The present value is the amount of cash needed today to generate a specified payment in the future at the prevailing risk-adjusted market return. Because of the ability to self-generate the future payment with the current cash, one is said to be indifferent between a future value and a present value. The formula that calculates the present value is

$$V = \frac{C}{(1+R)^T},$$

where V is the present value, C is the future cash payment, R is the prevailing periodic risk-adjusted return, and T is the number of periods until the cash payment is expected. This formula is the bedrock tool for financial valuation. Finance people call it the *present-value* or *discounting* formula. Such calculations are called *present-value calculations* because they reduce the value of an expected future payment stream to a current present value.

Profit. A company's profit is a measure of the difference over a period of time in the magnitude of revenue bringing money into the business relative to the magnitude of costs taking money out of the business. The term *profit* is synonymous with the *income* or *earnings*. When profit is positive, revenue exceeds costs. When profit is negative (commonly called a loss), costs for the period exceed revenue. The net between the revenue and costs is the profit of the business over a period of time—say, a year. There are different definitions of profit based on what category of costs is included. *Gross profit* refers to profit that includes only the direct costs of producing the products sold. For example, gross profit is equal to the revenue less the direct cost of goods sold (COGS). The terms *operating profit* and *operating income* refer to profit defined by including all the operating costs of the business (including the indirect costs associated with the overall business operations). The terms *net profit, net income,* and *net earnings* refer to profit defined by including all the costs of the business, including the financing costs such as interest expense and income taxes paid to the government. Since interest expense has been deducted, net profit is a measure of profit that goes only to equity holders. In contrast, operating profit is a concept of profit that is available to both debt holders and equity holders, since interest expense is not yet subtracted out.

Profit and loss statement (P&L). *See* income statement.

Profit margin. Profit margin measures the amount of profit generated as a percentage of the sales price. Its magnitude is determined by the relation of business costs to sales. If the sales price is high relative to the per-unit cost, then the profit margin is high. If total revenue is low relative to total costs, then profit margin is low. Profit margins may differ widely across businesses. For example, some businesses may operate at a high margin by pricing their goods or services at 50% above their costs, whereas other businesses may operate at a low margin by pricing their goods or services at 10% above their costs. The profit margin can be thought of as the percentage of the sales price that represents profit to the business. Profit margin can be determined based on various definitions of profit as in the above description. As such, profit margin can be defined based on *gross margin* (using gross profit), *operating margin* (using operating profit), or *net profit margin* (using net profit).

Property, plant, and equipment (PP&E). A business's PP&E refers to the cost of all the long-term tangible assets the business owns; an alternative name for PP&E is *property and equipment (P&E)*. These assets include the cost of the land the company owns, the cost of the buildings the company owns, and the cost of all the long-term equipment the company owns. All these long-term assets are considered *tangible assets* (i.e., there is a physical thing one can handle). By the conventions of accounting, PP&E is listed at cost (how much it historically cost to acquire it) and not at its prevailing market value. The verb *capitalize* means to put an asset on the balance sheet. For example, if a business needed to repair a piece of equipment, the manager would either capitalize the repair costs by adding the costs to the equipment and then expensing (depreciating) that capitalized cost over several years, or the manager would *expense* the cost by running it immediately through the income statement as a repair charge. If the cost is expensed, it might appear on the income statement as a sales, general, and administrative (SG&A) expense.

Real rates. *See* nominal rates.

Receivable days. *See* days sales outstanding (DSO).

Receivables. The term receivables is used to refer to bills that the company is owed. Companies often sell their goods and services to customers on *credit*. For example, they deliver a load of goods and leave an invoice stating that the customer has 30 days to pay for the goods. This invoice is a receivable for the seller. The seller expects that the receivable will eventually be turned into cash when the invoice is paid, but for the time being, the company tabulates the asset as a receivable. Suppose a hospital treats a patient for a broken arm. Once the broken arm is repaired, the hospital issues a bill to the patient's health insurance carrier for payment for its services. Until this payment is received, the hospital will list the expected payment among its assets as a receivable. In issuing the receivable, the hospital is extending credit to the patient and insurance company by waiting for a later payment.

Required return. When making investment decisions, investors weigh the expected return on investment (ROI) with the risk associated with the investment. The required return is the expected ROI that compensates the investor for the risk they are undertaking. The higher the risk, the higher the required return. Because of the importance of this concept in investment decision-making, there are many terms for the required return. These synonyms include the *opportunity cost of capital*, the *cost of capital*, the *hurdle rate*, and the *discount rate*. All these terms refer to the benchmark rate that distinguishes returns on investment that are good (above the benchmark) from those that are bad (below the benchmark).

Return on equity (ROE). *See* return on investment (ROI).

Return on investment (ROI). Finance language includes a lot of terms to describe the returns that are expected or realized on investments made. In general, ROI is defined as the gain investors receive divided by the investment money they put up. Finance people use lots of terms for this concept because it is so important. ROI comes in two forms: (1) income and (2) price appreciation, or *capital gains*. Suppose that Eleanor has invested USD100 in Jumbo Airlines by buying a share of its stock that is currently trading at USD100 per share. Eleanor has done her homework on Jumbo Airlines and believes that the expected return on the stock is 9%. If, over the first year, Jumbo Airlines pays a USD10 cash dividend and the stock price remains at USD100, Eleanor has made a return of 10% on her USD100 investment—a bit better than expected. This 10% comes from the income gain of USD10 plus the price appreciation of USD0. The combined USD10 gain divided by the USD100 investment gives the 10% return. Over the second year, Jumbo Airlines pays a USD10 cash dividend and the stock price depreciates to USD90, so Eleanor has made a return of 0% on her USD100 updated investment. This 0% comes from the income gain of USD10 less the price depreciation of USD10. The combined USD0 gain divided by the USD100 investment gives the 0% return. While Eleanor anticipated a return of 9% on the stock, her realized returns were somewhat different. She earned 10% over the first year and 0% over the second year, for an overall annual return of 5% over the two years. Note that rates of return are by convention quoted in annual terms. While Eleanor in fact earned 10% over the two years, her rate of return is quoted as 5% because that is the average return she realized on an annual basis (5% per year). ROI is important to finance people because it measures the annual gain investors get on their investment. There are many different definitions of ROI based on the definition of the annual gain and the definition of the investment. For example, *return on equity (ROE)* measures the gain that equity holders receive through their equity investment; it is defined as net profit divided by the amount of investment that equity investors have made through owner's equity.

Risk-free rate. The term risk-free rate is used to denote the return investors can achieve without bearing risk. In the risk-return graph (see **Figure 6.1**), the risk-free rate is the y-intercept of the risk-adjusted benchmark line—the amount of return investors require for investments whose risk is zero. The risk-free rate is a baseline rate, as other required rates of return should always be at least as high as the risk-free rate (since that is what you get without bearing any risk). Government bond yields or interbank rates are rates used in practice as examples of risk-free rates. To obtain an estimate of the required rate of return, one commonly adds a relevant risk premium to the prevailing risk-free rate.

Risk premium. Finance people believe that investments with more risk need to earn greater return than investments with less risk. They call this the *risk-return relation*. The risk premium measures the steepness of that relation. The risk premium is the amount of additional return that is required with greater risk. As an example, stocks have historically earned greater returns than bonds when examined over long periods of time. This additional return makes sense to finance people because of the risk premium. Because stocks are considered riskier than bonds, the additional return associated with investing in stocks is considered an example of a risk premium. Finance people say "the greater the risk, the greater the return" to emphasize the concept of the risk premium. A subtle point to appreciate is that the concept of a risk premium is true only in expectations—before the outcome. Since higher-risk investments are, by definition, riskier, they may or may not pay out with high returns. This is the risk of a high-risk investment—you expect higher returns on the investment, but there is no guarantee. If you want a guaranteed return, you'll have to forgo the high-risk premium associated with high-risk investments and accept a low-risk premium on a low-risk investment. The mechanism for achieving the risk premium is the market price of the investment. Low-risk investments tend to be attractive to investors, so their prices will be bid up such that the subsequent returns will be relatively low (because investors have had to pay so much). On the other hand, high-risk investments tend not to be as attractive to investors, so their prices will be bid down such that subsequent returns will be relatively high (because the investors have had to pay so little).

ROE. *See* return on investment (ROI).

ROI. *See* return on investment (ROI).

Securities markets. *See* financial securities.

Selling and administrative (S&A) costs. *See* income statement.

Selling, general, and administrative (SG&A) costs. *See* income statement.

Shares. *See* financial securities.

Stakeholders. *See* corporate governance.

Stock exchange. *See* financial securities.

Stocks. *See* financial securities.

Systematic risk. Systematic risk measures susceptibility to common risk factors. A firm is considered to have high systematic risk if it is highly susceptible to the risk factors that affect other firms. A firm is considered to have low systematic risk if it is not all that susceptible to the risk factors that affect other firms. As an example, firms that are highly affected by bad world outcomes such as military conflicts, pandemics, or energy shortages are considered to have high systematic risk. Firms that are minimally affected by these bad world outcomes are considered to have low systematic risk. Common alternative terms for systematic risk include *market risk*, *covariance risk*, and *beta risk*. These terms are used interchangeably in finance. *See also* idiosyncratic risk.

Tangible assets. *See* property, plant, and equipment (PP&E).

Tax shield. Government tax policy commonly subsidizes certain actions by reducing business or individual taxes in order to encourage or subsidize certain activities. The value of the reduction in taxes from such tax policy is called a tax shield. One type of tax shield is associated with debt financing. In order to stimulate the acquisition of assets, governments commonly allow individuals or businesses to deduct their interest. Because of this ability to deduct interest payments from taxable income, the cost of borrowing is reduced. For example, suppose that Jumbo Airlines buys some assets using debt financing and pays USD1 million in interest. Since the interest payments Jumbo makes are tax deductible (meaning Jumbo is able to reduce its taxable income by the amount of the interest payments), the net cost of the debt financing is less than the interest payment. Instead, the true net cost of the debt is equal to the amount of interest paid less the tax payments that the interest deduction saves the company. The value of the tax savings from interest deductions is the value of the tax shield.

Terminal value. A common approach for estimating investment values using discounted cash flow (DCF) analysis is to forecast the expected cash flow over a specified planning horizon and then to use a terminal-value assumption to capture the value of the investment at the end of the planning horizon. Suppose the management team at Jumbo Airlines is estimating the value of acquiring a new plane. To do this, it estimates the value of the expected incremental cash flow Jumbo will be able to generate over a 20-year period. To estimate the remaining value, the team estimates the expected market value of the plane in 20 years. This is the terminal value. By adding together the present value of the cash flow associated with the planning horizon with the present value of the terminal value, the team is able to estimate the total expected value of investing in the new plane.

Total capital. Total capital represents the total amount of money that investors have invested in the business to acquire the buildings and equipment associated with fixed assets and the inventory and receivables associated with working capital. Total capital differs from total assets in that total assets represent all the assets of the business, whereas total capital represents all the assets that are financed by investors. Accounts payable, for example, represents a source of financing provided by the business suppliers. The portion of the total assets that is financed by the suppliers is included in total capital. Total capital is commonly equivalent to *net assets*.

Trade credit. Trade credit is a form of financing that is offered between buyers and sellers. A typical business sale includes multiple negotiated items: the price, the delivery, and the payment. Trade credit occurs when the payment date differs from the delivery date. If the seller allows the buyer to pay for the product 30 days after delivery, then the seller has extended 30 days of trade credit to the buyer. Trade credit is like bank credit in that both types of credit are contracts for a future delivery of payment. Sometimes sellers provide a discount incentive to pay early. The contract term "1/10 net 30" (pronounced one ten net 30) means that the buyer must pay for the product in 30 days but will get a 1% discount on the price if the payment is made by the 10th day. Trade credit is used to stimulate sales (it is one of many things that affect sales). For example, a business may stimulate more sales by offering customers 60 days of trade credit than by reducing its prices a certain amount.

Volatility. Volatility is a measure of risk. It considers the amount of variation in performance outcomes. Statistical measures of volatility include *variance* and *standard deviation*. To calculate the variance of a set of outcomes, one calculates the average of the set and then adds up the squared differences between the outcome and the average and divides by the number of observations less 1. For example, if the set of goals in two games are the numbers 3 and 7, then the average goal is 5 and the variance in goals is 8. This variance value of 8 is calculated by first finding the variation between each number of goals and the average number of goals, as follows:

Game 1 variation: Difference between outcome of 3 and average of 5 is -2.
Game 2 variation: Difference between outcome of 7 and average of 5 is $+2$.

Next, we square the values of the two variations to get numbers that are always positive, and add them up. By squaring the -2 and $+2$, we get a positive measure of variation that we add up to get 8 $[8 = (-2)^2 + (+2)^2]$. To calculate the standard deviation of a set of outcomes, we calculate the square root of the variance. In the above example, the square root of 8 is 2.83. Thus, a measure of volatility for the number of goals in two games (3 and 7) is variance 8 and standard deviation 2.83. These statistics provide a measure of risk or volatility. If, alternatively, the set of outcomes are 1 and 1, then variance is zero and the standard deviation is zero. This set of numbers has no variance or volatility.

Wages payable. *See* payables.

Working capital. Working capital—or, equivalently, *net working capital*—refers to the net difference between a business's current operating assets and its current operating liabilities. It can be calculated by adding up the operating cash, receivables, and inventory, then subtracting the operating accounts payable and wages payable. This difference is a measure of the net amount of the current assets the business has less the current liabilities it owes. Because we generally think of having lots of stuff as a good thing, it is common to think that businesses want lots of working capital. But finance people recognize that lots of working capital is costly because investors have to finance it all, and so they tend to prefer low, efficient amounts of working capital (i.e., inventory that moves quickly and accounts receivable that get collected quickly). Since working capital is a measure of the amount of funding required to finance the business's net current assets, that funding requirement should be minimized as much as possible. For example, if working capital is equal to zero (e.g., accounts payable offsets accounts receivable and inventory), investors don't have to come up with the money to fund the company's current operating assets; the generosity of suppliers and employees of the company (by not demanding immediate payment) is large enough that it completely funds all the cash, customer credit, and inventory. If working capital is greater than zero, then investors finance the working-capital balance.

Yield. Finance people use yield to describe returns on debt. Suppose Eleanor purchases one Jumbo Airlines bond for USD950 (the USD1,000-face-value bond is trading on the over-the-counter bond market at a price of USD95 per USD100 of face value). The Jumbo Airline bond has a promised interest rate (*coupon rate*, in bond language) of 6%. This means that Jumbo Airlines will pay USD60 [6% of USD1,000] every year to each bond holder. Since Eleanor doesn't expect the bond price to change that much, the yield or expected return is 6.3%, which equals USD60 divided by the USD950 investment. *Yield to maturity* is a term used to calculate the average annual yield that bond holders expect to achieve if the bond holder holds the bond to maturity, collecting all the promised interest (coupon) payments and receiving the face value of the bond of USD1,000 at maturity.

Yield to maturity. *See* yield.

The Math of Finance

This appendix provides common math formulas used in finance. Please know that this is not a comprehensive list, but it does include many of the most common math equations.

COMPOUND RETURN FORMULA (FUTURE VALUE FORMULA)

The compound return formula helps moves values across time. If you want to know what something is worth in the future, you could move that Time 0 value to Time T by multiplying it by $(1 + R)^T$, where R is the relevant risk-adjusted discount rate and T is the number of time periods. The discount rate should be in the same units of time (i.e., monthly time needs monthly rates; annual time needs annual rates). This formula is also called the future value formula because it moves value into the future.

$$\text{Value in Year } 0(1 + R)^T = \text{value in Year } T.$$

Doug is saving for a trip retirement. He has saved up USD100,000 so far. If he invests that money at an annual rate of 5% for 10 years, how much should he expect to have?

Using the compound return formula, Doug can multiply the value of his savings now of USD100,000 by $(1 + 5\%)^{10}$, which is the 5% return rate compounded 10 times. The calculation will tell him that he can expect to have USD162,889 in 10 years at a 5% investment rate.

COMPOUND ANNUAL GROWTH RATE (CAGR) FORMULA

This formula helps calculate an annual growth rate or CAGR (often pronounced *cay-grr*) over several years. The value T represents the number of years, and the $1/T$ represents the Tth root. Notice that this equation is actually the same as the compound return formula, but it has been rearranged to solve for R, the rate that moves the values across time.

$$\text{CAGR} = \left(\frac{\text{value in Year } T}{\text{value in Year } 0} \right)^{1/T} - 1.$$

Suppose that the number of people in your community has grown from 200,000 to 300,000 over the past five years. You want to calculate what the compound annual population growth rate has been over the past five years. To calculate the CAGR, divide 300,000 by 200,000 to get 1.5. Then take 1.5 to the 1/5 power. This is the same as taking it to the 0.2 power. Once you do this, you'll get the value 1.084. Subtract the 1 and you have a CAGR of 8.4%. This means that the compound annual population growth rate for your community has been 8.4% per year. If you want to test your knowledge, use the compound return formula to extrapolate your community's population for 10 years using the 8.4% rate. You should find that it grows to 672,069 people. Compound growth adds up quickly!

VARIANCE AND STANDARD DEVIATION FORMULAS

These two formulas are ways to describe the variation of set of values. The formula calculates how much the data tends to differ from the average value. In the variance formula, N is the number of observations, x_1 is the value of the first item, x_N is the value of the last item, and $\bar{x}$ is the average value. The ... symbol means that you repeat the pattern in the calculation for all items from the first one to the last one. The standard deviation is defined as the square root of the variance. It is rare that people actually use these equations to calculate these values; normally they will use a computer to do it for them since it can be tedious.

$$\text{Variance} = \frac{1}{N-1} \left[\left(x_1 - \bar{x} \right)^2 + \cdots + \left(x_N - \bar{x} \right)^2 \right].$$

Standard deviation = square root of variance.

These formulas are used all the time to calculate the variation or risk of something. Say you wanted to get a sense of the variation in high temperatures in the place you live. To do this, you could find the high temperatures for every day over the past year, and use that data to calculate the standard deviation. Suppose that your temperature standard deviation is 5 degrees, and a friend who lives in a different state does the same thing and gets 1 degree: it is clear that the weather where your friends lives is much less volatile than it is where you live.

CAPITAL ASSET PRICING MODEL (CAPM) FORMULA

This formula is used to estimate the required return associated with a risky investment. The formula suggests that you can calculate the required return for any risky investment if you know three things: the risk-free rate, the beta, and the market risk premium.

Expected return = risk-free rate + beta risk of investment × market risk premium.

Suppose you are trying to establish a benchmark hurdle rate for investing in your brother's business, which makes airplane seats. You find that airplane seat investments have a beta risk measure of 1.2, the prevailing risk-free rate is 6%, and the market risk premium seems to be 5%. Putting all that in the CAPM (often pronounced *cap-em*) formula, you'll find that the relevant benchmark rate is 12%. Finance people love this formula because it is simple and is backed up by some really interesting finance theory that argues for how investors should think about risk.

THE ACCOUNTING EQUATION

This equation forms the basis of double-entry accounting, which is the way that financial statements are created. The idea is that all assets have two parts: the physical part and the claims associated with that asset. The balance sheet uses this equation by saying that the investment in the asset is associated with an identical financing claim.

$$\text{Assets} = \text{liabilities} + \text{equity.}$$

PROFIT EQUATIONS

There are lots of ways of calculating profit for a business. These equations show the differences between some of the most common definitions of profit.

Gross profit tells you the profit after all direct costs have been subtracted from revenue.

$$\text{Gross profit} = \text{revenue} - \text{cost of goods sold.}$$

Operating profit tells you the profit after all operating costs have been subtracted from revenue.

$$\text{Operating profit} = \text{revenue} - \text{operating costs.}$$

Net profit tells you the profit after all costs have been subtracted from revenue.

$$\text{Net profit} = \text{revenue} - \text{all costs.}$$

RETURN ON EQUITY (ROE) DECOMPOSITION OF FORMULA

ROE is a really common financial ratio because it tells what returns equity investors are getting on their investment. It is defined as profit divided by equity. This formula decomposes—or splits out the calculation of ROE—into multiple aspects of ROE. In the formula below, ROE is divided into three aspects: profit margin (defined as profit/sales), asset turnover (defined as sales/assets), and leverage (defined as assets/equity). Using this decomposition, one can identify the source of variation in ROE, since any variation in ROE must be due to at least one of these three aspects.

$$\text{ROE} = \frac{\text{profit}}{\text{equity}} = \frac{\text{profit}}{\text{sales}} \times \frac{\text{sales}}{\text{assets}} \times \frac{\text{assets}}{\text{equity}}.$$

Suppose Keith is figuring out the ROE for his business. He finds that the ROE has suddenly dropped from 10% to 5%, and he doesn't know why. Since Keith's shareholders will want to know what is going on with their ROE, Keith has to figure this out. To do so, he turns to the ROE decomposition formula and looks at what has happened to the three aspects of ROE. He finds that profit margin has stayed constant at 5%. He finds that leverage has stayed constant at 1. He finds that asset turnover has dropped from 2 to 1. Aha! He now knows that a decline in asset turnover is the cause of his ROE troubles. With that understanding, he can call up the plant manager and see what is going on with asset turnover.

CASH FLOW FORMULA

Cash flow is the money that goes to investors. There are many different variations of cash flow formulas. The following are some examples of different formulas for calculating total cash flow or free cash flow to investors:

Cash flow = profit − investment.

Cash flow = net operating profit after tax (NOPAT) + depreciation and amortization − capital expenditures − increases in net working capital.

Cash flow = NOPAT − changes in net fixed assets − increases in net working capital.

PRESENT-VALUE FORMULA

The single-payment present-value formula helps move a single value across time. If you want to know what a value in the future is worth today, you could move that Time T value to Time 0 by dividing it by $(1+R)^T$, where R is the relevant risk-adjusted discount rate and T is the number of periods of time. The discount rate should be in the same units of time (i.e., monthly time needs monthly rates; annual time needs annual rates).

As an example, Doug is saving for retirement. He needs USD500,000 to retire in 10 years, so he needs to know how much he needs to invest now if the annual investment rate is 5%.

This formula is also called the present-value formula because it moves values from the future to the present. If you look carefully, you'll notice that it is closely related to the compound return formula.

$$V = \frac{C}{(1+R)^T},$$

where V is the present value, C is the future cash payment, R is the prevailing periodic risk-adjusted return, and T is the number of periods until the cash payment is expected.

Using the present-value formula, Doug can divide the USD500,000 value he needs in the future by $(1+5\%)^{10}$, which is the 5% return rate compounded 10 times. The calculation will tell him that he needs to have USD306,957 today, if he is investing at 5% for 10 years and expects USD500,000 at the end of that 10-year period.

PERPETUITY FORMULA

Perpetuity. A perpetuity is a promised payment of expected cash flow that repeats at a regular interval forever. An example of a perpetuity is a promise of a USD100 payment every year forever. The formula for calculating the present value of a perpetuity is

$$V = \frac{C}{R},$$

where V is the present value, C is the promised payment or expected cash flow, and R is the risk-adjusted discount rate. As an example, suppose that Jumbo Airlines is considering offering new flight service between San Jose and Santo Domingo. Jumbo expects that the service will generate USD1 million of cash flow per year. Since Jumbo has no expectation for ending the service, investors might expect that the USD1 million cash flow will to go on forever, so they will value this business opportunity as a perpetuity. If the relevant discount rate is 10%, the formula for calculating the present value of the San Jose–Santo Domingo business is

$$V = \frac{\text{USD1 million}}{10\%} = \text{USD10 million}.$$

If you think about it, a value of USD10 million seems reasonable, since if an investor had USD10 million and invested it at an expected rate of return of 10%, the investor would earn USD1 million each year forever. In effect, a sum of USD10 million allows one to home cook an annual USD1 million payment for forever. Finance people also commonly use an alternative present-value formula that accommodates cash flow that is expected to grow at a constant rate (instead of being constant). The present-value formula for this growing perpetuity is

$$V = \frac{C_1}{R-g},$$

where V is the present value of the growing perpetuity, C_1 is the first promised payment, R is the risk-adjusted discount rate, and g is the expected growth rate for the cash flow.

ANNUITY FORMULA

An annuity is a promised payment of expected cash flow that repeats at a regular interval and then ends at some defined point. A loan is a common example of an annuity, where the borrower agrees to make a specific payment every month for a specified number of months. The formula for calculating the present value of an annuity is

$$V = \frac{C}{R} - \frac{C}{R(1+R)^T},$$

where V is the present value of the annuity, C is the regular promised payment, R is the risk-adjusted periodic discount rate, and T is the expected number of periods until maturity. As an example, suppose that Ingrid has agreed to make payments of USD290 per month to her bank for five years to finance USD15,000 of the classic antique car she is buying. If the prevailing annual interest rate for car loans of this type is 6%, is the loan fair for both Ingrid and the bank? To do this, we first note that Ingrid has agreed to pay a monthly annuity to the bank. If the annual relevant risk-adjusted rate is 6%, then the monthly periodic rate is 0.5% (which comes from 6.0%/12 months in a year). The number of periods to maturity is 60 months (because 5 years × 12 months per year = 60 months). Inputting the appropriate values into the annuity present-value formula, we get a present value of USD15,000:

$$V = \frac{USD290}{0.5\%} - \frac{USD290}{0.5\%(1+0.5\%)^{60}} = USD15,000.$$

Since the present value of the annuity is equal to USD15,000, the bank's willingness to offer Ingrid USD15,000 seems appropriate. The terms of the loan seem fair for both parties.

CASH CYCLE FORMULAS

The cash cycle or cash conversion cycle formula calculates for a business the time between when cash leaves the business (when a purchase is paid) to when cash returns to the business (when a bill is collected). The cash cycle is equal to the number of days that inventory tends to stay in inventory (DIO or inventory days) plus the number of days that accounts receivable tend to take to be collected (DSO or receivable days) minus the number of days that accounts payable tend to take to be collected (DPO or payable days).

$$\text{Cash cycle} = \text{DIO} + \text{DSO} - \text{DPO}.$$

The components of the cash cycle are computed as below. In each case, they represent the number of days based on the current level from the balance sheet and the amount of volume from the income statement.

$$DIO = \frac{\text{inventory}}{\text{cost of goods sold}} \times 365 \text{ days.}$$

$$DPO = \frac{\text{accounts payable}}{\text{cost of goods sold}} \times 365 \text{ days.}$$

$$DSO = \frac{\text{accounts receivable}}{\text{revenue}} \times 365 \text{ days.}$$

Index

Note to readers: A page number in **bold** indicates a definition of the indexed term; a page number in *italic* indicates a figure or a table; a page number in the form 26n12 indicates a footnote. Review questions and their answers in **Appendix I** are not included in this index. Unless a term shows up only in the glossary, **Appendix II** is not included in this index. However, the formulas in **Appendix III** are included in this index.

About the Author

MICHAEL J. SCHILL is the Sponsors Professor of Business Administration of the Darden School of Business at the University of Virginia. He has long taught the core finance curriculum to MBA students and appreciates engaging both those students who are eager to be in a finance classroom and those who are apprehensive about it. He teaches a finance elective designed for students with no interest in a career in finance. His research spans empirical questions in corporate finance, asset pricing, and international finance. He coauthored the case study book *Case Studies in Finance: Managing for Corporate Value Creation*. He has been on the faculty at Darden since 2001 and was previously with the University of California at Riverside, as well as a visiting professor at Cambridge and Melbourne. He is the author or coauthor of over 60 cases, technical notes, and simulations. Prior to his doctoral work, he was a management consultant with Marakon Associates in Stamford and London. He received a BS from Brigham Young University, an MBA from INSEAD, and a PhD from the University of Washington. When he's not thinking about what finance people think, he enjoys endless hikes, heart-pounding paddles, and perfect cups of fresh-pressed cider. He got a C in his first finance class.